Perfect Love

A Hero's Journey

Written By: Ann Lenaers

Front Cover Photo By: Sharon Pittaway
Courtesy of www.unsplash.com

Back Cover Photo By:
Ann Lenaers

Unless otherwise indicated, scripture quotations are from the King James Version of the Bible, or KJV.

Scripture quotations marked NIV are taken from the Holy Bible, New International Version®. NIV®. Copyright© 1973, 1978, 1984, 2011 by Biblica, Inc.™ Used by permission of Zondervan. All rights reserved worldwide. www.zondervan.com The "NIV" and "New International Version" are trademarks registered in the United States Patent and Trademark Office by Biblica, Inc.™

Page 51 – Illustration and Art Design by David A. Henderson & Johanna Henderson// Illustration of Armor of God Artwork is Cover Artwork for Armor of God Bible Study found at www.DevotedToMaker.com// Artwork Inspired by Nephilim The Remnants Book found at www.NephilimTheRemnants.com// Copyright 2018 by David A Henderson

All rights reserved. No part of this publication may be reproduced, stored in a retrieval system, or transmitted in any form by any means – for example, electronic, photocopy, recording – without the prior written permission of Ann Lenaers. The only exception is brief quotations in printed reviews.

Self-published through Create Space. www.CreateSpace.com

Disclaimer: The words of this book are written from my personal perspective (Ann Lenaers). I recognize that the events described may have been viewed differently from the perspective of others involved. Sharing this story is intended to provide insight for healing to anyone facing similar challenges and is in no way intended to harm the real people involved.

Copyright © 2018 Ann Lenaers
All rights reserved.
ISBN-13: 978-1723244513
ISBN-10: 1723244511

Table of Contents

Laying Foundations……7

Part 1

1. The Call to Adventure……………..20
2. Refusal of the Call………………….30
3. Supernatural Aid……………….......36
4. Crossing the First Threshold……….54

Part 2

5. The Belly of the Whale……..………..82
6. The Road of Trials…………………103
7. The Meeting with the Goddess……..227
8. Woman as Temptress……………….227
9. Atonement with the Father…………240
10. Apotheosis………………………..255
11. The Ultimate Boon………………..264
12. Refusal of the Return……………..267

Part 3

13. The Magic Flight………………...272
14. Rescue from Without……………..293
15. Crossing the Return Threshold…….298
16. Master of the Two Worlds………...303
17. Freedom to Live…………………..327

Heavenly Father,

I ask for your guidance and blessings as I try my best to help people find greater understanding in your Word. Let the Holy Spirit help us cultivate the desire and ability to walk in your divine ways. Allow your truth, wisdom, and grace to shine forth from these pages and draw your people closer to you. Light the spark of your joy in their hearts and nourish it through every passage.

Create a feeling of peace, calm, and safety as we all work to face ourselves in the mirror and refine our imperfections for your glory. Have mercy as we progress through the journey, forgiving our failings and helping us up when we stumble. Teach us to discern clearly when we are in the presence of the influence of the enemy, and protect us from their attacks so we can focus on you with perfect trust.

We love you and thank you for all you have done, are doing, and continue to do for us and through us!

Amazing grace, how sweet the sound,
that saved a wretch like me.
I once was lost, but now am found,
was blind but now I see.
Twas grace that taught my heart to fear,
and grace my fears relieved.
How precious did that grace appear,
the hour I first believed.

I send up this prayer in the spirit and name of Christ.
Amen!
3-3-18

Laying Foundations

*And they that shall be of thee
shall build the old waste places.
Thou shalt raise up the foundations
of many generations,
and thou shalt be called
the repairer of the breach,
the restorer of paths to dwell in.*
Isaiah 58:12

Start to finish, the Bible is a redemption story. It started when God created the world, and *it was good* (*Genesis 1-2*). The Old Testament teaches law, order, and reasoning skills. The New Testament gospel focuses more on the application of love, grace, and forgiveness. The perfect balance of law and love - *a healthy use of compassion* - is the whole of the developmental story in the Bible, teaching us the exact skills necessary to conquer the duality of man through peace in our daily lives instead of butting heads in conflict (*Proverbs 11:1 & 20:23, Isaiah 40:12*).

Embracing this journey develops our minds and hearts. It presents us with real life examples that compare a moral code to immorality. In the search to understand God's will for us, first we must identify what it looks like to do things wrong and avoid following suit. Then we must also observe what it looks like to do things right and imitate it. This narrows life down on both ends in a dual refinement process. Even the very middle of the Bible, *Psalm 117*, says *O praise the Lord, all ye nations: praise Him all ye people. For his merciful kindness is great toward us, and the truth of the Lord endureth forever. Praise ye the Lord.* There is compassion, smack dab in the middle.

That is the narrow path to heaven (*Matthew 7:13-14*), following in Christ's footsteps (*Luke 9:23*). Boundary lines have to be drawn about what is considered acceptable behavior, but we can learn how to enact all things through love so that we are *choosing* the acceptable behaviors instead of being forced into them. There is no law against the fruits of the Spirit (*Galatians 5:22-23, James 3:17, 1 Corinthians 13:4-7*). Force will always breed contempt, conflict, and rebellion without fail. However, the Holy Spirit aids in convicting us to be better people once we accept that we've been in error (*John 16:7-8*).

The Old Testament says fear is the *beginning* of the wisdom and knowledge of God (*Proverbs 1:5-9 & 9:10*), The New Testament verse that should pair with that says there is no fear in perfect love (*1 John 4:18*)! The highest command we were given was to love God with all our hearts, souls, and minds. The second was to love our neighbor as ourselves (*Matthew 22:36-40, Galatians 5:14, Romans 13:8-10*). We are told that **all** the law and prophets hang on these words. *How do we get from fear to love?*

These passages when pulled together express a need for healing and growth, but we don't often give focus to the middle ground of faith. We focus on accepting Christ and see leaders who are well seasoned, but we don't typically shed much light on the journey in between. We can't fulfill those commands until we can clearly define what perfect love *looks* like from every angle. Once we do, we can use that as a launching point to move past our fear of punishment as a motivator and into the journey towards living in love, being partakers in the divine nature (*2 Peter 1*).

That doesn't mean we will stop fearing God. To fear God is a virtue (*Psalm 31:19 & 112:1, Ecclesiastes 8:12-13, Luke 1:50, etc.*). This process will help define fear through the lens of love so it takes on a healthy tone of sincere respect for His authority. What you once called fear will translate into things like reverence, obedience, humility, and submission to God in a way that you are prepared to choose. *The fear of the Lord is to hate evil: pride, and arrogancy, and the evil way, and the forward mouth do I hate* (*Proverbs 8:13*).

That is the spiritual journey I seek to take with you in this book, to help you try and paint a clearer picture of what perfect love looks like using the Bible so new personal goals can continually be set and pursued. We will attempt to lift words off of the two-dimensional pages and paint a three-dimensional, 360 degree view of love as a whole concept in our hearts and minds.

We live in a time where people will say they love a pair of shoes, a song, a toaster strudel, a pet, a friend, a parent, a spouse, and everything in between! I believe that makes it necessary to reflect upon its true meaning in order to reclaim its deeper truth. Real love is deep, not cheap. If emotion is an ocean, remember that Christ walked on water (*Matthew 14:22-36, Mark 6:45-56, John 6:16-24*). Hopefully, by the end, you will find the message of love and peace in the Bible more understandable and actionable in the modern world. We will work to understand its depths without drowning in it.

This is not a book about religion (*James 1:27*). It's about faith and our hearts, shifting our focus upwards to fulfilling our spiritual needs rather than just our base line physical needs. I will present thought provoking questions to encourage you to go deeper within yourself as you develop your faith and look towards the mentality of one who is part of the kingdom of God. There will be no judgment of where you came from, what denomination you practice, or what doctrines you've been told. This is also not intended to create new doctrines. We will only be evaluating scripture as believers who seek the truth (*2 Thessalonians 2:9-10*).

I definitely don't want to fulfill that traditional image in your mind of a Bible thumper who chucks verses at you like bullets, but it has been my experience that if you cannot cite your source for your viewpoint, it is not deemed a credible perspective. Therefore, as I cover these basics, all verses will be appropriately cited for your benefit in study and nothing more. You don't have to look up every single verse cited to get the point, but they are provided if you want to study any certain point further. This is a workbook, so I encourage you to highlight and mark it up as much as will benefit you!

I have also opted to abandon traditional quotation mark procedures. Anytime you see a verse quoted, anything in parenthesis, any quote, or any title it will instead be italicized to easily visually identify it as separate from the main flow of the text. This looked less clunky in my opinion and is easier to reference quickly in study. Some words are also italicized simply to place emphasis in the sentence. I wish that was something they could have done when the Bible was written. Moving the place of emphasis in a sentence can change the entire meaning!

I will also reference Strong's Concordance for clarity as needed. First published in 1890, James Strong wrote *Strong's Exhaustive Concordance* as a collection of all the original Hebrew and Greek words from the Bible organized in alphabetical order and paired with their root word definition. Each word was assigned a number for easy reference. This is not a perfect resource when used by itself since in the Koine Greek of the New Testament the full meaning of a word reflected its context in the sentence, but it is also widely respected.

That is why I love using *Bible Hub* online, because it brings together many resources. When you look up one of these words there, you can find the number of times it was used in scripture, a list of every verse it was used in, and a side-by-side comparison of up to twenty-five different translations. You can click through to see the exact original words in their sequence which it was translated from. Lexicons and a stack of commentaries are referenced as well. They also share snippets from a few major English translations of each verse so you can see how it was used in context.

This is not designed to tear into the Bible and say it's all wrong. It is meant to help us regain our clarity interpreting its original message and navigate better, sort of like helping us imagine hearing the tone of voice and seeing the body language. It amplifies the richness of the text. Like the Holy Spirit does from inside us, it helps fill out what is missing in written communication as an external physical tool.

Another act of due diligence behind this writing is related to authenticity and purity. It has been made clear as we have found a few of the oldest copies of scripture that a few things have been added over the last 2000 years which weren't original content. For example, while we all know and love the story where Christ defends the adulterous woman by saying *let he who is without sin cast the first stone*, it is not reported to appear in any manuscript until around the 5th century, though it was alluded to as early as possibly the 2nd century. That is still over a century after the life of Christ and the apostles where it was not even discussed, let alone part of canon. It was missing from three texts and out of place in a fourth, being tagged onto the end of the book of *John*.

None of us was alive during those times. We can only look at history objectively and do our best to compile an honest understanding of it as we pray and meditate on the Word. Out of respect for this information, I have not referenced any of those few verses or passages that are questioned as not having been part of the original manuscripts to support this overall message. *It is possible* they were divine revelations or oral traditions intended to be in the message. There are many possible explanations. I'm just going to be honest that nobody alive knows for sure. All we know is what is documented in history. It is worth noting that these discrepancies are few and far between, though. The large majority of manuscripts found all match up, which is a testament to the solidity of the Word.

I will also acknowledge that there were books in the original manuscripts that have since been removed and categorized as apocryphal, which basically means for some reason or another there was doubt about their authenticity or authorship. This includes but is not limited to books such as *Tobit, Enoch, Judith, 1 & 4 Maccabees,* and *Wisdom,* though some Bibles have kept them. There are many other works considered apocryphal that were not compiled in the early Bible such as *the Secret Book of John, Pistis Sophia, Gospel of Thomas,* and others. There are still further works that derivate from Abrahamic faiths such as *The Zohar, Sefer Yetzirah,* and others.

    I will not be pulling references from any of these books. I have not read them all, but what I have read thus far has involved a blend of information, some of which I agree with and some of which I do not. If you'd like to do a study on any of them for yourself, feel free. Just wait to do it until you have developed a strong understanding of the core Biblical message. Use that foundational knowledge to discern the truth in what you are reading.

    The good news is that even in all that study, all of this information essentially changed nothing about what I originally set out to share here. Most Christians believe the Bible was made perfect over the course of time by God's influence through man and that its current state is the way God wanted it. In all of my study, I would have to agree. Everything you need to know is in there if you trust the Spirit to guide you in understanding it. That's why this comprehensive study is kept to what is in the canonical scripture. You might utilize other tools for better understanding, but the Bible is all you truly need.

    This has been a difficult undertaking, so I have taken the precaution of comparing a wide array of perspectives on a subject before voicing an opinion about it. Know that this effort reflects a sincere desire to speak only truth when studying the Bible. I do not wish to guide anyone to false understanding. That does not make me infallible. I try to be sharp, but I accept the reality that I can only try my best. True humility demands that we accept our ability to make mistakes even with the best intentions. It is *always* advisable to do your own studies, fact check, and pray for discernment. God *is* infallible.

    This approach is about laying out a path you can walk today so that you're able to follow in the footsteps that Christ left along the beach of life as closely as possible (*Matthew 16:24-26*). We may not be perfect, but we should still always try our best in life. Through sharing my humble perspective of trying to do this for myself, this book will share what this journey has looked like for me. It is my hope that my life lessons can provide you with further insight.

There's a saying that a fool learns from his own mistakes, but a wise man will learn from the mistakes of others. Experience is a slow teacher at the cost of making many mistakes along the road. If I can help you learn a few lessons from reading instead of experiencing them the hard way, it is worth the effort. I lived in sin, but through faith God managed to help me heal it. Once I truly accepted Christ in my heart, he helped me learn the error in my ways so that I could **repent** (*meaning to express sincere regret for one's actions, to turn away from sin or evil, to change*), **atone** (*meaning reparation for a wrong, to pay back or make amends*), and **forgive** with the same grace used to forgive me.

He turned my mistakes into blessings by helping me learn the lessons they brought me. He made riches feel empty and poor feel unlimitedly wealthy. He brought peace to my soul and taught me how to trust through his truth and wisdom. He poured Spirit into my heart and showed me real love. After being saved, he inspired me towards growth just like I have seen so very many others testify (*Hebrews 10:24, Ephesians 2:10*).

Hopefully it will bring depth to your understanding of my favorite passage, *Colossians 3:11-17*. Go look this one up! This one flows best in the NIV translation, but it's interesting to compare how different it sounds in comparison to others. I find there is a certain power in turning to the passage and seeing it's words like facts right there on the page. It reinforces that I'm not just pulling this stuff out of a hat, and helps the Spirit be heard. *2 Timothy 3:16* tells us *All scripture is given by inspiration of God, and is profitable for doctrine, for reproof, for correction, for instruction in righteousness.*

My studies for very many years prior to accepting Christ were of science, psychology, health, and even some other world religions. Once I began to dig deep into the study of Christ, I also evaluated how this information cross applied and what perhaps didn't line up so well. I will not turn to it much, though, because this is about developing emotional intelligence through the Word. We can't try to science our way out of the natural growth process God has provided. Some things have no shortcut, and you simply must go straight through them.

It is in our nature to want to be in control of things. Having been made in God's image, that only makes sense, right? A desire for order is instinctual. Plus, control feels like safety to many people. It's the chaos of uncertainty that tends to strike nerves. Know that I understand this feeling. I wouldn't judge you even if you stood directly in front of me, but I hope you will keep in mind as you read that I can't possibly be judging your actions when I've never met you to know any of them. It is important to me that I don't just share the gospel of peace, but I do my best to live it with integrity. That means I acknowledge who has the authority to judge you, and that is not anyone other than God (*Matthew 7:1-5, Luke 6:37-42, James 4:11-12, Romans 2:1-3, etc.*).

    I only seek to be a catalyst for the necessary healing process to begin in each individual who reads this book so that in turn we can all work together to help heal the world. There are simply certain questions we need to be asking ourselves, and once we have answered them, we need to be certain we are living in a way that is not hypocritical to our beliefs. *Who am I to myself? Who am I to others? Who am I to God? What needs to change about my answers?* (*Isaiah 55:7-11, Lamentations 3:40, Romans 7:15-24*)

    After all I have seen and experienced, I am 100% a believer without an iota of doubt. I would like to think of myself as a modern disciple. Christ said your love for one another will prove to the world that you are my disciples (*John 13:35*). I try to share all the love I can. I am also of the belief that the time of Revelation is upon us, and we should proclaim that Christ is coming! I certainly don't want that to be a fearful thought for anyone. It's supposed to be an overall positive thing where true evil is finally purged and God's kingdom is instated (*Revelation 21:4*).

    That being said, I know how finicky some people get hearing this terminology. Many are afraid of false prophets as we have been warned would come in these times (*Matthew 7:15 & 24:4-5, 2 Timothy 3:13*), so again, I certainly encourage you to study and pray over everything I share. I will spark the thought process, but Christ should rightfully be doing the teaching. (*Matthew 23:1-12*)

    I am a woman speaking up for God, and there will be some who shun this entire message solely based on that alone. *I know you can't win them all.* I refuse to turn away from what I feel has been placed on my heart to share (*Isaiah 61:1, Matthew 10:27*). The Bible tells of many women who were used for the glory of God. Some examples can be found in *Deborah in Judges 4-5, Luke 2:36-38, Romans 16:1-7, Philippians 4:3, Acts 13:49, 2nd John*, and others.

Acts 2:17-18 says both men and women will prophecy. He does not call the qualified - He qualifies the called.

Basically, as long as God's message echoes through me, I don't care what you call me. Saying I'm a penguin wouldn't magically turn me into one, nor would it change anything I have said here. I think this is part of why God referred to Himself as *I am that I am* (*Exodus 3:14*). He didn't care what He was called as long as the message was clear. Labels don't change who you are. There are many things that God is, but it seems He wanted us to know Him by His character.

Ultimately, I acknowledge your free will to believe as you so choose and pray that I will receive that mutual level of respect. **Your soul is your responsibility, and I cannot decide beliefs for it**. I can only lovingly share with you what has helped and guided me. Even if you disagree with my words, I hope they at least serve to be thought provoking.

My biggest pet peeve is hypocrisy - people who say one thing yet do another. Rather than be angry at the problem that has clearly arisen from poor communication skills and emotional suppression, it is my hope to help people develop their emotional intelligence. Stop allowing people to think that strength is suffering in silence! It takes much more strength to speak and to do it with loving wisdom guiding your words. There are certainly going to be times where silence is appropriate, especially if it allows you to think *before* you speak. It simply isn't meant to be perpetual. That is balance in action.

We must incorporate the Word in the foundations of self to heal this. Our primary focus here will be on the behavioral aspect of the message and how it applies to our communication skills. This is all about answering the question of what comes *next* after you feel you have accepted Christ. How do we proceed? We will dive into understanding how we grow as well as how communication is the root cause and solution to most problems.

Remember - God the Father represents *law*, and Christ represents *love*. Well the Holy Spirit is the next step in the path of humanity's evolution of spiritual expression from thought to word to deed - the Holy Spirit represents the ***action*** that results from the internal character built in our thoughts and words! It is how God reveals Himself to us in a more intimate way as we learn to live lives that are holy in His sight. The Holy Spirit indwells within us (*1*

Corinthians 6:19), and greater is He that is in us than he that is in the world. (*1 John 4:4*)

Understand that when Christ was alive, the New Testament was being written, and every time he references *scripture,* he is talking about the Old Testament. For those who are unaware, the *Torah* or *Pentateuch* of Jewish faith is the first five books of the Bible (*Genesis, Exodus, Leviticus, Numbers, Deuteronomy*). Christ said in *Luke 24:44*, *These are the words which I spake unto you, while I was yet with you, that all things must be fulfilled which were written in the law of Moses and in the prophets and in the Psalms concerning me.*

If you would like to hear a remarkable testimony from a man who was once an Israeli Jew who, like many, refused to read the New Testament or *Isaiah 53*, there is a video called *Jesus in the Old Testament* presented by *Amir Tsarfati*. He shares about his journey of identifying Christ as the Messiah of the Old Testament more thoroughly and beautifully than I can possibly imagine replicating. ***To find this video and many others I think you might enjoy that relate to or expand on the topics covered here, I have created a playlist on YouTube by the same name as this book. I do not necessarily agree with every single word or thought presented in each video. I have done my best to accumulate videos I agree with for the most part to help you branch out in your study. Practice your discernment.***

Here we will dive into unifying the Bible in its current structure as a whole utilizing the ten commandments in the Old Testament and the gospel message, especially the sermon on the mount. It focuses on how we were *all* called to repentance for the forgiveness of sins, which is clearly stated in *Luke 24:44-49* and *Acts 17:30*. Repentance is a two-fold concept that reflects not only an expression of sincere remorse for your sins, but it also requires you to forsake or turn away from that sin. I can only hope that my efforts help rejuvenate the message and will benefit anyone, whether they come from any Abrahamic religion or are even atheist. There is a powerful behavioral message here that will benefit all with ears to hear. The differences are important though, so study before making decisions about them.

We need ways to see what we normally would not see. Just like you look in a glass mirror to pop a pimple for example, studying the Bible provides us a spiritual mirror so we can see more clearly to purge the spiritual dirt from our lives. It is healthy to ask yourself how your mind is filling in that 93% of missing data as I communicate with you right now. You are reading my words, but what does my voice sound like in your head? What inflection are you putting on sentences? Is there a different way to read it that would change the meaning? I try to choose vivid language that is difficult to misconstrue, but it is still possible to do. Be sure that as you read, you are aware that my tone is always *intended* to be peaceful, calm, positive, and to encourage you to reflect. If you're not hearing it that way in your mind as you read, that is coming from you.

As far as where I derived the outline for this journey, one of the biggest claims to fame for Joseph Campbell was that he identified what is called the **hero's journey**. He outlined three major parts which break down into seventeen subcategories outlining a road map that he felt more or less encompassed every major heroic tale. He derived it from the study of mythology and psychology in the same school of thought as Carl Jung. For now, I'm just providing an idea of what to expect. The call to adventure will sound later.

Just to be crystal clear, I am NOT regarding the Bible as mythology by applying this process to it. I do believe the Bible is all real and true. These documented events happened in real life. We simply live in a time where people idolize superheroes. I believe we can each be even better heroes than those we have admired in movies when we model our lives after a truly great hero - Christ. While the heroes in movies win battles with violence, Christ taught us to fly above the storm as eagles do and win battles with love and wisdom.

On a final note, I will not be tainting the delivery of this message by talking about hell here. It would veer too far away from the main point. This book is geared towards forward progress, getting away from fear towards love. The thought of hell breeds fear. Focus on your relationship with God breeds love. Part of this journey is about developing trust that you are redeemed (*Isaiah 43:1-2*) and the endurance not to lose faith. If you follow the process laid out here with sincerity and truth in your heart, hell should not be a concern. You will have made strong and sincere effort, learned how to follow Christ's footsteps in intimate detail, and been encouraged to apply it to your life.

Before the call sounds, I invite you to take a moment of ***honest*** reflection. On the following page, write who you feel you are right now. What do you feel you know about God? In what state is your relationship with Him? What questions or concerns are you struggling with? Do you believe in truth in your heart that you have already received salvation? Do you feel you have work you need to do or would like to pursue? What are your strengths and weaknesses? Lay it all bare on the paper, then go to a quiet place and pray about it. Ask God to accompany you as you continue your journey through this book. There are no wrong answers when it comes to how you feel about yourself. Tell God how you feel, and ask Him from the bottom of your heart to help guide you to deeper understanding. This will prepare you to hear the call to your personal adventure and leave you a point of reference in the future to see how far you've come.

*Part One:
Separation
(aka Planting a Seed)*

1. *The Call to Adventure*

Awake! Awake!
Put on thy strength, O Zion;
put on thy beautiful garments,
Jerusalem, the Holy City!
For the uncircumcised and the unclean
will no longer enter you.
Shake thyself from the dust;
arise, and sit down, O Jerusalem.
Loose thyself from the bands of thy neck,
O captive daughter of Zion.
For thus saith the Lord,
Ye have sold yourselves for nought,
and ye shall be redeemed without money.
Isaiah 52:1-3

There are a multitude of ways that you can first come to hear about the Bible. Maybe you saw a cross and wondered what it represented, or your parents took you to church as a child. Perhaps you saw a Bible in the library or took a religion class in college. Did someone make a joke or reference to God on tv? Maybe you even encountered a bold soul who asked you if you had yet accepted Christ as your personal Lord and Savior, and you looked at them blankly in confusion. However it happened, that first time the Bible was brought into your awareness, *you were called* to this adventure (*Isaiah 42:6-7*).

The seed was planted, and you'll never be able to remove your knowledge of its existence from your awareness. You had no idea who Christ was, maybe even no clue about religion or God. Then suddenly the information was presented, and your heart and mind were forced to reconcile the information. This is our first encounter with cognitive dissonance in faith among what will be many more. *Cognitive dissonance* is best described as that moment when you receive new information that is contradictory to what you believed to be true. Suddenly you must decide if you were right or wrong. Is there really more to learn than what I thought I knew or is this new information a lie?

There are people who will receive more tangible and pointed

callings from God if they are to fulfill a specific task for Him. You may have experienced that as well. However, we are focusing on the development from day one here, and everyone is called in some way or another (*Jeremiah 31:34, Hebrews 8:11, Matthew 24:14*).

Humans are instinctively afraid of things we don't understand. In *Hebrews 5:13-14* those who do not yet understand how to distinguish good from evil are compared to an infant who must drink milk because they are not yet ready for solid food (*see also 1 Peter 2:2-3*). A strange social stigma has arisen surrounding the notion of attempting to come to faith or understand righteousness and live by it. People seem to feel judged when they don't think they meet someone else's standards, though that certainly shouldn't be the case. Fear and being defensive of their position is often the resulting action.

There is a saying that your opinion of me is a reflection of you, meaning what you attack me for is about you more than it is about me. I am not your enemy for seeking truth and wanting to share it with you. I find that the only way to advance to solid food in scriptural study is to accept that we are in that aforementioned time where great deception is prophesied to occur, and that the masses will follow it. This means it's not intended to be offensive when someone disagrees with you. It's just something we must work through because we desire truth (*Galatians 4:16*). It is the truth that sets us free.

In the grand scheme of humanity, we are equivalent to an eighteen-year-old who graduated high school and goes out to live on their own for the first time. We are hormonal and afraid, yet also impulsive, and think we know so much more than we do. We feel unbreakable! It seems like our general mentality is that if we can hold a rectangular piece of metal and glass in our hand and access the entire internet, then what could we possibly not know yet?

We are afraid to be honest, to speak our truth, and to accept how people respond to it. Fear of conflict creates suppression and manipulation. We are afraid to be wrong, even though being deceived makes us the victim, not the offender. We start fighting so hard to be right that sometimes we forget why we were fighting in the first place *or* go the opposite direction and abandon seeking truth because it feels easier than change. We have to work towards overcoming our *fight or flight* response before growth of any value can occur.

Humans were given free will to live this experience. God said seek me out with your whole heart and you'll find me (*Jeremiah 29:13*). If we are told to *seek* God in order to find Him and *choose* to accept Christ into our hearts, then there must be other decisions God will not make for us.

This doesn't exclude predestination. It is clear that some people are called and led. *Revelation 7 & 14* speaks of a large group of the elect who are foreknown by God and cannot be deceived (*Romans 8:28-30*). Their appointed destiny is considered unavoidable. God lives outside of time in eternity, so it would make sense that He has already seen all of time occur. I imagine there is some blend of free will, divine destiny, and guiding hands that lead us to the right place. Maybe God sees all possibilities and knows what is most likely to occur, giving Him the ability to interject and guide towards certain outcomes.

Anxiety, stress, suffering, and feelings of lack have become a normal state of being in this day and age. I think this results from trying to handle *everything* ourselves instead of asking God for help. It leads to a state where we feel being defensive or offensive is the only way to be. In truth, center is the best place. Sometimes we step up to the plate of responsibility, and other times we lean on God. **Grace** reflects a fluid blend of both which requires a certain level of wisdom and understanding. That's where peace resides and the bigger picture is not just understood but lived. Until we begin to learn and appreciate how to balance all areas of our lives through God's guidance, we can never know perfect love.

Note that there is a huge difference between being lukewarm versus being balanced and peaceful. Christ warns us that if we are lukewarm we will be spit out of his mouth (*Revelation 3:16*). Personally, I won't drink room temperature water. It's gross. It has to be a cold beverage like ice water or tea, or it has to be hot like cider. I feel this is in reference to being lazy and indecisive, specifically in regards to following the path he laid out for us. We must make good choices and live life in the action of honesty, not rest on our laurels (*James 1:23-24*).

Being balanced, however, is a distinct choice made daily requiring a willpower which only faith has ever provided me. It means we identify the weight of our personal responsibilities and needs while still accounting for the feelings and lives of others. What God wants from us is the filter through which we handle both sides.

In a conflict, we can acknowledge all sides to the story hold at least partial truth based on the idea that someone legitimately *experienced* something they believed to be true. If their experience was based on false information, we are then able to identify it.

Identifying balance is a necessity for following God. We just have to know the difference between true and false balance so we are not indulging evil (*Proverbs 11:1*). We are balanced in the will and goodness of God, not balancing good with a blend of evil. There is a difference, and we will explore that in detail here.

Love is such a grand concept that it is a scale or spectrum of experiences. One end demonstrates the lack of any love and the other end lacks any restrictions. We have to cut off and discard the outlier behaviors a bit at a time as we focus in on the middle until the middle is what is left.

That doesn't mean we accept bad behaviors or allow them to continue. Keep the good, drop the bad. *Zechariah 13:7-9* and *Ezekiel 5:12-13* allude to this concept, and *Revelation* also talks about things being divided into different sections of thirds in many places. The negative extreme is represented by fire and the positive extreme is represented by water. The true balance is represented by spirit, because it guides us to that life. I believe this is why we must be baptized in fire, water, and spirit (*Matthew 3:11, Luke 3:16, John 3:5*). This will be discussed more later.

Negative Extremes	True Balance	Positive Extremes
Strict Legalism	Law & Grace	Strict Antinomianism
Judgment	Compassion & Mercy	Forgiveness
Hate	Wisdom & Respect	Love
Slavery/Oppression	Teamwork & Friends	Free Will/Chaos
Anger/Fear	Peace & Reason	Charity/Trust

That list could go on forever. We must have both mercy and justice to maintain a true balance. Isn't that what has defined a fair and just ruler throughout history, a reflection of both? Knowing this, consider for a moment what it would mean for Christ to be the Word of God. He had to speak in a human body in order to share the gospel, right? Where is your voice box? It falls directly in between your mind and your heart. They must both be working in unison to understand the concepts Christ taught. Even his words were spoken from a place of balance. To be all mind is robotic, and to be all heart is chaotic. When you utilize both, you either get pure insanity by pulling each to the outer extremes of their potential, or you come to the center in a balanced harmony.

Both sides of the spectrum hold some benefit in healthy application. God encompasses all things on the spectrum, but He reflects all that is good about them. A dose of fear is sometimes the only effective motivator to change negative habits. Free will is great if we draw reasonable boundaries around it, thusly providing that small dose of fear through things like laws and moral codes. They wall in the ego and heart which can become a beast within us if left unchecked. The downside there is that they must be enforced, otherwise they are useless. A law without a consequence for breaking it is nothing more than a formally worded suggestion, a wall made of paper instead of concrete. Basically, the thickness and stability of your walls of law revolve around your willpower and self-control. These are very mind centered things.

If we had unrestricted free will which is tied more to the impulsive nature of the feeling heart, then it would end up looping back around to falling under the fear category, because you would never feel able to trust that someone else wasn't going to harm you. People would constantly be defensive or offensive motivated by paranoia and self-preservation. *Nobody wants chaos any more than they want slavery.*

The interesting part is that when we analyze love we find many spectrums within it. Every personality trait can be expressed in either a loving or hateful way. My favorite metaphor for this involves light. When you shine white light through a prism, it creates a rainbow. We have determined that this means white light contains all those colors within it. *1 John 1:5* tells us that God is all light with no darkness in Him whatsoever. This says to me that the love of God when put through the prism of life on earth can create every color.

These colors are symbolic of personality traits, giftings, strengths and weaknesses (*Isaiah 11:2-3*), and each one falls on its own spectrum of shades from dark to light based on the free will choices made by each soul. Just like the parable about the talents (*Matthew 25:14-30*), you decide whether the gifts you are given are used wisely or foolishly. In our journey to understand perfect love, it will be necessary to at least have basic understanding of how to be bright and loving with each color or trait, eventually allowing us to live in the presence of that white light of God again when we exit the prism of this life and enter the kingdom.

This is the life long journey we all embark upon of identifying how to live happy, healthy, fulfilled lives as individuals without hurting anyone else in the process. It's a daring goal to attempt to leave the world in better shape than you found it! We must embrace traits like kindness, understanding, empathy, forgiveness, and much more that require us to sacrifice of ourselves to the benefit of others. It means we must learn gratitude and appreciation and find joy in living caring lives instead of feeling hurt or obligated by the needs of others who equally want the same fulfillment in life that we ourselves do. We must be able to honor the free will of others to choose for themselves while prohibiting dangerous actions and still doing what we believe is right, *aka righteous*.

Every culture has some concept of the scales of justice, trying to balance good versus evil. Egyptians spoke of weighing the heart against a feather, the Bible talks about the measure of a man, and so on. The scale is even used as a symbol to represent our legal system where we have trial by an unbiased jury, and a verdict and sentencing are issued based on weighing all the evidence presented. All of these are representative of the idea that what you do in life matters and you will be held accountable for the whole of your choices, which admittedly for some people can be scary (*2 Corinthians 5:10*).

Eventually we realize two things if we care enough to try to understand the human experience. **One**, love covers a multitude of sins. (*1 Peter 4:8*) The King James Version says *charity* in that verse instead of *love*, and others say *grace*. The original word these translations are based on is *G26 - agaph* - which means love. The Greek had six words for love. This particular one means love for everyone, so it has a more universal context. Note that a *multitude of sins* is different than saying *all sins*. **Two**, we need to stop worrying about being measured on the scales of judgment which breeds a feeling of competition or comparison to one another and *instead* try to understand how to be more in line with what set the balance in the first place - God.

It occurred to me one day there is only one thing that is fully selfish, fully selfless, and fully Godly all at the same time - PEACE. Think about it for a minute. Isn't that the only thing that benefits everyone? It appears to be the ultimate pinnacle expression of love. As you start walking that tightrope on the narrow path of the gospel of peace, you may fall off many times. That is normal, and it's where we learn the lessons that help us polish the journey further.

Mistakes are opportunities to learn, so don't beat yourself up about them. Just work through the process of forgiveness and grow from them. I may be trying to help you avoid some mistakes, but I can't help you avoid them all. Some things just have to be experienced to reach our hearts on the level God needs us to understand in order to fulfill His plans for our lives.

Don't skip the part where you learn from it and apply the lessons to your life! It is important when we work on self-development to look in the mirror with honesty, but it is equally important not to judge ourselves too harshly (*James 1:22-25*). Growth should never create unhealthy feelings of depression, even though it can certainly be a saddening shock when we crack our ego wide open and first realize we have flaws. Don't let it intimidate you. Let self-awareness *inspire* you. Personal growth can be a fun project if you allow it.

Just acknowledge that the goal is change, and that is something that takes time and patience. There will be guidance and support as long as you ask for it. Pray daily! With time and practice, you will become a pro! You will walk that tightrope just as well as you can walk down the street. You'll be able to do tricks on that tightrope, flips, balancing acts, you name it!

This calling is important! There is a spiritual battlefield in our hearts and minds, and if the enemy wins, they take your soul. My purpose here is to engage in an adventure with you, where you learn how to throw on the armor of God and realize how heroic it is to be devout in faith with thought, word, and deed being in unison with God's will for us! It's not just about achieving the bare minimum of saving your soul. Here we will focus on growing into a more Christ-like person, healing, and eventually leading others *by your example* with love and forgiveness in your heart. I want you to live the truth of love, not just think about it.

There will be many trials along the way, but Christ promises to grant the overcomers with many rewards! Be careful, though. It is my belief that utilizing rewards like this as your motivator has the power to corrupt people. They are a reward to be made aware of, not your driving force. In fact, once we dig into the study of the behavioral message, it will become clear that if they are your motivator for being a good person and following God, then it may go so far as being greed and idolatry. I have stated it here for the sake of awareness and to keep in line with the hero's journey trope.

How do we claim victory? The original Greek word used for *overcome* in these promises is G3529 - *nikao's* or *nike*. That same word is used for *overcome* in *1 John 5:5. Who is he that overcometh the world but he that believeth that Jesus is the Son of God?* This means to complete the quest and receive the promises, we must seek out Christ and accept him completely in our hearts, believing no matter what trials we face.

How do we know we have truly 100% accepted him in our hearts? In *John 14:21*, Christ tells us *He that hath my commandments, and keepeth them, he it is that loveth me: and he that loveth me shall be loved of my Father, and I will love him, and will manifest myself to him.* We will study the transition from the law of sin and death to the law of liberty (*James 2:12-13*) to having true divine nature with grace as your character.

I am fascinated with numbers. It is apparent when you get into Biblical study that they hold symbolic meaning which will be referenced in this book from time to time. I personally theorize that if we can create coding for all software using 0 and 1, then maybe God created everything in the universe using 0-9. That is part of what makes the Hebrew language so fascinating. The characters can represent both numbers and letters, the balance of order and expression. The same character is both qualitative and quantitative.

I find it intriguing that the most important divine numbers always seem to be primes. That doesn't mean all primes represent good things, but all the good ones are frequently primes. That means the number is only divisible by itself and *one*, indicating a certain strength or unshakeable prominence that only God or the concept reflected by the number itself could destroy. Primes are always odd since all even numbers are divisible by two, so feel free to take it as a compliment if you're ever called odd.

I bring this up because I read a book once called *The Biblical Meaning of Numbers from One to Forty* by Dr. Stephen E. Jones. He believed the prime number seventeen represented victory, which is exactly what I hope you will receive through this! Seventeen steps in a hero's journey in order to obtain victory feels quite appropriate.

Furthermore, when you add the numbers 1-17 together

(*1+2+3+4... etc.*), you get 153 which is specifically stated as the number of fish the disciples caught when they followed Christ's instructions to fish from the right side of the boat instead of the left where they were catching nothing. (*John 21:1-14*) Throughout the Bible, the left side or path is symbolic of legalism, severity, and fear. The right side or path is symbolic of love, grace, mercy, and forgiveness. *Ezekiel 4:4-6* implies that Israel is the left side and Judah is the right, but you will find many passages that detail both sides.

Christ was telling them they would bring more people to God, or catch more fish, by fishing from the right side with love. However, it is important to identify that both the left and right side are part of the *same* one boat floating in the *same* one spot, implying that this was a lesson in *how* to deliver the information, *not* that the message of God's will itself has changed. Christ is a repairer of the breech, and we are all supposed to be one through him. He tore down the wall between the Jews and the nations and invited them in. You don't get rid of the left side of the boat just because you're standing on the right side. That is a sure way to drown.

Write below what you remember about the first time you heard about the Bible. Do you remember how you felt, or what your first impressions were? What happened? Be honest. Explain in your own words what you are being called to learn and understand through this particular journey.

_____
_____
_____
_____
_____
_____
_____
_____
_____
_____
_____
_____
_____
_____
_____
_____
_____
_____

2. Refusal of The Call

*Many shall be purified, and made white, and tried;
but the wicked shall do wickedly
and none of the wicked shall understand;
but the wise shall understand.*
Daniel 12:10

Is God real? It's certainly a doozy of a question to wrap an analytical mind around once it has been opened to the possibility. Think for a moment about how difficult that question is to objectively answer in the year 2018AD. The New Testament is over 2000 years old and the Old Testament can date Job back to around 1500BC. Time has made us far, far removed from knowing any of the people who lived in those times directly. Record keeping wasn't nearly as pristine then as it is in the technology age. Languages used then are not commonly used today, so there is a language and translation barrier to sort through. Science cannot yet prove God is real but has many *theories* of how things exist without being divinely constructed. Historians still search to validate the vast wealth of information presented in the Bible. We have seen countless world religions that seem to contradict it.

The modern world can be overwhelming for someone seeking to honestly learn about faith. The language of so many different Biblical translations could easily confuse anyone. We are warned in scripture that we live in the time of the great deception (*Matthew 24:4-5, 2 Thessalonians 2, Acts 20:29, 2 Corinthians 11:13-15, etc.*). It's valuable to differentiate that *deception may be the fault of the deceiver, but seeking truth is the responsibility of the believer.* Awareness of the problem is only the first step. Professional opinions fall all across the board, and times are just way different than they were 2000 years ago. It can be difficult to sort through all the varying and contradictory information available to us at the touch of a button.

Believe me, being able to write this book took years of digging and sorting through contradicting beliefs and plenty of prayer. Writing wasn't my original intention for doing the study. It just became the fruit of a heart and mind that do not believe truth should be withheld regarding such crucial concepts. So many times I thought I had it figured out only to be corrected again. It has most certainly been a refinement process, but eventually it all leveled out and I felt peace in it.

Some days it feels like the only thing that is working in God's favor is the Bible. Do you follow Occam's Razor that the simplest answer is the correct one? In that mess, nothing sounds like a simple answer, so even that could be difficult. *Or* do you take a chance and try to understand the pile of prophecies and personal testimonies collected into this one book?

While we all value honesty, I feel it is a concept that is dying in the thick of a competitive society. Nobody wants to be lied to, but plenty of people seem fine with telling lies. This behavior over long periods of time has eaten away at what was once known as *trust*. Most people when confronted with any specific situation would caution you to be wary of others. It's common knowledge that the world can be a dangerous place. We have identity theft, fake news, robberies, cheaters, and plenty of people willing to manipulate and twist the truth for their personal benefit. If we truly live in a time of great deception, then truth may be the most valuable characteristic there is!

When you combine all of these problems, it would only be natural for any person to look at the Bible with doubt, fear, confusion, and uncertainty. What makes this one book more than just another book full of stories? *Faith* is what fills the space between what we know and don't know. It is the distance between facts and our questions about the unknown. It is the most fundamental thing Christ asked of us, the first step we take, and something we must hold close to our hearts for our entire lives. *Hebrews 11:1* defines it so eloquently - *Now faith is the substance of things hoped for, the evidence of things not seen.* Read that verse a few times over, and really digest what it means. Read the rest of *chapter 11* for a wonderful list of people who triumphed in faith. *By faith* all things are possible (*Matthew 19:26*).

When you are first confronted with the Word, it will require a leap of faith to take it seriously. I would like to say it's easy to come to faith, and for some people it is. For most people though, that would be sugar coating the truth in a way that creates unrealistic expectations. You can't bottle it or buy it. It's invisible, but when it is real in your heart it feels tangible. It cannot be given, but you must choose to accept it as something you cherish.

You could be someone who sits in a state of disbelief for a very long time. My parents both involved me in the respective churches they attended when I was a child. One was northern Methodist, the other southern Baptist. I taught Sunday school in high school, sang, and even accompanied on the piano and organ for church for several years. I actively participated in multiple youth groups which I became very engaged in. Yet even after all that, when I went out into the world on my own, I wasn't yet convicted in my belief enough and slowly strayed from anything that resembled faith I might have had.

Over many years I sought answers everywhere else. My brain just couldn't process the reality or priceless value of the Bible. I lived in sin without truly realizing it, justifying my actions through science and attempts at logic. I thought I was relatively smart and had a good heart and hoped that was all that mattered at the end of the day. There was just always something missing...

I often had moments of feeling disconnected or numb. I battled depression, serious obesity peaking at 345 lbs at 5'9", and often lacked that sense of purpose we all desire out of life. Accordingly, I surrounded myself with many people who felt the same. These people only reinforced the distance I felt from faith, and it dwindled down to just a tiny flickering ember of hope that there was something more. That ember was buried where it would rarely come to the forefront of my thoughts. It was drowned out in my concerns over finances and general life issues. I was still trying to be a good person and make good choices, but life was enough to face without adding this confusion to the mix. At least, that's how it felt then.

When I step back and look around at the world today, I see so much hurt and suffering. *Don't you?* I can't help but notice that while many choose to deny faith all together, the common denominator I see is that they often tend to be the same people who express a feeling of something lacking in their lives constantly. They always express feeling a hole in some part of their hearts that nothing seems to fill, a missing piece. In my humble experience in this life, I have found the difference to be that people of faith have somewhere to turn when they feel like they're at the bottom of the barrel. People without faith see darkness and nothingness when they hit that point. *How lonely is that?* It's a matter of what perspective you see when you look into the unknown. It changes a person's entire personality when you see the mystery of God there instead of nothing.

In all my efforts to understand the workings of the human mind and emotions, I have never found anything more perfect than the Bible. I believe that from a psychology standpoint it exhibits genius far beyond anything humanity has ever demonstrated being capable of concocting on its own. I mean, let's be honest, if we as a species even followed *one* of the ten commandments - *thou shalt not kill* - we would have world peace, or at least a solid foundation to it.

Why do we oppose developing our peaceful nature? *Human* nature leans more towards the animalistic, Darwinian behavior and chooses to be driven by fear, but *divine* nature is led by love. The Bible gives extensive clear examples of what you should or should not do in a peaceful society, like learning to turn the other cheek (*Matthew 5:38-45*). Eventually when you realize that, your motivation to follow it is because you love the message and what it represents, not that you are afraid of judgment or punishment.

Wouldn't it take an eternal, infinitely wise God who created us to be able to put that all in one book with so much precision? Plus, even if you studied the scripture and fully accepted and implemented its instructions into your life but still felt confusion about whether God was real or not, you would still be contributing to building a better society as a whole and have accepted divine character in your heart. I can't imagine anyone doing all of that and not becoming convinced in the process that God is *real*.

Therefore, maybe there is no better instruction manual to life than the map laid out for us in the Bible. It is healthy to be humble enough to accept a good example when it's set and learn from it. It is also healthy to remember that some of the examples in the Bible are meant to teach us what not to do, and we shouldn't judge the book until we have read and understood it. Wouldn't you rather do that with some faith in your heart and a belief that your prayers are answered? I think yes, but to each their own.

While choosing Him every day builds a deeply beautiful relationship, we also have the ability to not choose Him, whether it be for one day or all of them. He has allowed that experience to occur. Any good parent knows *anything I do for you, you do not learn to do for yourself.* Sometimes out of love, we give a hungry man a fish. Other times, it's more appropriate to teach him how to fish. Yet other times, it is more valuable to let a man figure out how to fish on his own and nudge him in the right direction if necessary. God knows what approach is best for each individual's greatest good in each situation, and I believe He answers every prayer accordingly.

This has been demonstrated through the eras as well. God gave us the sustenance of the commandments through Moses, then Christ taught us to be fishers of men with truth and grace, then we entered this age of the Spirit where He is behind the veil (*John 1:17*). It makes me think of teaching a child to ride a bike. First you get them on the bike. Then you hold the seat so they find their balance, walking with them as they start to pedal forward. Eventually you have to let go so they do it on their own, and you wave and smile. They look at you for that boost of encouragement to know they can do it! If they fall off, you kiss the booboos and clean it up, then help them get back on the bike and try again. Eventually they ride that bike straight back into your driveway and give you a big hug.

I have found that I can usually look back down the road and see clearly why things happened as they did. Some things are only clear in hindsight. Sometimes in order to move on to better blessings we must go through the pain of separating from something no longer meant for us. Many things won't make sense in the moment, but that's ok. We live, and we learn. It's time to do some learning now.

Advancing from your first reaction to hearing about the Bible, what were your second and third? As your curiosity started generating questions to which you wanted answers, what kind of picture started to form in your mind as you collected information? What has been the hardest thing for you to process about the concept of God? Did you experience deep trauma in your life and find yourself asking why God wasn't there for you in your time of need? Are you just too skeptical to find something supernatural to be credible? Did you grow up in an environment that did not support or teach faith? Did you grow up in an environment that did teach faith but made you feel unwelcome? Write all the things that have been holding you back from God.

_____
_____
_____
_____
_____
_____

3. Supernatural Aid

Trust in the Lord with all thine heart,
And lean not unto thine own understanding.
In all thy ways acknowledge him,
and he shall direct thy paths.
Proverbs 3:5-6

What must happen to push you over the edge to be a serious seeker of the truth and wisdom of God? What gets you over the hump of disbelief to the *need* to know and seek God with your whole heart? Once you have committed to taking up the quest, what tools should be in your arsenal to prepare you for a journey of this nature before you depart? How will God help you along the way?

Testimony

My very first encounter with what was undeniably a supernatural experience was not a positive one. Looking back, there may have been instances prior to that, but I chalked them up to imagination or coincidence. The year was 2010. I was in my early 20's and had been spending time with a friend. He and I were slowly splitting a bottle of blackberry wine and playing video games. We didn't even finish the bottle, so we weren't anywhere near drunk. He started to act somewhat tired and set down his controller to lay down on the couch, so I kept playing by myself.

After a few minutes he stood up and walked to the opposite side of the room. I then saw him contort, bending over backwards in an almost disjointed way that I don't think a person should be able to bend. He started making these low, growling noises. Eventually he stood back up and walked towards me slowly, speaking in a language I have never heard before in that low, growly voice far from his own. He stopped a few feet in front of me, looking at me like he was inspecting me while moving around in a sort of animalistic shiftiness.

I froze. I mean I was caught completely off guard. We had just been laughing and having fun a few minutes prior. I had no clue what to do or how to respond to this, so I did the same thing they suggest you do when approached by some kinds of bears - I sat completely still and tried to stay calm. I stared at him for a few moments, and he stared at me. Even in my memory, I just don't feel like the *he* that was staring at me is a memory of my friend. Then he moved slowly towards the couch, laid down, and went to sleep. He woke back up about ten minutes later.

When asked if he remembered what had just happened, he was completely clueless. The last thing he remembered was setting down his controller and laying down to rest. I wasn't sure how to take this, and my mind kept chalking it up to a *very* well executed prank, but deep down it started to solidify a feeling that the supernatural realm was real.

In the end of September 2012, my four year old daughter walked up to me out of nowhere, locked eyes with me, and in a tone with maturity well beyond her age she said, *"You will not be lost anymore."* Then she just walked away and played. I had been sitting silently on the couch, just relaxing when she first approached, so I couldn't for the life of me figure out what would have prompted such a statement out of nowhere. I even made a social media post about exactly how weird it was.

A little over a month later, I ended up on a road trip to California to help a dear friend who was struggling to overcome drug addiction. It's hard to explain, because something like that was not in my normal nature. When he asked me to go with him, I felt like something inside said yes for me, even when my brain was saying no. I believe now that it was an experience the Holy Spirit was nudging me to have, because on that trip I came back to belief in God.

My daughter stayed in my mother's care while I was gone for about a week. From the outside, I knew this trip looked irrational and mischievous. Through my eyes this journey was led entirely by fate and part of God's design in reply to our cries for answers. Sometimes we are lifted up from the ashes, and sometimes we fall and learn priceless lessons from the experience. I can find no logical way to explain many of the things that happened beyond that. It's only in looking back many years later that things started to make any kind of sense. I have only been able to conclude that trip was meant to happen exactly as it did, right down to coming six inches from a car accident.

When we were about forty-five minutes from arriving in Santa Cruz, I hit my breaking point. I had been driving for almost two solid days on about one hour of sleep and needed rest. The interstate had concrete divider walls. They must have been at least eight feet high. I was in the far left lane thinking about whether or not I should stop for gas since I had a quarter tank left. My body felt weak. Heavy eyes would blink closed for a moment, then I'd remind myself to stay awake. Eventually my eyes closed for what I only knew was longer than a blink. It was suddenly dark, warm, and calm... Out of the dark a person-shaped figure made of pure white light emerged from what felt like behind me. I clearly felt its right hand firmly but gently grab my right shoulder, shake it twice, and a loving male voice pointedly but calmly said *wake up.*

When my eyes opened, the car was drifting hard left at about sixty-five mph, within six inches of crashing directly into the median wall. I *instantly* corrected back into my lane. Every other driver was staring at the road like they didn't even see me. There was about a solid half mile radius of clearance from all but one other car. It seemed lucky. Then I became aware of the song on the radio and identified that I had missed about 15-20 seconds of it while my eyes were closed. *How could my eyes have been closed for so long?*

I turned to my friend and started to thank him for waking me but found that he was still sound asleep. In fact, he was lightly snoring. I knew without a shadow of a doubt someone had physically touched my shoulder and woken me up, but the only other person in the car was most definitely not conscious when that happened. I knew I'd felt a guiding hand on that trip, but until then it had been completely metaphorical to me.

This was certainly a lot to process. It's one thing to imagine that maybe there is an invisible force that moves in our lives. This experience was about me seeing the divine with literal form and voice. After what I had seen, I could no longer rationalize around it, and I stopped denying that these things are real. A few days later walking along the beach was when I accepted it as truth.

There was so much running through my mind. Far too much had happened leading me there for this not to have been fate. It appeared that my life had been guided to take this trip then saved from what would have been a deadly car accident. I was meant to come to that beach and stand there, staring at my toes as each step passed. Something or someone made sure it happened at that point in my timeline exactly the way it did.

Footprints came to mind. In this story, a person was walking along the beach with God and saw two sets of footprints in the sand. When the person looked back on their life, they noticed in their times of struggle there was only one set of prints, and they angrily asked God why in their darkest hours He abandoned them. God replied *During your times of trial and suffering, when you see only one set of footprints, it was then that I carried you.*

    I looked down seeing only my footprints lining the beach. Looking back on other times in my life where I'd visited a beach with family, I had never recalled seeing two sets. I thought to myself that a fact and science person would say it obviously just meant I was walking alone as the person in the story assumed. However, I could feel at that moment that I wasn't. I hadn't just come to this beach, I had been led. There was a pull on my soul, a presence.

    I came back to my faith that day, determining that perhaps one set of footprints had meant God had carried me every step of the way (*Isaiah 46:4*). It wasn't about labels or doctrines or churches. Truly I wasn't worried about what to call it. In that moment I felt it was about having faith again, believing there was more than just existence. I imagined God cared far more about faith and living through love than anything else. What would matter going forward was my words and actions. I felt the dying ember reignited in that pure moment. It wasn't immediately important what I labeled myself or my faith, only that I had faith again. I *felt* faith.

    I was thankful for having met this friend. Our conversations over the previous few months were what woke me up to notice my own spiritual needs and surroundings in the first place. I'd become so absorbed in my responsibilities for so long, not wanting to let anyone down, that I neglected to nourish my own soul until it felt unquenchable.

As I continued walking, I came to a rock face. It went up maybe sixty or seventy feet and had a small sort of cliff side. All I knew when I saw it was how much I wanted to be sitting at the top. I found footings, scaling barefoot up and along the side until I reached the spot that caught my eye. I sat with my feet hanging off the edge and felt like I'd found a piece of heaven.

All of the elements flourished together simultaneously in this one spot. The rocks and dirt were below me, strong no matter how long or hard the water crashed into its edges. The massive ocean emanated exquisite shades of blues and greens, sparkling in the sunlight. It was constantly moving and ran deeper and further than I could possibly imagine. The air was fresh and cool with a light breeze carrying it, and I felt grateful for the sun's warmth. It was a constant burning blaze of light, a metaphor for a beautiful soul that ran so deep and fiery that it lit up the entire world. I was awe struck. Elevated into the center of everything, I had found a picture of perfection in this spot.

I closed my eyes to take it all in, marking for myself that this was one of many moments I classify in my heart and mind as a *forever moment*. From then on, whenever I wanted calm perspective and clarity in my life, I would remember that place where I felt alive and connected with faith. My happy place was not a figment of imagination, but a fixed point where I had felt inner peace and experienced living on a whole new level.

The rest of the trip was profound but personal. The details aren't relevant in this context. What's important is that we both came back from Santa Cruz with a renewed sense of self, and a desire to take control of our lives from new perspectives. I determined I wasn't happy living where we did anymore. I felt like a robot just scraping by as a single working mom, and that place held emotional baggage for me that brought up memories every time I saw the places attached to them. There had to be a way to live a happy and fulfilling personal life in balance with my parenting responsibilities. I identified that I needed to find that balance.

There were other spiritual experiences over the years that followed. I also faced many trials, which I will share more later on. Let's just say I can definitely relate to the book of Job. I could sit here listing off all these events individually, but this book is not about showing all kinds of signs and wonders. It's about how God instructs us to live as our best selves through love. I shared these examples, because for me, they were experiences of supernatural aid that made me come back and take the call to faith more seriously.

Over the years as I started researching these experiences hoping to understand them better, I started finding others with intervention stories. You can find many videos about the saving power of Christ in the playlist I created. If you look, you can find testimony after testimony after testimony from people who claim to have encountered angels or even Christ himself. All of these people testify to the positive transformation that happened in their lives once they accepted Christ. Not once ever have I seen someone say a demonic entity did not respond to the authority of the name of Christ. These people are all complete strangers. It would be nearly impossible for them all to collaborate to create fictional agreeable stories, yet they all overlap. Seek these testimonies out for yourself if you need the evidence. It's there. That can be your sign of supernatural aid.

I would like to think that everyone will get at least one moment like that, where the divine makes itself known to them personally in an undeniable way. I also know there are plenty of people who would miss some signs right in front of their face, so not everyone is going to recognize an experience like that. Further still, I think some people are shut off from the idea that something like this could ever possibly be real. They put up a barrier that doesn't allow it to happen for them. If you want to find God, you have to be open to how He communicates. Don't get in your own way with doubt. Shutting yourself off from possibility guarantees it not to be possible for you.

Prayer

While we aren't meant to go seeking signs all the time, if you really feel you need one, start praying and *ask* for it. When I first started to get serious about prayer, I would go off on my own and pray out loud about a topic, going as deep and honest with it as I could put into words. Christ said in the sermon on the mount that it is best to pray in private, not feel the need to be showy in public (*Matthew 6:5-8*).

The next day, I would be looking for an answer to pop up somewhere that didn't come, so I would shrug it off. At the end of the second day when I had practically forgotten I prayed, it would fall right in my lap. Somehow I would be led to a Bible verse or repeating message or some pointed situation that felt like an answer. Something would give me that light bulb moment where the thing I was struggling with made more sense.

The more frequently I prayed, the faster I started getting answers. I certainly didn't get answers to everything, but far too many things appeared that were specifically relevant to what I prayed in private for it not to merit my attention. Eventually I even had moments where I felt like my prayer was being answered while I was praying it.

There was one day I was getting ready to leave for work and my driveway was buried in snow. Our shovel was terrible, and it would have taken me over an hour of the most annoying work ever to clear enough of the driveway for my car to get onto the street. I seriously almost considered calling in sick. Instead, I chose to pray. As I paused and thought the words *Lord, please help me*, I heard my neighbor's driveway around the corner begin to be plowed by a truck. I ran around quick and waved at him, at which point he gave me a thumb up and promptly pulled around to clear my driveway. It only took him ten minutes, I wasn't late for work, and he didn't even want my money. Of course I gave the man my genuine thanks, but that really just felt like an instant blessing.

Prayer is powerful! God wants to talk with you. If you're nervous at first, keep in mind that even if you had no faith, it is beneficial to be able to voice your thoughts out. It's therapeutic and releases some internal pressure, so there's nothing to lose by doing it. If you ask me, the ability and desire to pray is the first *work* that demonstrates the sincerity of your faith. It's one step closer to God than you were before, showing your desire to form a relationship. It's really one of the best places to start. Initiate the conversation (*Matthew 7:7-11*).

Please, don't think you have to follow some prewritten prayer. I fully believe God wants us to pray the sincerity of our hearts and say how we truly feel. There is a relief that accompanies openly expressing your thoughts and feelings to God. It takes them out of your head and turns it into a conversation. Sure, the Lord's Prayer (*Matthew 6:9-13*) is a good one to throw in your rotation occasionally, but it shouldn't be the only one. It was more of an outline in my humble opinion.

The important thing to remember when praying is what it

means to say *in Jesus name we pray, Amen* at the end of it. There are many people who will give you a funny look if they don't hear it said. I don't feel that was meant to be a line you necessarily had to say out loud. Rather, it was intended to be something you felt on the inside. There are several points where Christ tells us that whatever we ask the Father for in his name will be done. (*John 14:13-14, 15:16, 16:23-24*) Prayer was certainly never intended to be used as a vending machine for expensive items and a way to win the lottery. The movie *Bruce Almighty* did a wonderful job of showing why that isn't realistic.

Other times when Christ commanded us to do things in his name, they were actions such as to gather (*Matthew 18:2*), to give a cup of water (*Mark 9:41*), and to believe we have life (*John 20:31*). During Biblical times, to ask people to do something in your name meant to ask them to do things in line with your character. Your name represents you, and thusly the whole of your personality is associated with it. It was like saying take my behaviors unto yourself and do as I do. All of these things are to be done the way Christ would have done them, including prayer. This also implies that what you do is done in his authority.

Christ prayed to the Father as though they were one (*John 17:21*), So we are to pray to the Father as though we are one with Christ who is one with the Father, using the Holy Spirit that indwells within us. This is your lifeline. If you don't feel your prayers, or if you are just reciting words you think you're supposed to pray, try once more with feeling, *please*. When you do encounter a prewritten prayer, this experience will often deepen the meaning of why the writer chose those words. The phrasing they chose starts to make sense, like unlocking a new understanding.

Author *Daniel Henderson* speaks on the subject of improving our prayers to more closely follow the model Christ gave us. He suggested a structure that consists of *reverence, response, requests,* and *readiness*. Don't forget to thank God in your prayers for His many blessings and tell Him you love Him (*Psalm 136:26, 1 Thessalonians 5:18*). These are things you would do for a friend or family member standing right in front of you, so why wouldn't you do it for God?

Also, make sure you're not always praying just to ask for something. If you only talk to me when you want something, I'm probably not going to enjoy your company very much, so why would we treat God that way? Lastly, try asking for guidance more often than you ask for solutions to be resolved a certain way you want. Value God's counsel. *Not my will, but yours, Father.*

So, do you absolutely have to say *in Jesus name we pray*? No, I don't think so. It's more important that you feel the connection to your prayer on a personal level, as though the Holy Spirit is with you. That being said, most people don't really see it this way. So as a courtesy not to offend people, I will often end prayers that are in the presence of others by saying *I send up this prayer in the spirit and name of Christ!* Plus, *amen* actually means *so be it*, so you're basically saying *let this be done*. What are you asking God to do? Do you understand the gravity of your requests (*Matthew 7:7*)?

It's not going to hurt you to say these words, and verbalizing it can be a good way to reinforce the feeling you are meant to have behind your prayer. Just keep in mind it's your heart that matters most. Align the intentions behind your prayers to be more like the intentions Christ had in his heart which can be clearly identified by his character. When you look at it from this perspective, it makes prayer a form of supernatural aid that you can carry with you everywhere you go. Never forget this is amplified when we have fellowship with other believers. Prayer with others at church, in meet-ups, study groups, and even online can be powerful! Take full advantage of *Matthew 18:20*.

With time, I have come to treat all thoughts, words, and actions as a form of prayer. God can see our hearts, right? Nothing is hidden from Him, so I keep myself aware of that and have worked each day to make all the things He sees pleasing by simply reminding myself that it will all be communicated to Him. It takes time to get to the place where that is comfortable, so don't pressure yourself. Just know that life is a prayer. Pray without ceasing (*1 Thessalonians 5:17*).

Gifts of the Spirit

Faith can move mountains (*Matthew 17:20*), and prayer enacts what lifts them. Be aware that the Holy Spirit bestows gifts as well, and I always see them develop in people the stronger their prayers become. They are clearly outlined in *1 Corinthians 12*, and include things like healing, faith, wisdom, the ability to perform miracles or prophecy, and even the gift of tongues.

Let me be clear about the gift of tongues. In scripture it states that this gift allows you to speak and/or understand languages you do not know. It's like a universal translator, breaking down the barrier instated at the Tower of Babel. Think of it like the babel fish in *Hitchhiker's Guide to the Galaxy.* They put it in their ear and are suddenly able to understand and speak all languages. Its purpose is for spreading the gospel, ministry, and I have seen people whose prayers turn to angelic tongues as well. *Acts 2:4 & 19:6,* and *1 Corinthians 14* are a few places that talk about it in more detail. Don't just babble nonsense sounds until it becomes a message.

I discussed the gifts of the spirit with a friend in ministry who said they feel we should seek after everything God has for us. I agree! If God has gifts in store for us, we should want and seek all of them with open trust. However, we should never forget that He decides what gifts we get and what ones we don't, and I don't personally believe any of us get every single one until heaven. I do not believe as some people do that you are only truly saved if you speak in tongues, simply because there is nowhere in scripture that says that is a requirement to be able to enter heaven. It says it is a gift.

The Holy Spirit will choose what gifts are for you and what aren't, so don't try to force it. You will receive gifts other people won't have, and they may have ones that you don't. I like to use the analogy of the human body. We have twelve systems that keep our body running such as the lymphatic system, nervous system, or the circulatory system. Each has a purpose that serves the whole. Your heart does not do the same thing as your brain or your lungs, but you need them all to live. Embrace what you were created to contribute to the body, and celebrate what others are able to contribute.

Trying to force these gifts is what borderlines on magic or sorcery, so let's create a line of differentiation between the supernatural aid gained from the gifts of the Spirit and doing witchcraft. The gifts of the spirit are subtle. They are holy, *not* harmful, and they require nothing more than great faith and prayer. Perhaps the Spirit will grant you the knowledge to know how to use herbs for medicinal purposes. You're not a witch just because you have a green thumb and know herbal remedies. That is a kind of healing gift, though I do believe laying of hands is another kind. Laying of hands is something not only Jesus, but all the apostles did (*Matthew 10:1, Acts 8:17-23, etc.*).

However, at the point where you are reciting spells or using totems, blood, sex, or any other objects in order to influence the world around you, then you have most likely crossed into witchcraft. *What about crystals, aren't they in the Bible?* The Bible does speak of the stones of the ephod both in Aaron's time and in the New Jerusalem to come as well as the use of the urim and thummim to communicate with God. If you really wanted to explore stones from a Biblical perspective, go ahead. I have just come to realize over time that the strength of your faith is where the true power lies. The gifts and talents granted us by the Holy Spirit can do all things that are good, pure, and holy. Anything it cannot do likely has a very good reason behind it.

God condemns sorcery and says those who practice it will not be allowed into the kingdom of heaven (*Revelation 22:15*). From what I can see in my study, I believe this is because it is a form of force. By using magic to change circumstances you are taking away free will and a level playing field, unbalancing the scales. You tip them in your favor at the cost of others. Plus, it tends to involve the worship of beings other than Him. Any one of these reasons should be sufficient, so the fact that there are many should be a strong deterrent.

A sorcerer is also someone trying to override God's authority by changing things to be the way they want them to be. Casting a spell is like saying you know how the world should work better than God. It says to Him that what He has given you isn't good enough for you, and you needed to take matters into your own hands even though He has provided you the Holy Spirit who can accomplish anything and everything you could truly need. Take a moment to realize that even demons can be cast out in the name of Christ, the name above all names (*Philippians 2:9*). There is no authority higher than what was bestowed upon him by God. The Holy Spirit is an extension of that to you. You don't need anything else.

Fasting

Fasting is also something I would qualify as a form of supernatural aid. Pairing it with prayer is one of the most powerful tools in our arsenal! There are many ways to fast, and they aren't always about abstaining from food. Anything you withhold from for God's sake for whatever length of time you set is a fast. I often see people fast from tv or social media for a period of time.

However, this section is about fasting from food. There seems to be something extra special about this kind of fasting, so I want to give it due focus. It's something I get questions about often due to participating in this practice. It develops willpower, strength of faith, and is an act that demonstrates our trust in God to nourish our needs just as Christ did when fasting forty days in the wilderness. (*Matthew 4*) During this time, the devil himself tried to tempt Christ into eating and into testing God, but these temptations were overcome through the faith and understanding of God's will that Christ followed diligently while setting his perfect example.

This practice is finally starting to gain scientific credibility as well, but in truth it has long been one of the few things almost every world religion encourages universally. Studies have shown that at least a seventy-two hour fasting period can give a reset to your immune system (*Valter Longo, University of Southern California*), especially given how closely it is tied to our digestive system. During fasting your white blood cell count decreases, but when you eat again it increases again. This suggests that your body replaces the old ones by producing new ones. Fasting also gives your body time to focus on the backlog of things it's too busy to handle when dealing with our daily eating habits and energy use. It's like spring cleaning or catching up on the to do list that stacked up over time.

Of course, you *might* lose weight as well, but that should ***never*** be your motivation for fasting, only a bonus. It is not healthy to starve yourself for body image or shaming purposes. This is the foundation of developing anorexia which is classified as a mental health condition.

Given the recent increase in attention on the subject, I wanted to share my personal perspective and some tips from experience. I do a three day fast once in the spring and once in fall, both for physical and spiritual health reasons. I also periodically fast on the Sabbath one day a week. At first, I did it every week for many months, but eventually I scaled back to a more occasional practice once I felt the important lessons had been learned. I treat this as penance for past gluttony, a deeper honoring of the meaning of resting on the Sabbath, and a chance for my body to catch up on its many processes from a week of eating. This has not only benefited my body, but it has deepened my relationship with God and built a willpower that carries into every act in my life. It provides thorough practice of the ability to say *no* to temptation, and that is *powerful* when applied to your life past just overcoming hunger.

If you have never fasted before, don't dive in head first. *Ease yourself in and pray as you go!* Start simple, perhaps skipping one meal one day a week, or maybe only eating between certain hours of that day. Your first major goal should be one full day.

In ancient times, some people would still consume certain herbs and vegetables during this time. I have also seen some suggest that 200 calories per day or less still counts as fasting. In modern times, you will typically hear people reference either water fasting or dry fasting, which is exactly how it sounds. It's the differentiation between whether you allow yourself to drink water or have nothing at all.

I preference towards water fasting but not ingesting anything else, because that water is what helps carry toxins out of your body in urine. I have met people who allow themselves to have coffee or tea, so I think ultimately what's most important is that you outline your parameters in advance and do it safely. Determine what will be allowed and not allowed as well as how long you will participate. *Then stick to it!* If you are concerned about what might be safe, consult your physician, especially if you have a preexisting condition. Obviously someone who has to monitor their blood sugar for example is not a prime candidate for this.

With time, you will find it easy and seek to challenge yourself further. Your energy level will not be as high as normal, so I sometimes push myself by being a little more active such as going for a walk with family. We are told not to look somber while fasting, so it is not obvious to others (*Matthew 6:16-18*). I recently stepped up to trying dry fasting, and of course longer periods of time will hold their own challenges.

You may notice odd things when doing longer fasts like your tongue turning white or breath stinking strongly. That is normal, but again, consult a doctor if anything concerns you. Truthfully on my first three day fast, I was so sure that the third day would be the hardest, but the first day ended up being hardest from psyching myself out about how difficult I thought it would be. Once you get past the first steps of establishing a fast, it gets easier as you go. I have a goal to someday complete a twenty-one day water fast, but that will be something done when I can take the time off work, be loosely monitored by someone, and have previously completed a seven day fast successfully.

      When coming off of a fasting period, it is not wise to binge eat. It might sound like a good idea to make up for lost eating, but I don't recommend it. Not only does that defeat the purpose of developing self-control, but it can be hard on your stomach. Also, avoid heavy foods like meat or sweets. Ease back in with smaller portions of fruits and vegetables and increase gradually back to your normal healthy eating habits. There are plenty of YouTube videos and blog articles available on the internet from professional sources if you'd like more information.

      We have programmed ourselves to eat daily and often, even if we can survive without eating every three hours as personal trainers and dieticians recommend. There are reasons fasting can be challenging thusly allowing us opportunities to grow. *Following are some examples of things that you go through in your mind when fasting and ways to counter them:*

*You make waffles for your kids for breakfast and get a small drop of syrup on your finger. Don't lick it off. Wash your hand.

*You feel bored and instinctually open the refrigerator wanting a snack. Don't forget that you are fasting. Leave yourself a note on the fridge, or tie a string to your finger that you will clearly see when food is brought towards your face as a reminder. It may sound silly, but it can be easy to forget you're fasting and eat without realizing it until you're chewing on something.

*You are preparing dinner for your family and are unsure of the balance of your seasonings. Don't taste test it. Ask someone else to try it. They are who you are cooking for anyway.

*It's your only chance to go grocery shopping. Don't impulse buy out of hunger or torture yourself in the dessert isle. Take a shopping list and stick to it.

*A friend invites you over and offers your favorite treat that you know they rarely make. Kindly decline. Use it as a chance to express you are fasting for spiritual reasons and allow it to minister in a way where someone is asking you questions instead of you leading with it. This always sparks some interesting conversations and sets a positive example.

*You ask someone else to prepare food for the family so you're not tempted, but it smells good, your mouth waters, and you have a headache. You may even be forced to watch them eat without you.

Don't give up! Obstacles happen in life. They are pauses, not stops. Drink a glass of water instead that has no caloric value. Pray for stronger willpower.

*You might get bored at some point, and ultimately end up sitting around counting the seconds until your fast is over. Don't torture yourself! Instead get your hands busy either praying, doing volunteer work, or catching up on clearing up clutter in your life. Be productive (*without overdoing it*) and positive during this time, and you'll get through it just fine.

The Armor of God

The last piece of supernatural aid I would like to offer you is the armor of God. It is outlined for us in *Ephesians 6:10-18*. This is the item we will seek to obtain in our quest and is a spiritual parallel to the physical armor in *Exodus 28*.

*Finally, be strong in the Lord and in his mighty power. Put on the full armor of God, so that you can take your stand against the devil's schemes. For our struggle is not against flesh and blood, but against the rulers, against the authorities, against the powers of this dark world and against the spiritual forces of evil in the heavenly realms. Therefore put on the full armor of God, so that when the day of evil comes, you may be able to stand your ground, and after you have done everything, to stand. Stand firm then, with the **belt of truth** buckled around your waist, with the **breastplate of righteousness** in place, and with your **feet fitted with the readiness that comes from the gospel of peace**. In addition to all this, take up the **shield of faith**, with which you can extinguish all the flaming arrows of the evil one. Take the **helmet of salvation** and the **sword of the Spirit, which is the word of God**. And **pray in the Spirit** on all occasions with all kinds of prayers and requests. With this in mind, be alert and always keep on praying for all the Lord's people.*

Notice salvation is the helmet of the whole armor. It protects your head, but I wouldn't want to end up in the middle of a spiritual battle wearing only a helmet. The item that protects your heart is the breastplate of righteousness, so it would be silly to suggest our behavior doesn't matter to God. Righteousness protects your heart which we will discuss later in more detail (*Proverbs 4:23*).

Armor of God

{ Put Your Armor On! }

"Therefore take up the whole armor of God, that you may be able to withstand in the evil day, and having done all, to stand firm."
Ephesians 6:13

A study of the Armor of God from Ephesians 6:10-18

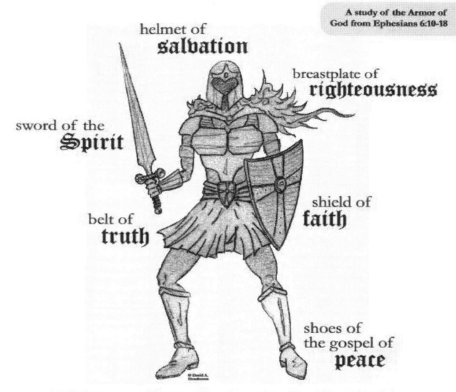

helmet of **salvation**

breastplate of **righteousness**

sword of the **Spirit**

shield of **faith**

belt of **truth**

shoes of the gospel of **peace**

{ WRITTEN & DESIGNED BY JOHANNA HENDERSON | ILLUSTRATED BY DAVID A. HENDERSON }
© 2014 by Johanna Henderson and David A. Henderson | www.NephilimTheRemnants.com

Think of putting it on the same way you would build a character in a role playing game. The difference is these are all things you wear on your spirit, not necessarily your physical body. No worries, you won't have to go around wearing medieval armor like the knights of the round table who quested for the holy grail. For you to be able to equip these items to yourself as the hero on this quest for all that is holy, you will start out with this basic setup which is the knowledge of this passage.

As you continue through this journey down the road, remember this armor. You will begin to strengthen the concepts attached to each piece of accoutrement, thusly upgrading them to better quality gear. By the end, you'll have top notch armor! The first fifteen minutes of your day sets the tone for the entire rest of it. Take a few minutes each morning praying for help in putting this armor on and for getting you through the day. Verbally acknowledge that you carry all these things with you!

In the space below, share any supernatural aid or experiences you may have encountered before. Identify whether you feel it was a positive or negative encounter and why. If you don't feel you've had this happen to you, write a prayer requesting for God to make the blessing of His presence known in your life. Your other option would be to share an experience you heard about from someone else that spoke to your heart. Once you have done that, summarize how you will be equipping yourself for this journey. What is important that you feel you need to remember from this section down the road? Pray about the struggles you listed in the previous section, and ask God to help you work through them as you continue this journey.

_____
_____
_____
_____
_____
_____
_____
_____
_____
_____
_____
_____
_____
_____
_____

4. Crossing the Threshold

*Behold, I stand at the door and knock.
If any man hear my voice and open the door,
I will come in to him, and will sup with him, and he with me.*
Revelation 3:20

It's time to stop being lukewarm. Here is the point where you decide to take a leap of faith and accept Christ in your heart. His grace will guide you to truth and wisdom, and you will come to understand more clearly through that why his name means *salvation*. For now, just declare what you know will be true. Claim your victory in advance!

This is where salvation falls. I see accepting Christ in your heart as conception. Being led by the Spirit to follow him is like being in the womb. It's where we grow through repentance, forgiveness of our past, and learning about Christ. It burns away the dross and leaves us pure and refined (*Isaiah 1:25, 1 Peter 1:7*). Then we are born again once we emerge from water baptism, having been washed clean, developed true understanding, and implemented it in our lives. As long as you don't abandon that faith and keep following, you'll be fine.

It can be so easy to doubt how God could possibly see us as worthy. By this point in life we are typically aware that we've made a lot of mistakes, and we can feel too imperfect to be accepted. There is a song by *Point of Grace* called *Who Am I* that embodies this delicate feeling of insignificance quite beautifully. This song along with a few of my favorites from other artists are on the playlist previously mentioned. If you like these musicians, I encourage you to support them financially by purchasing their music. This list is intended to connect you to things you may like in a recommendation capacity, *not* take away from their livelihood.

It's just not true that we are insignificant though! That is just what the devil wants you to believe. It's a virtue to be humble, but it is equally valuable to know your worth. Coming to that understanding about yourself is such an integral part of what makes Christ your Savior and helps you identify God. He will forgive who you were and work to mold you in his image like clay. You will want his grace to be covering you through this adventure. Trust that

God won't let you down!

There is a Japanese practice called *kintsukuroi*. This word means *to repair with gold*. It is the art of repairing pottery with gold or silver lacquer and understanding that the piece is more beautiful for having been broken. This is honestly *exactly* what I imagine is the result of truly accepting Christ (*Revelation 3:18*). Eventually the process breeds deeper faith for those who are redeemed, which is more valuable than gold (*1 Peter 1:7*). He comes in and helps guide you through honestly repairing your life, and it becomes more beautiful. Know that there is boundless joy in heaven over even one soul coming to repentance (*Luke 15:7-10*)!

Looking back on your strife, you will learn to appreciate the lessons you learned through hardship. He will help you become aware of the root cause of your problems and make you wise so you can do your best to avoid pain in the future. He will slowly show you that love is a verb, and it is something that operates at peak efficiency and success when it is chosen. You will see the truth and logic that can be infused into emotions and acknowledge that law needs some love in it as the essence of his pure divine character starts to become one with your own (*Isaiah 40:31*).

You will feel things more deeply. You will cry a little more often, but you'll find sometimes they are this new kind of tears of joy over something so seemingly small and insignificant to the person next to you. You'll see deep beauty in a small moment, and it will move you to tears.

Know that this step of crossing the threshold is the bare minimum requirement. Right now, in this moment, accepting Christ - that is Biblically considered the bottom line. Scripture says if you do not deny his name, he will not deny yours (*Matthew 10:33, Mark 8:38, 1 John 2:22-23 & 3:36, etc.*). The Bible states that you *cannot* be saved if you do not accept Christ. God sent him for this purpose. That doesn't mean you have to immediately be a perfect person. You'll spend years incorporating his behaviors into your personality! Take your time with each of these steps. This is not a book you breeze through in a couple days.

If your heart is still struggling with questions, I understand. You'll see no judgment here. It took time for me, too. I was too afraid of being deceived, and it held me back. If that is the case, it might benefit you to read a few more sections then come back to this. ***But*** it is my obligation to be clear that this step is the *most* *important one*, and it is the *bottom line*. We are saved by the gift of grace which is bestowed through our faith. You must *believe and accept the truth* which Christ embodied.

Christ frequently insisted in scripture that strong faith is the source for miracles. (*Matthew 8:5-13, Mark 2:1-12, etc.*). There is one story that really brings this home. Christ was in a crowd of people, so clearly he was making physical contact with many of them. A woman who was sick believed if she simply touched his robe that it would heal her, so she did. He then asked who had touched him, because he felt the power leave him. When he identified who had touched him, he told her that her faith had made her well (*Mark 5:25-34, Luke 8:43-48*). *Your faith has saved you, go in peace.*

Again in *Matthew 14:22-36* Christ walks on water. When the disciples saw him, they were afraid it was a spirit at first, but Christ told them not to be afraid. Peter then asked Christ to bid him to walk on the water too if it was really him. So he did. At first Peter walked towards him, but as he noticed the boisterous wind around him, he began to sink. Christ had to reach out a hand to save him as he cried out for help. Christ's response was *O thou of little faith, wherefore didst thou doubt?* It was his faith that was allowing him to experience this miracle. When he allowed the outside world to cause him to doubt his faith is when he began to sink. Faith is a powerful thing!

This brings us to the other side of the coin of faith. I have seen a great deal of heated debate over the question of whether salvation can be lost or not and what is asked of us to maintain it if anything. There is so very much scripture about this subject that it could probably fill another book. I am going to cite some of the more commonly referenced passages here and discuss them in order to convey my perspective.

While this will only scratch the surface of what the Bible says on the topic, hopefully it will give you a solid approach on how to study this further and convey what the conversation has looked like in my experience. Please also know that none of what I'm about to share is intended to diminish love, create fear, or cast judgment on you. Mercy triumphs over judgment (*James 2:13*). This discussion will eventually work to strengthen love giving it definition and standards. I try my best to speak all truth in love, but I also cannot abandon reason in order to do so. As we progress through the hard bits of discussion, keep love in your heart.

The people who say salvation cannot be lost will lean very heavily into *Ephesians 2:8-9. For by grace are ye saved through faith; and that not of yourselves. It is the gift of God. Not of works, lest any man should boast.* Yes, we are saved by the grace granted through our faith, but this is a topic that runs deep. They believe this to mean works don't matter, only accepting salvation through grace does. While that may seem cut and dry, you must ask yourself - do you truly have faith in Christ if you do not try your best to follow his commands?

Are you honestly expecting a free gift of salvation to be a free pass to continue in sinful behavior? I believe we aren't just being saved from damnation and hell, but also from the darkness in ourselves. Transformation is essential, which is what people would discover if they continued reading this passage into verse *10. For we are his workmanship, created in Christ Jesus **unto good works**, which God hath before ordained that we should walk in them.* After accepting Christ, we need to work through stopping our sinning and add good works/behaviors/faith-inspired-actions to our lives.

Continuing on, *Hebrews 10:26-29* says *For if we sin willfully after that we have received the knowledge of the truth, there remaineth no more sacrifice for sins, but a certain fearful looking for of judgment and fiery indignation, which shall devour the adversaries. He that despised Moses' law died without mercy under two or three witnesses: Of how much sorer punishment, suppose ye, shall he be thought worthy, who hath trodden under foot the Son of God, and hath counted the blood of the covenant, wherewith he was sanctified, an unholy thing, and hath done despite unto the Spirit of grace?* In a nutshell, this is saying the forgiveness we receive is granted because we were born ignorant to the truth and didn't really know any better.

However, once you've been shown the truth and fully understand it, you are accountable for your actions going forward. Mistakes made still require repentance. Again, this takes time and will not occur overnight. I see it as the difference between making mistakes in ignorance and making choices with intent. Christ backs this up from his own mouth in *Matthew 7:21-23. Not everyone that saith unto me, Lord, Lord, shall enter into the kingdom of heaven; but he that doeth the will of my Father which is in heaven. Many will say to me in that day, Lord, Lord, have we not prophesied in thy name? And in thy name have cast out devils? And in thy name done many wonderful works? And then will I profess unto them, I never knew you: depart from me, ye that work iniquity.* Other translations use the word lawlessness instead of iniquity, meaning for all intents and purposes the same thing.

We are told that faith without works is dead (*James 2*), because even though we are saved by grace through faith, it is our works and behaviors that are the supporting evidence that our faith is sincere. Faith is a foundation that should influence your decisions. To follow Christ implies a desire to have your character molded to be more like his own. If you choose to deny the instructions that came directly from the mouth of Christ, then you are not following him. You are trying to mold him into what you desire him to be instead of letting him mold you into his likeness. For some that is a piece of cake, and for others it will be a tough pill to swallow. No matter which response is yours, God loves you and wants to help you get there.

Another common argument you'll see regards *Romans 8:1-2*. This passage says *There is therefore now no condemnation to them which are in Christ Jesus, who walk not after the flesh but after the Spirit. For the law of the Spirit of life in Christ Jesus hath made me free from the law of sin and death.* I understand how this could easily be taken out of context, especially when most people who fire this one off only share the first thirteen words.

There are two things to point out here. First, this verse identifies the stipulation that this lack of condemnation is for those who walk not after the flesh but after the Spirit. That is describing someone who turns *away* from sin in their walk in life to follow the convictions of the Spirit. To follow implies many footsteps, not just one. It's ok to be in the journey for a long time. It's not ok to ignore what the Spirit says to your heart. Secondly, it clearly states that there is a law of the Spirit of life in Christ. That is reiterated in *Romans 7:2-4* using the analogy of marriage. We were released from one to the other through Christ in order to bear fruit for God.

What you will realize in this study is if you are following Christ's instructions and example, you are already following the old law beyond bare minimum. He upped the ante when he demonstrated love and grace in its application to the concept of law. Accounting for emotions and intentions when it comes to reason is a higher enactment of the law than a simple pass/fail, an upgrade or evolution of it if you will. The law of the spirit of life in Christ has color and shading instead of being black and white.

If you go back just a couple chapters in *Romans* to *6:12-15*, it is pretty clear Apostle Paul knew that just because we are under grace does *not* give license to sin. Grace isn't grace if it is not good and upright. Evil grace is *disgrace*. Grace is a word that reflects how love makes good behaviors feel more effortless, loving, and free. It flows. The definition is *simple elegance or refinement of movement*. The commandments define what God sees as sinful, and therefore are still relevant. We will cover in detail later how Christ expressed this. What I have shared here is a common example of how people will lift verses out of the Bible which distorts them out of context thusly supporting their alternate perspective.

Also, in *Revelation 3:5* Christ says *He that overcometh, the same shall be clothed in white raiment; and I will not blot out his name out of the book of life, but I will confess his name before my Father, and before his angels*. He makes it clear that he can not only add names to the book of life but remove them. This is reiterated in many other passages throughout the Old Testament as well, including but not limited to *Exodus 32:33, Deuteronomy 25:6 & 29:20,* and *Psalm 9:5, 83:4 & 109:13*. I do not believe this would have been stated if it weren't possible to lose salvation.

That being said, I don't think salvation is handed out just for saying a few words and attending church. Once received I also don't believe it can be easily lost. Scripture says once you have true salvation you can never be *taken* from His hand (*John 10:28*). That doesn't mean you personally can't give up your salvation by abandoning your faith. Here we are again, addressing the balance of things. I have seen many people become so comfortable and complacent in the certainty of their salvation that they slowly lose their dedication and backslide into old habits until they lose the faith completely. Don't let anyone take your crown (*Revelation 3:11*).

It reminds me of the parable of the virgins who didn't have enough oil for their lamps (*Matthew 25:1-13*). Like faith, oil keeps the fire burning. If you run out, you lose your light. The authenticity of your faith is intended to match the authenticity of Christ's love and truth. Faith is not a season of temporary interest in God. It is a lifestyle choice that will overflow with joy when you embrace it for the long haul.

Matthew 10:32-33 also states that those who acknowledge

Christ before men will be acknowledged to the Father, and whoever denies him will be denied. If you are willing to deny Christ to others, then it is nearly impossible to say that your faith is sincere. Your insides need to match your outsides. Changes that are too easy to acquire are just as easy to lose. Does this help narrow the scope of understanding? Process exists for your benefit, to solidify your faith and make it sturdy, unshakeable. I don't believe grace makes abrupt changes. It transitions.

    The strongest argument *against* the law which so few people bring to discussion unless they are advanced in study is *Galatians 2*. Paul sums up in verse *21* saying *I do not frustrate the grace of God, for if righteousness come by the law, then Christ is dead in vain.* His point in this passage was if we could follow the law and get into heaven that way, then Christ's sacrifice on the cross was for nothing and we didn't need his grace and salvation. Again, this same man said we still don't have license to sin, so what did he mean here? What we must understand is that we receive something we didn't have before when we accept Christ into our hearts, and it is a pivotal gift. We are not just forgiven. We receive guidance and blessings.

    A big part of faith in Christ is our willingness to admit that we need God's help to become better people. We may think we have wisdom, but God is exponentially and eternally wiser. Saying we must accept salvation causes us to admit that we needed saving in the first place - a crucial ego check. That is hard for some people to do, because it requires us to see inside ourselves from outside ourselves. Look at how much power God has placed behind that moment of humility, though! He gives us so much when we accept that truth (*Matthew 6:33, Luke 12:31*).

    When we had the law in the Old Testament it lacked the finesse of love and kindness in execution even though that was its original purpose, and very few ever met the standard. The ones that came close were painted as heroes! Most people were blind to the error in their ways. Look back now and much of their error seems easy to spot, but hindsight is 20/20. The truth and grace given to us when we accept Christ enables us to succeed through the personal guidance of the Word and Spirit. That is what Christ's death gave us - a chance we never had before to really get it right. It was an act of God's grace, and we *must* accept it. We then honor that gift with our better behavior as we learn and grow.

    Later in Galatians *5:3* we are told if you follow one Torah law you must follow them all. *James 2:10* then supports this by saying if you follow them and break one, you are guilty of all of them. What I hope you're starting to realize is that those who follow all the instructions of Christ in the sermon on the mount and gospel teachings will already be following the true intended spirit of all of the Torah. You will soon see the tremendous amount of overlap between Old and New Testament commands. Just keep in your heart that you are following Christ and his instruction. Accepting Christ is the path or the *way* we follow from one state of life to the next - from sinner to saint.

Accepting him is the enactment or beginning of the process of repentance. Following him going forward is the completion of that process. After we receive that gift of approval, we are in Christ, so we begin to adopt his divine character as our own. We begin to heal. His character in scripture revolves highly around the fact that he perfectly followed the law. Of course he did, because he *is* truth and would know no other way!

It is a simple reversal of process. Instead of a system that told us to *follow the rules or else*, we enter a new system with Christ focused on choosing to embrace the divine nature that resonates from the law which defines what righteousness is in the eyes of God. Instead of following the law in fear to determine if we merit heaven, we are given the promise of salvation up front as a gift of love that guides us towards developing the divine nature that polished the law of life in Christ. Instead of feeling oppressed, we feel uplifted. No longer are we made to feel we aren't good enough. Instead, we are welcomed in and guided with love, understanding, and patience, because we accepted we had growth to do and we needed his help to do it.

For Christ, following the law was natural to him, because it was intrinsic to who he was on every level of his being. It just flowed from him. That again is the essence of truth and grace. We begin to see through Christ's eyes and learn how he made it look so effortless to obey God. If your faith is sincere, you will be transformed, born again into a seemingly new person (*2 Corinthians 5:17*). Yet you still hold the power to reject it as I have seen some people do.

It may ultimately come down to whether your initial acceptance of Christ is authentic in your heart or not, but the overall point still stands. If he calls us friends, then ask yourself a simple question. If you no longer talk to or see your friend for ten years, are you still friends? All relationships require nourishment and upkeep, even the one you have with Christ. I don't want you to meet him at the judgment and hear him say he never knew you, so let's get familiar with him.

An interesting point I want to bring to the table here is whether this was really a new concept or not. *1 Corinthians 10:2* tells us that all the people Moses led were baptized into him in the cloud and sea. In addition to that, *Isaiah 43:25* and *Ezekiel 18:21-31* blew my mind wide open when I first read them. There is so much talk about how the message of the New Testament was a new covenant, even reference to it in places like *Hebrews 8:13*, but read that passage from Ezekiel here. It would be impossible to deny how familiar it sounds to the New Testament and explains what example Christ set.

But the wicked will turn from all his sins that he hath committed, and keep all my statutes, and do that which is lawful and right, he shall surely live, he shall not die. All his transgressions that he hath committed, they shall not be mentioned unto him: in his righteousness that he hath done he shall live. Have I any pleasure at all that the wicked should die? saith the Lord God, and not that he should return from his ways and live? But when the righteous turneth away from his righteousness, and committeth iniquity, and doeth according to all the abominations that the wicked man doeth, shall he live? All his righteousness that he hath done shall not be mentioned: in his trespass that he hath trespassed, and in his sin that he hath sinned, in them shall he die. Yet ye say, the way of the Lord is not equal. Hear now, O house of Israel; **is not my way equal? Are not your ways unequal?** *When a righteous man turneth away from his righteousness, and committeth iniquity, and dieth in them, for his iniquity that he hath done shall he die. Again, when the wicked man turneth away from his wickedness that he hath committed, and doeth that which is lawful and right, he shall save his soul alive. Because he considereth, and turneth away from all his transgressions that he hath committed, he shall surely live, he shall not die. Yet saith the house of Israel, the way of the Lord is not equal. O house of Israel, are not my ways equal? Are not your ways unequal? Therefore I will judge you, O house of Israel,* **every one according to his ways***, saith the Lord God. Repent, and turn yourselves from all your transgressions, whereby ye have transgressed, and* **make you a new** *heart and a new spirit: for why will ye die, O house of Israel?*

The icing on that cake is when you add in other passages. *Jeremiah 17:10, 1 Chronicles 28:9, Psalm 139:1, Matthew 16:27, Romans 8:27, and Revelation 2:23* all talk about searching hearts and minds and rewarding according to works. *Ephesians 4:22-24, Matthew 9:17, John 3:7,* and others talk about casting off the old self, being born again in the new. It is something said uniformly across both testaments. We have always been called to repentance, even if the structure of the covenants or delivery style of the message were modified. God wanted us to have a standard based on loving one another. I accept, respect, and *appreciate* that.

The last thing I want to point out here is the description of the judgment and heaven. Every person will face judgment, even those who accepted Christ. In *Revelation 16:7 & 19:2* we are told that many will praise God's fair and just judgments and that any punishment administered will be righteous. *Revelation 21* also discusses New Jerusalem, the city that will descend from heaven. *Verse 4* states *And God shall wipe away all tears from their eyes; and there will be no more death, neither sorrow, nor crying, neither shall there be any more pain, for the former things have passed away. Verse 8* also tells us *But the fearful, and unbelieving, and the abominable, and murderers, and whoremongers, and sorcerers, and idolaters, and all liars shall have their part in the lake which burneth with fire and brimstone, which is the second death.* Clearly the kingdom of heaven has standards.

Further, we are told in *Luke 17:20-21* that the coming of the kingdom of God cannot be observed because it is inside you! Changing our behaviors to be in line with God's will by following Christ's example helps us become members of the kingdom on an internal and spiritual level, which will then manifest in the physical as more and more people begin to accomplish it. The whole book of Revelation happens inside us in a metaphorical parallel *before* it happens in the physical where you can see it. Even that evolves from thought to word to deed, causing our inner world to become the outer world.

Know that God's clear desire is for all to come to repentance and be saved (*1 Timothy 2:4, 2 Peter 3:9, Ezekiel 18:23, Matthew 23:37*). He does not wish to see a single soul be lost. However, if we are truly given free will, then there will be those who choose ignorance and refuse to change. At the end of the day, we are free to choose, but not free from the consequences of our choices. Rest assured we are promised that all the world will know the truth and have a chance at redemption before the end comes. (*Matthew 24:14*). I believe this is the reason His judgments will all be considered fair and just. We will all get plenty of time, plenty of forgiveness, and a clear shot to get it right.

How you behave as a person *is your works* that make your faith alive instead of dead, not just cookie cutter good deeds or hollow financial donations. Nobody gets to buy their way into heaven. You can donate money to causes out of *sincere* desire to help, and that is a good work that demonstrates your faith (*Mark 12:41-44, Luke 21:1-4*). There just isn't a list of things or threshold of spending that will get an evil heart into heaven.

While grace alone is what gives us that second chance salvation and forgives us as we learn and grow, to deny God's instructions for our behavior after receiving salvation because you believe it is not necessary is not a belief that can be justified through scripture. To deny the law of the spirit of life would be to deny God's eternal and steadfast character. That contradicts the idea of loving Him with our whole heart, mind, and soul.

Focusing on developing healthy behavior and naturally strong moral character is a happy middle ground between law and love. Cling to that desire to be a good person who gives their best self to the world, and do it in the name of Christ. The grace of Christ places emphasis on what flows from of us naturally like water being poured into a glass. Yet even the glass is there as walls that reign in the water like rules reigns in our behavior. When you fill that glass, do you dump the whole pitcher all at once? Do you pour in little dribbles at a time? No, of course not! One way is messy and likely wasteful, and the other way would take forever! You fill the glass at a steady pouring pace that you can manage.

It takes time for changes to become our nature, and we can only succeed in the long term when motivated by love. Christ wasn't just perfect at following the law. He found the perfect way to execute it with ease and joy. He lived it just as easily as he breathed, even when persecuted. Someone who devoutly follows Christ for life will eventually just radiate the nature of heaven while here on earth (*Daniel 12:3, Matthew 5:15-16*).

God is our Father, and we are his children when we are in Christ (*Galatians 3:26-29, John 1:11-14*). What father doesn't discipline his children? We certainly don't have to spank or be violent with them, but we do have to establish house rules and enforce them as our kids grow up, otherwise they'll walk all over you, right? If you let a child climb wherever they want and eat whatever they want and say whatever they want without manners, then what will that produce? Most kids will become diabetic because candy was every meal, they'll break your expensive flat screen tv, and you'll get notes home from school that your kid is mean.

Would it change the way you looked at God if instead of calling him Father you called Him parent? God is a parent through providing and enforcing morality! I appreciate the wisdom imparted by my parents when I was younger. Granted I didn't get to spend tons of time with either one, but I certainly respect that they had to say no and enforce it sometimes. As a parent myself now, I see how much children benefit from structure reinforced through love. So once we are saved by grace, the Holy Spirit will begin to convict us in order to correct us. These corrections are based in the standard of divine love and happen because of it.

Hebrews 12:7-9 says *If ye endure chastening, God dealeth with you as sons, for what son is he whom the father chasteneth not? But if ye be without chastisement, whereof all are partakers, then are ye bastards, and not sons. Furthermore we have had fathers of our flesh which corrected us, and we gave them reverence. Shall we not much rather be in subjection unto the Father of spirits, and live?* If you believe you accepted Christ and are saved but have never experienced a moment of conviction to follow the Bible more closely, then ask yourself how sincere you were in your salvation moment.

If someone had looked at your heart right then and there, would they have seen a door truly open to being a disciple of Christ, or would they have seen you just going through the motions? I think it matters. (*Revelation 3:20*) So we have identified that we are meant to make our best effort to follow the commands of Christ, and it's important to take the time to understand it as best we can in our heads and hearts. We have also identified that faith and love are of the highest importance.

Some people believe all Old Testament law is no longer valid after Christ fulfilled it. Christ tells us, however, that not a single bit of the law will pass away until heaven and earth disappear (*Matthew 5:17-19*). He says from his own mouth that those who break the law and teach men to do so will be lowest in heaven, while those who do follow and teach the law will be the greatest in heaven. Does that mean we have to follow all 613 of the Torah laws? That's a decision you have to make for yourself, and digging into the covenants is a wonderful study.

It is my personal belief in that verse Christ was referring to the law of the spirit of life which he declared at the sermon on the mount and clarified in his other teachings. It mirrors the scene when Moses gave the ten commandments on the mountain, and later people had the rest of Torah law as clarification. The best analogy I can think of is the way our own government is structured. We have the Constitution which all laws hang on in a timeless way. Then we have amendments and others laws that clarify intent. Some stick and others change with the times. The ten commandments are like God's Constitution, and the rest of Torah is like our laws.

For example, the Old Testament had a rule about tithing 10% of your income. Do I tithe? I guess technically yes I do, but it's not specifically because I'm adhering to that law. It's because in following the spirit of Christ's teachings about love, it is in my character to be giving. I actually give way more than 10% when I have the resources available. If that fell out of my nature, that law would be sitting there still to remind me not to fall below a standard. However, I also don't allow it to restrict me from giving more.

I also recall a government class in high school. Our teacher was the mayor of a small town who later went on to work in the House of Representatives. He told us once there was a law in his city about not spitting on the streets, because there was a time where it was a serious and disgusting problem. However, now that people stopped doing it, the law was frivolous. It's still sitting there, but it's not even enforced. Nobody is getting tickets for it if they do it.

The truth is the truth. There's no denying that, BUT what is true about *you* can change! For example, it used to be true that I had not accepted Christ. Now it is true that I have. Both are true statements, but when I changed, the truth about me changed. Universal truths like 2+2=4 will forever and always be unchanging fact. Feelings can change with time though, and they effect behavior which the law was all about.

I think that is why Christ who is truth can offer forgiveness. He wants to see a better future truth exist, to see us grow into more loving and peaceful people. He paints the picture of the better truth inside us and guides us towards it like a beacon of light.

The Jewish people have what is called the *Halakhah*. This word means *the way*, and it is all about the deeply detailed answers to following Torah law to the letter. However, a big point Christ made is that when we super focus on the details we can lose sight of the big picture which we will see in later sections. Should we follow the way? Yes! That is Christ! But the way is not only truth. It is *life*. It is not just a list of instructions. It is the essence of love. The law is the foundation of developing character, so it had to be super detailed in the beginning. However, I think anything Christ didn't reiterate in his life on earth likely reflected our growth towards love. To me, the New Testament *is* the only *halakhah* I need when I follow the Spirit.

Whether you follow Torah or not, I hear many people complain that 613 laws is just too much. The way we are approaching this study will be about archetypes, so it will consolidate and solidify your understanding down to major concepts to make things easier. Apostle Paul hit the nail on the head when he said ***love is the fulfillment of the law*** (*Romans 13:8-10*).

However, it is interesting to note that there are so many laws on the book for the United States even on just a federal level that we don't even bother to count them. I have heard claims that there are 20,000 laws just pertaining to guns. Back in 1982 the Justice Department spent two years attempting to count the total number of criminal laws. At that time they compiled a list of roughly 3,000 laws. To say that 613 is just too much but still follow all the law you are currently required to as an American citizen is a poor reasoning to justify not at least trying to study and understand them.

The portion of Old Testament law that we will study in this book is the ten commandments (*Exodus 20:1-17*). When we do that, we will extract the major principle being expressed and address for each command what the New Testament says about the concept to see how it is still relevant in Christ's message. If you master the concepts we are about to explore, the details will flow naturally with the grace you are given when accepting Christ.

The goal here isn't to bog you down in law and legalism, but instead to wrap our heads and hearts around more archetypal principles of divine nature so we can see love clearly through the eyes of God instead of man. That doesn't mean details don't exist or that my perspective about the covenants will necessarily match yours. It just means it is your responsibility to continue your study as the Spirit moves you beyond what is covered here.

The ten commandments were the only Torah law written in stone by the hand of God Himself, and Christ later directly referenced them at the sermon on the mount. He states what we had heard before and tells us how he wants us to do it even better instead of giving bare minimum effort. (*Matthew 5-7*) They were basic truths that described how God wanted a good person to behave. Each was a clarification of how to choose life when faced with conflict.

We were supposed to identify them as liberating, not oppressive. In fact, it is counted as loving God to follow them without regarding them as difficult (*1 John 5:2-3*). You are told that you are blessed for following them (*Revelation 22:14*), that they outline the vision that will give us peace and long life (*Proverbs 3:1-2 & 29:18*), and that they allow us to partake in the divine nature (*2 Peter 1:2-4*). Sign me up for that, please!

Just to really drive the point home, have you ever asked yourself what the satanic perspective is about the law? Satanists follow the law of Thelema, which states *do what thou wilt will be the whole of the law*. While you as a good-hearted person might look at that and think *no worries, I choose to be good*, there are problems with that. First of all, it sets no moral standard for what is considered good. That means you end up basing your decisions on how you feel in each moment of your fluxuating emotional state instead of having a standard you follow. What happens when you have a moment of rage and think the good option is to kill the one who hurt your feelings?

This also leaves the door wide open to people with evil hearts to do whatever they want. Purely unrestricted free will becomes more and more chaotic as you add more people to the situation. If you want to kill, it's not against the rules. If you want to destroy property, steal or lie, it's not against the rules. There are no rules. Do you really want to follow a principle like that in a world that exceeds a population of 7.5billion? We need order. I really don't think anyone wants to be on the receiving end of unbridled chaos just so they have the right to dish it out. To be lawless is the most opposite of Christ one can be, so it should be clear that if someone is teaching you there are no guidelines they are following the spirit of the antichrist (*2 Thessalonians 2:8*).

When you look at the concept of the Biblical law through the lens of Satan, it changes the way you see this movement of antinomianism. If the law was truly abolished and Christ knew enough about the future to know his death was coming and prophecy the end times, do you think perhaps he would have directly stated at any point in his life even once that he was abolishing the law? He didn't. He only instructed and clarified how to follow it in everything he said.

That doesn't make legalism the answer. The answer is to repair the breach by restoring the proper balance (*Isaiah 58:11-14*). When you follow Christ, God writes the law on your heart of stone, the Holy Spirit convicts you of what you need to work on changing and leads you to truth, then love draws the waters of life forth from it like a beautiful spring (*Psalm 40:8, Hebrews 10:16, Jeremiah 31:33*). Eventually that heart of stone is replaced with a soft heart of flesh (*Ezekiel 36:25-27*).

I definitely feel the commandments of God are things that were meant to be both positive and eternal. Anything written in stone is symbolic of permanence. The idea of removal of the law is supposed to imply that you eventually no longer need rules and punishment to be a good person, because these things become intrinsic parts of your personal moral code. Your character becomes like Christ (*1 John 3*). However, they never actually go away. That would be like abandoning your standards. Your instinctual behaviors will slowly gravitate towards purity and truth when you have a loving relationship with God, exhibiting the essence of divine character. So very long story made short - God has standards and that is a good thing. Christ helps us meet them with healing and joy.

Here we find an interesting number correlation. If you add the ten Commandments of the Old Testament to the two highest stated by Christ in the New Testament, you get *twelve* official commandments. There are plenty of commands in the Bible about behavior outside of these, but they pretty much all emanate from the twelve. You might be thinking wait, that's not a prime number as mentioned earlier, and you'd be right. However, Christ is returning for his bride, so I see the union of two prime numbers, like 7 representing the bridegroom and 5 representing the bride, a marriage of law and love. It's certainly an interesting theory to ponder.

Twelve is a number constantly found in the Bible to describe governmental perfection and the structure of New Jerusalem. There were twelve tribes of Israel, each of which fulfilled a different role to serve the whole just like the twelve systems of the human body

(*Genesis 49, Revelation 7*). Christ had twelve apostles. In *Revelation 21*, we are told New Jerusalem has streets of gold and twelve gates that are twelve pearls, and there are twelve gemstones in the foundations. This parallels to the fact that there were twelve similar gemstones on the original ephod of the high priest in the time of Aaron (*Exodus 28*). The ephod was the breastplate of the high priest, and there were also twelve stones set in gold, one for each of the twelve tribes.

12,000 people from each of the 12 tribes make up the 144,000 of Revelation. In my study they appear to be people who will be made both kings *and* priests in the order of Melchizedek under the leadership of Christ, doing his work and following him wherever he goes (*Revelation 14:4*). This also seems to be supported by the promises to those who overcome. This group of people will likely also be forerunners for Christ, establishing the standard of the kingdom of heaven to come, essentially laying the foundations.

Twelve is clearly a number that is important in the structure of the divine plan. My personal viewpoint is that these twelve commands are what we are supposed to focus on mastering. As I have said, if we do, the rest of the details should come fairly naturally. I started playing around with a theory that each stone in the foundation of the city represents these twelve concepts we must work towards mastering, personality traits. When it says the streets are paved with gold transparent as glass, that may also be a metaphor for the road we must walk to develop these traits in purity and faith.

In *Matthew 5:20,* Christ states to the people during the sermon on the mount that if your righteousness does not meet or exceed that of the scribes and Pharisees, that you will never enter the kingdom of heaven. It implies that leaders of God help set standards. So again I will repeat, while our initial salvation is by grace alone, it is clear that standards are still in place which we must each do our best to reach through the conviction, support, and guidance of Christ and the Holy Spirit. When you receive the Spirit and it says *you are enough* and *you are capable*, it is best to believe it and run with it.

I promise, there's a point to sharing all of this. We must be able to clearly identify the objectives and parameters of this journey before setting out on the thick of it. This is the foundation of why I chose to write this book the way that I did. This may all sound like simply a neat correlation, but there is a short video on the playlist from a man who really brought it together for me. He was studying the names of the 12 tribes in the book of Revelation, and he noticed they were not in proper birth order. *They are as follows*:

1. Judah = I will praise the Lord
2. Ruben = He has looked on me
3. Gad = Given good fortune
4. Asher = Happy am I
5. Naphtali = My wrestling
6. Manasseh = Making me to forget
7. Simeon = God hears me
8. Levi = Attached to me
9. Issachar = Purchased me
10. Zebulon = Dwelling
11. Joseph = God will add to me
12, Benjamin = Son of His right hand

This man realized perhaps that new order was intentional on John's part. To decode the message, he took the meanings of the names and contributed a few filler words to fill out the sentences. I will bracket the words he added: *I will praise the Lord [for] He has looked on me [and] given good fortune. Happy am I [because] my wrestling, [God is] making me to forget. God hears me [and] is attached to me. [He has] purchased me [a] dwelling [and] will add to me the Son of His right hand.* I believe this is the theme and message of the new song that will be sung by the 144,000 (*Revelation 14:3*). The song is like a swan song, the one that defines their journey and experience with the Lord. It will express the deep feelings of joy they gained through surviving their trials and keeping faith in God, feelings so overwhelming they must sing to release them.

It will be a story nobody else will be able to replicate but that is consistent for every one of them, and it will be at the foundation of their ministry. That implies to me that again, perhaps they will have to earn each stone in the breastplate through working to master how to fulfill the twelve concepts, or perhaps that each group focuses on a different element of faith. Beyond the 144,000 we see reference to a great multitude (*Revelation 7:9*) who come out of the tribulation. So don't worry, even if you do not end up as part of the 144,000 first fruits (*Revelation 14:4*), I do not believe it will disqualify you from the kingdom the way some other people do, and this is all still relevant information. If it wasn't, then there would be no need to say first fruits and imply there are second fruits.

Scripture is clear about the predestination of the 144,000. They are chosen and elected by God (*Matthew 24:31, Romans 8:28-30 & 11:2-7, 1 Corinthians 2:7, 1 Peter 1:2, etc*). The quantity of the great multitude does not appear to be predetermined, though, and is the group of those who *choose* to follow God.

Obviously God knows that change takes time. I'm a believer that ripping the Band-Aid or going cold turkey to change creates too much pressure and can actually make things worse for some people. Transitional change in steps over time tends to produce more lasting success in the long term. Prayer brings strength, help, hope, and forgiveness as we work through the walk to repent and atone. You have to turn away from sin in your heart, and that's a process. This means motives not only matter, they might mean everything! Pure intention is necessary and can be learned with time if we stop to analyze our lives with more self-awareness, studying the great handbook that is the Bible. It just requires you to feel the conviction to want to change. Find your conviction with the Holy Spirit, and God will help with the rest.

Why do I think someone can learn pure motive? *Colossians 3:11* tells us that Christ is all and is in all! There is a divine spark in each of us that gave us life. In *John 14:20,* Christ tells us that he is in the Father, and we are in him, and he is in us. It will be a realization we have when we identify that he walks with us in Spirit. If we all carry that speck of the divine, then it must be possible for every person to awaken it in their hearts to guide and purify them. This does *not* mean we are all God. I do think it means we are all a grain of sand that forms the shoreline of the beach, though, or perhaps a drop of water in the ocean. That is the context I feel is most appropriate for *John 10:30-38 & Psalm 82:6*. These two verses are ones that get wildly distorted out of context by certain people in the new age movement. Always be sure to keep your ego in check.

This might explain how God is capable of being omniscient (*all knowing*) and able to read hearts and minds. Jeremiah 17:10 says *I the Lord search the heart, I try the reins even to give every man according to his ways, and according to the fruit of his doings*. This concept is repeated throughout the New Testament as well, citing many times Christ knew the hearts of the people and confronted them about it. Basically it says you will reap what you sow, meaning you get what you give, a concept of honest equivalent exchange echoed in many other passages (*James 3:17-18, 2 Corinthians 5:9-10 & 9:6, Galatians 6:8, Proverbs 14:14, Luke 6:38, etc*).

If God can see inside you, then you cannot hide the truth from Him. Knowing this compels us to purify ourselves with sincerity according to His ways, not only to avoid wrath but to receive the incentives. Either path is intended to lead you to Him. Would you rather be led by fear and punishment or love and reward? Following Christ's path is the only way to the Father, but that doesn't mean there aren't many ways we are brought to Christ. He leads us to the Father with love *and* reward.

We must see past the threat and lean on the promise. That is how we gradually pull away from fear towards love. With time and effort, we end up metaphorically killing off the ways of the old self being born again. Eventually, though, you feel so wrapped in His safe, loving arms that you lose the fear entirely as well as the feeling of need for the reward. You feel strengthened and empowered by the Holy Spirit, and that will feel like enough of a reward. It will fill you with joy just to be able to walk out in the fresh air, take a deep breathe, and feel the breeze and warm sun on your face. That is the point where *2 Corinthians 12:8-10* becomes so clear. Grace is sufficient because strength is made perfect in weakness. Let that sink in…

It keeps going from there though! Christ shared a parable about the pearl of greatest worth. (*Matthew 13:45-46)* Pearls are formed over time in darkness and under pressure. Yet they come out white and shining. There is a simple, elegant beauty to them. In the parable, the kingdom of heaven is compared to a merchant seeking pearls. He finds one of great price and sells everything he has to buy it, implying its extremely high value.

It doesn't matter which angle you interpret this parable from. The kingdom is a pearl, and we must be willing to live in the world but not of it, focusing on God's will and love and turning from man's desires. We then purchase the pearl with our lives (*Romans 12:1*). On the flip side, Christ gave his life, and his blood purchased us at a great price to be part of this kingdom (*1 Corinthians 6:19-20, Galatians 3:13-14, Colossians 1:1-24*). When we are covered in the blood of Christ (*the Lamb*), we belong to him. He makes a point to say, however, that he will no longer call us servants, but we will be called his **friends** (*John 15:15*).

What makes someone a pearl of great worth? In my humble opinion, it is someone who truly goes beyond a life of reciprocity. The pearl of greatest worth is someone who has *completely learned the meaning of love* through trials and perseverance (*Luke 3:16, Matthew 3:11-12, Hebrews 12*) and appreciates living that way. They don't require fear or reward to motivate them. Instead they are driven by real love. Therefore, they love everyone they meet in the Spirit of Christ, reflecting his divine nature. They are the ones who were caring for *him* by caring for even the least of their brothers and sisters (*Matthew 25:32-40*). It is someone willing to sacrifice for others, even if it may cost them their lives, because they want to do what they believe is right for God and the greater good. *Greater love hath no man than this, that a man lay down his life for his friends (John 15:13)*. It is someone who will do all of this without desiring a reward, because successfully helping someone in need is reward enough.

I must be incredibly clear about the concept of self-sacrifice. The willingness to die for what is right is noble, like jumping in front of someone to take a bullet for them. Sending people on suicide missions in order to kill as many innocent people as possible is *not* in any way Godly (*John 16:2-4*). If you want to help God, then help people change their hearts, don't kill them. Self-sacrifice is a defensive or protective move, not an offensive one. To suggest otherwise is to claim that God contradicted Himself when he commanded us not to kill.

Have you ever had someone give you something without wanting anything in return, who just helped you out of the goodness of their heart? I believe that special, joyful, tangible feeling you get in your chest when a kindness like this happens is you feeling the Holy Spirit move in your lives. Christ says wherever two or more gather in my name, there I'll be (*Matthew 18:20*). He never stipulated that he's only present when you are praying together. Sometimes it's just about loving interactions.

A pearl is someone who is humble enough to realize power isn't all it's cracked up to be, but knows peace is everything and that leading others to it requires a special kind of strength that draws from the well of love. Perfect love lives in someone who gives of themselves without requiring anything in return, here or in heaven (*Matthew 6:1-4*). They just choose to be good because *that is their nature* to unconditionally love. *That* is why pearls are often associated with wisdom. You can read as many books as you want, but wisdom can only come from the experience of applying that knowledge to how you live your life.

That kind of person is a true hero, and exactly who Christ teaches us to be. He will teach anyone who takes up the quest, even Paul who literally helped bring Christians to their death before he became one! ***All*** *who have sinned are called to redemption.* (*Luke 5:32*) The question is who will answer the call? Even if this all sounds at first like it is dramatic change with too much pressure and maybe further than you think you could go, don't pressure yourself into a panic attack. Christ will hold your hand as you strive to take each step. Trying to work your way through growth is better than not trying at all. God's timing is perfect with a season for everything (*Psalm 37:7-8, Ecclesiastes 3:1-8*). Change won't be overnight, but the pivot from choosing sin to doing your best to choose God *must* happen. It is part of your salvation.

I think the pure desire to leave the world better than you found it is the spark needed in our hearts. If you have that, then giving you knowledge of the truth will mold you in Christ's image. If that isn't in your heart, you really need to ask yourself *why*. What could make you desire to do harm rather than make amends peacefully? Peace allows everyone to be happy instead of just you. That is something that can be healed, but no problem can be addressed until it can first be identified as a problem.

On the subject of church...

Maybe accepting Christ is as far as you want to go right this minute. As long as God knows, that is what counts. However, you will feel great joy and reinforcement when you voice this in fellowship as well! Seek to be surrounded by Christian company at church. I'm sure they will celebrate with you, and the fellowship with other believers will make the presence of God feel more tangible to you. Take whatever steps from here that you feel the Spirit guides you towards.

Personally, I struggled for a long time to find a church that felt like the right fit for me. As John Muir most eloquently said, *I would rather be in the mountains thinking of God than in church thinking about the mountains.* That's how I felt, because God didn't really build me to stay put all the time. The earth is my church as it is his footstool and created by Him (*Isaiah 66:1-2*), and I can find fellowship with any believer in any moment shared. I find the deepest connections in one on one contact or leading small groups, and that still qualifies as at least two people gathering in his name.

That being said, I understand the value of church fellowship now that God led me to one that feels like home. It should feel like family! The structure and leadership it provides is so precious, *especially* in the earliest stages of your journey. I have encountered a few churches where the Holy Spirit is so clearly present that it can be felt in your chest and put tears in your eyes, because it is just so beautiful. I want to be there with my family in Christ all the time! Participate in fellowship in ways which you are led and are comfortable doing. (*Hebrews 10:25*) God will help that evolve over time and most likely lead you right through the doors of a lovely church home where you can not only learn but serve.

Be prepared that each church is different. You may have to look around a bit. They all follow different doctrines (*some much more strictly than others*) and have different practices at their foundations. Some will be very invested in doing volunteer projects, while others will focus on sharing the gospel outside the four walls. Some will have buoyant live bands and lead spontaneous prayer with the congregation shouting *amen* and *hallelujah*, while others will sit in pews and sing hymns and recite prewritten prayers as a group. Some will practice laying of hands or speaking in tongues, while others will view that as nonsense. Find one that fits your worship style and convictions and feels like *family*.

Some will follow different holiday traditions as well. There are seven feast days that were appointed by God in the Old Testament, and nowhere in the Bible does it say we are no longer to honor them. These are times such as Passover, Shavuot, and Yom Kippur. Hanukah is actually an optional eighth holiday. Other holidays like Easter and Christmas have emerged since the time of Christ. Even if you choose not to participate in these holidays, it is of value to study them. They all have rich meaning behind them that will deepen your understanding of scripture.

Different churches will have different perspectives on these holidays. They will argue about whose calendar is accurate, how to participate in each holiday, whether they are really Christian or pagan, and plenty of other things. There is an entire Roman infusion into Christianity that one must consider in the discussion about holidays if your intention is to live by the truth. This is another subject where the journey of researching for yourself deepens the conviction, so I'm not going to focus on handing out answers here. Whatever you do, check multiple sources, keep it faith centered, and let the Spirit guide you.

When it comes to holidays, I honor both sets. I see this as honoring that the story started somewhere and continued, so we have more things to recall. In truth, holidays are sticky territory, and scripture warns us about getting too immersed in traditions of men (*Galatians 4:10-11, Jeremiah 10:3-4, James 1:27, Isaiah 1:14-15*). The real purpose of a holiday is to be a remembrance of important things, not to be the only day that we honor our faith. They are also prophetic, and we are not to judge others for their practices (*Colossians 2:16-17, Romans 14:5-6*). I see every day as holy, so when I honor these days it's not a big show. It's a personal affair that is strictly about God.

Even when honoring the birth and resurrection of Christ, I have been pulling back from the eggs, bunnies, Santa, etc. Having a child, I didn't want to just pull the rug out from under her once I made this decision for myself, but she was told the truth about the holidays and we scaled back our involvement in the commercial aspects. This coming year we will adjust further.

Just to offer my two cents, I would be wary about any church who insists that to participate you *must* agree with any doctrine they share, especially if you feel it is blatantly *not* scripturally supported. Never follow the words of a church that contradict the Word. Anyone who tries to insist it is their way or the highway is likely missing the brotherly love and peace aspect of the gospel, and that is basically the whole gospel, the biggest point we are not meant to miss.

I've seen websites for churches that stated to join them you must agree with their view on the rapture, even though there are many prevalent theories. I have seen online videos of people being kicked out of their church for not agreeing with certain doctrine. You might as well not even bother going, because they don't want to hear it. No matter what else I liked about them, that pushed me away. Even if I had agreed with their perspective, they said I had to in order to participate with them. They put up a barrier instead of opening a door. I know church leaders are compelled to protect their flock, but confusion hits even the best of us in this imperfect world and that should be met with compassion, not aggression. The love of God is about choosing Him, not being forced or controlled. If that is how they want their congregation to be run, that's their choice. My choice is not to participate there.

If you find a church you generally like that has just one or two small issues, the best thing you can do is bring your concern privately to leadership. Don't be a gossip and infect the congregation with feelings of dissent. If they are happy there, let them be happy. The way the church leaders choose to handle your concern will be telling enough of whether you would like to be part of their congregation. It's about the difference between whether they acknowledge your concerns and try to help you understand and work through it, or if they say *because I said so* and shun you. Pray on it, and trust how the Spirit leads you.

It may be that it's easier for you to find a different church than for a whole congregation to change their position. We need to remember the only one who lived a perfect life is Christ. We are all capable of mistakes and believing a falsehood, even if we are in ministry. Getting into scripture is crucial to avoiding struggle with this as much as possible.

Only you can decide for yourself what you find tolerable and what you do not. God will sometimes plant us in a church for our own good and growth, and it is good to have roots. Just don't immerse yourself in a church that you feel will weaken your relationship with God rather than strengthen it. Remember that Satan is at the root of all struggle and conflict, and he can target anyone. I would rather see the church healed than abandoned, because it is all about our hearts in the end.

Ultimately I feel He would rather see us all fellowship together than fight over divisive doctrines between denominations. This is part of why I attend a non-denominational, Bible believing, openly welcoming church. Everyone can work to come closer to Christ, no matter what stage they are at in their faith. If the Spirit moves you to join a church, by all means do so. I congratulate you! A church always has been and always will be the *congregation*, not the building.

Things will certainly become clearer slowly over time, especially once you decide to walk past your fears and choose faith. Always be patient for God's perfect timing (*Ecclesiastes 3:1 & 8:6,*

Acts 1:7 & 3:11, Lamentations 3:25-26). While you continue through this path you will feel raw and exposed, and every emotion will surface. Christ brings you back to peace every time. Have faith!

Now that we have outlined what the path will look like going forward, it's time to reflect and prepare. In your own words, summarize that you have accepted the quest. Know that you will succeed if you seek God with your whole heart based on His promise that this is true, and commit to doing so on the paper. Own it! Declare it! Write it below. Who is he? You may even choose to mark down the date you made this decision. For me, I think the official date that I declared I would pursue a true understanding of Christ was 3-11-17, which I later realized was the parallel to my favorite verse *Colossians 3:11-17*. I feel like I was led to that verse as a special reminder of the day he brought me close to him and I brought him close to me. There was a feeling of acceptance and commitment on that day that has never been shaken away since. What are you accepting on your special day? When this has been written down completely, find a quiet place and pray it out loud. Let God hear your voice acknowledge your intention.

Part Two:
Trials & Victories
Of Initiation
(aka Growth)

5. Belly of the Whale

And he said unto me:
My grace is sufficient for thee,
for my strength is made perfect in weakness.
Most gladly therefore will I rather
glory in my infirmities,
that the power of Christ may rest upon me.
Therefore I take pleasure in infirmities,
in reproaches, in necessities,
in persecutions, in distresses for Christ's sake.
For when I am weak, I am strong.
2 Corinthians 12:9-10

Step five of our journey references a Biblical story. (*Jonah 1-2*). The *belly of the whale* is a very common phrase you will hear in regard to being thrown into the thick of a seemingly impossible challenge or consequence. This was depicted in the story of *Pinocchio*, but in the Bible, *Jonah* got his own book.

The Lord had called up Jonah, instructing him to go to Nineveh and cry out against their wickedness. Instead, Jonah tried to run away to Tarshish in fear. While on the boat to sail there, the ship encountered great turmoil on the waters. Eventually it was determined by the crew that God's anger at Jonah's disobedience was causing this danger. Jonah instructed them to throw him overboard so the affliction would end. Eventually they did, and God had planned ahead by causing a whale to come up and swallow him.

He sat inside that whale for three days and nights with all the time in the world to reevaluate his decision. Eventually he prayed to God and recommitted to following Him. God then instructed the whale to vomit him up on dry land, and again he was given the command to go to Nineveh. How do you imagine it felt to sit inside a whale, dark and wet for three whole days, not knowing if or when it would end?

With all my learning from the church up until I was eighteen, I was confident I knew all I needed to know in the Bible. I was baptized as a baby, confirmed in eighth grade, took communion a multitude of times, participated in groups, and knew what I thought was all of the Bible stories by heart. I started to notice when the pastor was cycling back through old sermons. This brought me into the depths of my journey with an ego that there couldn't possibly be all that much more to learn. I was blind but thought I could see.

Christ shattered that ego and opened my eyes in the spring of 2017. It really drove home *1 Corinthians 15*, where the Apostle Paul speaks of being sown in dishonor but raised in glory. My journey wasn't perfect, but God used my mistakes to teach me and bring me where I needed to be. Scripture hints that we can be sent into the wilderness intentionally to serve God's purpose (*Deuteronomy 8:2, Isaiah 40:3, Ezekiel 20, Hosea 2:13-16, etc.*).

How did I get there? After that road trip in 2012, I did eventually move to a new home with a friend in July 2013. He had children in the area he wanted to be closer to, and it was mutually beneficial for us to split a three bedroom house as roommates. A month after getting there, I was fired from my job for a reason they refused to give me. It was their legal right, but it had me super confused. I'd had no write-ups, and they knew I was new to the area still figuring things out and getting moved in, so I legitimately wasn't sure what happened. At the same time my daughter's dad was out of work and I was not receiving child support. On top of that, my roommate was hit with paying child support for two separate children, so our budget suddenly became practically nonexistent.

Somehow by the grace of God, we never lost our home. Time after time when we were scraping for pennies, something miraculously came through. I found work as a housekeeper that was perfect for me, and we started the path to get back on our own feet. After six months, my roommate became my boyfriend in January 2014.

I dove head first into repairing my physical health. Let me tell you, that's a brutal journey, but I trudged through it! From my peak weight at about 345lbs, I lost 111 lbs and was a distributor for the direct sales company whose products contributed to my results in addition to my diet and exercise changes. Around this same time, a strange phenomenon started to occur where someone I cared for passed away about every three months like clockwork. Three of them were suicides. (*National Suicide Prevention Lifeline is 1-800-273-8255, PLEASE have it in your phone at all times!*) One was an old friend from college, one was the friend I went on the road trip to California with, and one was my boyfriend's mom. There were also several losses to cancer including my grandpa and a couple friends.

I was so heartbroken by each one, over and over again (*Psalm 34:18*). There was so much going on in my life that I was scared to allow myself to have a breakdown. I didn't want my pain to negatively impact the lives of my family and friends, so I overcompensated by trying to live in the silver lining of passionately trying to help others with their physical health. I tried to use my pain to fuel my compassion.

The cycle broke when my dad had a heart attack in fall of 2015. Prayers were answered, and he survived! It pushed me over the edge, though, and I emotionally collapsed for awhile. I wrote a book about my road trip to try and process some of my grief, but ultimately it remained unpublished so my friend's legacy in life would not be of his moment of weakness. It could remain positive in the experiences remembered and lessons learned with him.

I spent all of 2016 focusing on mental and emotional health. I was trying to process my feelings and take more time for self care. I think every mom reaches a point in the modern world where she realizes she's taking on way more than she should as one person and starts learning when and how it is appropriate to say no or to delegate tasks. It is a mother's instinct to pour out all of herself for others, but that model cannot survive forever if she does not occasionally take time to refill for herself.

This is what got me immersed in the self help and new age culture. My desire to say goodbye to those I lost and make peace with their death begged the question of what happens when we die, thusly pulling me to develop my spiritual health. At first I was interested in reiki, mediums, channelers, and yoga. I'm not going to say I had a negative experience. I was attributing these things as gifts from the Biblical God in my head, not realizing what parts were scriptural and what weren't. I was in them more for the healing aspect and the psychology behind their presentation.

These things did help a bit, even though I still felt this need to keep seeking something. I just wasn't sure what and kept soaking up new information like a sponge. It kept me hopping around to understand varying perspectives. Unfortunately I wasn't yet convicted in my need to come back to study of the Bible. If I had been, I would never have gotten into these things. However, by doing them, I gained understanding of popular worldly perspectives I otherwise would not have understood. I believe we learn best through experience, and perhaps God knew it was necessary for me to have that experience so that when I came back to the Bible, I would end up with zero questions or doubts.

I explored the world then whittled it down to the truth rather than starting with the truth and following curiosity to wonder if there was more. Looking back, it feels now like the best was saved for last. In my head, I believed in the Biblical God, knew enough, and had seen proof that the supernatural realm was real. I just ran with it, like a baby eating solid food before they are ready.

In August 2016 I was in a car accident. I was not found to be at fault, but it started giving me anxiety driving through intersections when I realized if I hadn't slammed on my brakes exactly when I did, someone with me could have died or been severely injured. Rather than taking the anti-depressant and class IV substance for panic attacks that was readily thrown at me before I could voice my wishes, I requested a referral for therapy.

This provided the unexpected good fortune of having an insurance company cover the expense of professional counseling for a little bit. Consequently, that helped with far more than just the car accident, because I was able to speak to someone who held no judgment for me. She needed nothing from me. As someone who was constantly giving of myself and not asking for things in return, *it was nice*. She knew that reducing my underlying stressors would reduce my overall anxiety about driving, and it worked. At this same time, I was also taking my life coaching certification courses and engaging in study, so everything I was learning was being applied to my life.

Eventually after having many interesting experiences in that new age world, I wrote a second book talking about the path of self-development. It started at the base level of existence and believing in God. It then looked at physical health and self care, followed by emotional health. Once the healthy self was identified, it discussed communication skills and how that applied to relationships. Last it covered society and politics. I shared in every section how I felt both God and science tied into all of that.

My intentions were as pure as snow, but my execution lacked Christ, a well of knowledge I had no realization I was missing. Based on what I knew of the Bible, I thought of him as more of an ascended master among many who was just an epic teacher. That is how most people in the new age movement view him. The Bible was even directly referenced many times throughout that book to support my perspective!

I sold a handful of copies before pulling it from publication a few short weeks later. I had written it privately, not wanting anyone to try and manipulate my viewpoint to be more like their own. When it was finally published, most who read it truly loved it. However, when my boyfriend read it, he was seriously put off by some of my opinions and refused to finish even half of it.

I valued his opinion and didn't want to lose our relationship of three years because of it, so I pulled it from distribution to do further study. My initial intention was to find more reinforcing evidence so I could modify the phrasing, but now I see that listening to his concern may have been the catalyst for my true salvation (*Proverbs 12:15 & 15:22*). To be honest, in all that time of feeling like I had faith, I don't recall a single moment where I asked myself if I had received salvation. I was just living in the moment of the joy of faith.

The cognitive dissonance of it all sent conflict through my head about what I had written and my decision to pull the book. My pride was hurt, because I was so engulfed in the feeling of accomplishment from creating something and seeing it through to the end. I wanted healing to be found in my words because of all the healing I had gone through to be able to write it. I was the definition of a bleeding heart. My true, deep desire had been to help people with my words, not hurt them. I was in the middle of an emotional battle of asking myself if I had been wrong, and if so, how much. Now I know that conviction of the Spirit often begins with feelings of confusion that stem from cognitive dissonance.

On top of this, I had a lot of strange questions coming to mind leading me to study the book of Revelation. Let me tell you right now, that is not a book one should dive into without *strong* foundations. While it carries lots of positive promises, it also carries lots of threat of punishment. Once you start reading it, you are forced to decide where you fit in the big picture, because it is made clear every single soul will have a part. Some will lead, others will oppress (*Revelation 13:5*). Some will go to war, others will hide (*Revelation 13:10*). Many will be saved, but many will be lost (*Revelation 7:9*).

I've seen it happen to so many people. You start asking yourself how long you have until this happens and get sucked into trying to pin down dates which is only a distraction from the real point. You ask yourself who you are in it and where you will end up. *Am I ready?* It can create feelings of fear and paranoia if you aren't ready for it. There's a reason it's the last book in the Bible and not the first, and it's not just to be chronological. My advice - don't skip it, but don't lead with it either.

    I had picked up reading my Bible again over the previous several months in order to cite verses in the book I pulled from distribution. On 3/11/17 I had started finding information that led me to feel I had been manipulated in a spiritual sense for the previous year or two. I kept hoping it was illusion and praying for God to help me find clarity and truth. I committed that day to seeking Him in purity, and I think for the first time ever, my *whole* heart was in it - not half, or two thirds, or 90% - all of it. I just wanted the peace of truth.

    I recalled seeing the verse where Christ tells the apostles some demons can only be cast out by prayer and fasting, even though I later learned there is a debate about whether *fasting* belongs in *Mark 9:29*. In an effort to clear my mind, that is exactly what I did. I intuitively felt like I was being asked if I was ready to change. Nobody was literally asking me a question in spoken words, but it was a feeling welling up inside me.

    On March 17th, 2017 I started my first ever three day water fast. I committed that no matter what I would not eat a single thing from 7PM Friday until 7AM Tuesday, and I would pray through it all. I had gained some of my lost weight back, getting up to roughly 285 lbs, so I wasn't really concerned that I would wither away even though I had never fasted before.

    On the evening of the 18th between 11PM-midnight, I fell asleep and had a miraculous dream. The whole time my boyfriend had been sitting at the computer playing video games. In this dream I was transported to a large white room. There were just white walls in what I think was a cube shape, that's it. It's not like I had a measuring tape, but I would guess the ceilings were at least twenty feet high, if not more. In the center of the room appeared a floating, roughly person-shaped being made of pure white light. I couldn't make out the details of their figure, just saw the rough form of arms, legs, a torso, and a head in the center. Light was emanating from this being in all directions in both straight and wavy lines.

    Aside from what I could see with my eyes, I could also feel this being's presence. My senses were in overdrive (*I didn't smell or taste anything at all*). I don't want to say that it hurt, but I will say that it was overwhelming to my physical body to be in this being's presence. The light was almost blinding, and I had to shield my eyes with my forearm and turn to the right. Every cell of my skin felt it, every hair was on end. There was a loud sound covering a range of frequencies from somewhat low to *very* high. It wasn't any louder than the front row of a rock concert though, so I didn't feel concerned about covering my ears. The room was warm, but not hot.

The most important part to me was what I felt in my heart, literally in my chest. It was a deeper, fuller, more perfect feeling of love than I could have *ever* possibly imagined a human was capable of feeling. Suddenly the concept of love felt like a tangible thing I could pull out of my chest and hold in my hand. Any more of that swelling feeling and I think my heart would have simply burst! All of this was happening simultaneously over the course of less than thirty seconds. After I turned my head to the right, it went dark and blank, like closing your eyes and not opening them. There was a brief moment after that where there was a half second flash of some rolling green fields, but that's it. It felt like there was more to this dream, but I was not allowed to remember it when I woke up.

My eyes jumped open from this dream, glancing around the room as my body laid there, frozen. What I experienced felt more real than waking up in that room. It was confusing, disorienting, and some strange blend of brutal and beautiful. It took me a few minutes to work up the courage, but I eventually went back to sleep peacefully knowing it was time to be serious in my faith.

I have an obligation to be honest here. I cannot put an official name on what I saw. This being did not speak in the short bit that I remembered. Not then and no time since then have I been given a name for that being or been told anything about it. I was left to decide for myself what had just happened. I knew *2 Corinthians 11:14* said even Satan transforms into an angel of light, and that meant I should be cautious. I also couldn't rule out that it was just a dream manifestation of my subconscious, though I hadn't studied the transfiguration on the mount yet (*Matthew 17:1-8, Mark 9:2-8, Luke 9:28-36, 2 Peter 1:16-18*). I couldn't determine any basis at that time for that specific imagery to surface in such an extremely tangible way. If it hadn't felt so very real, I could have written it off as a dream, but it did, so I started trying to compile the possibilities and eliminate the variables.

There is an old riddle told in many variations. You might recognize it from the movie *The Labyrinth* which this situation brought to mind. You are walking along a path and approach two men guarding two doors. One tells only truth (*in this application, Christ*) and one tells only lies (*Satan is the father of lies*). We are assuming here that one door leads to heaven, and the other leads to hell. These two men appear identical, thusly mirroring the idea that even Satan can transfigure into a being of light the same way Christ did. Eyes and ears can be deceived.

In the riddle you only get one question to determine which one is which. The answer is to ask one of them which door the other man would say leads to heaven. It doesn't matter which one you ask. Both guards will point to the same door, which will be the door to hell. You choose the opposite door. *Why does that make any sense?* When you ask the liar, he will lie, saying the other man would point you towards the door to hell and call it the door to heaven. When you ask the truth teller, he will be honest that that the other guard will point you towards the door to hell and call it heaven. Either way, both identify which one is the wrong door.

It is a profound lesson in the importance of discernment. If someone is a liar, you can't just ask them directly for answers, because they will lie. How would you know? We must determine truth based on character. We need to know what both honesty and deception look like to find truth. Luckily for us, we have plenty of material in the Bible and time to study it to learn discernment by identifying the character of Christ versus Satan, so we can determine when we are being led by false prophets and when we are hearing truth. We get way more than one question.

I may not be able to name the being I saw due to lack of identification being provided, but I can tell you what happened as a result of it. You will have to discern for yourself, just like I did. It made me feel like the reason I wasn't provided a name was to alert me to my need to hone my discernment. It motivated me to study the character of Christ versus Satan in as much detail as I could. Figuring it out rather than being given the answer was an *irreplaceable* part of my journey. I mean, the whole point of this riddle is that I would have needed to do that anyway, right? If I had been told a name, wouldn't I have still needed to discern if it was true? Then again, if I had been given a name, would it have occurred to me to study this or would I have trusted it? It's hard to say.

I did end up completing the fasting period successfully, but through the rest of it, I almost felt like my inner conflict over my stack of confusion was trying to personify itself in my head through this riddle. My brain was collecting puzzle pieces and trying to fit them together. I was torn over what I thought about all of it and too scared to tell anyone in fear they would try to commit me like I was crazy. I think my mind divided the discussion as being between the devil and Christ and forced me to choose one.

It was only about a day of this. Don't think I just snapped and lost my marbles. In my attempt to paint a clear picture with only words on paper, it can certainly sound more dramatic than it is. Nobody knew how I was feeling on the inside. I just kept quiet for the most part in deep thought. I put on my smile and was living my daily life through this fasting period remarkably patiently. I even still went grocery shopping and cooked dinner for my family!

A house divided against itself cannot stand (*Matthew 12:22-28, Mark 3:25*), so I knew I had to get serious. On that Sunday afternoon, my family and I ended up at the park. I had been starting to feel peaceful, because *of course* I choose Christ! I walked off on my own to a small balcony that looked out over the water. As I stood there with my eyes closed, I could feel a small breeze on my face and the sun was lightly warming my skin. I could hear birds chirping and gentle movement on the water. Then it happened, just like a choice was set in stone. I started singing the first thing that came to mind. It just flowed out of my mouth like water from a spring.

> *Why should I feel discouraged?*
> *Why should the shadows fall?*
> *Why should my heart be lonely*
> *and long for heaven and home?*
> *When Jesus is my portion,*
> *A constant friend is he,*
> *for his eye is on the sparrow,*
> *and I know he watches me.*

As I finished, I reflected on the words of this song and felt what grace feels like. I felt like all my collective troubles that were being personified in the devil threw hands up and said *that's it, I'm done, I can't beat that*. They were gone. This was my heart song now. There has not been a single day since then that I don't feel that song just as deeply as I did in that moment. That was a *forever moment*.

No matter how perfect that felt, it didn't stop my mind from later working its way through the cognitive dissonance. I still desired to help people with my life, so it made me incredibly concerned with sharpening my discernment and making sure I was speaking real truth. I felt the weight of responsibility that comes with being influential in the world. I didn't want to speak a word of it until I was crystal clear what I felt it all meant.

Looking back, I think that when I saw that vision, my old self died. Then the seed of Christ was planted. This whole series of events was the pivot point in my life where I stopped trying to find God on my own and turned to Christ. I sought out truth with the pure and innocent curiosity of a child matched with the adult desire to understand what was happening. *That* is the feeling we all must embrace to begin that true relationship - *sincere curiosity* (*Matthew 18:3-4, Mark 10:15, Luke 18:17*).

I spent 2017 deep in the belly of the whale. For about six months I was studying nonstop, praying and seeking as much Biblical knowledge as my mind could absorb, following a crumb trail of puzzle pieces in God's perfect timing. I already had a large pool of information from my previous studies, so this part of my journey was about understanding how Christ fit into it all, truly accepting him, and forming the big picture with all my puzzle pieces. I was reaching out to people who were leaders of faith wanting to understand Christ from every perspective possible, even other religions. Who is he compared to how others view him?

If I wanted to sort out my spiritual experiences, I thought I would start by digging through what rational minds have to say about it. I again considered my mental health, but in all other respects I was fine. I was a responsible mom who worked and paid the majority of the bills, cooked, cleaned, and spent quality time with the kids, and none of that was interrupted.

I even honestly filled in a rather thorough online assessment meant to identify if you may be in the middle of a mental health crisis, and I easily passed it. All it said was that I may have mild stress issues. My mind was still in a rational place, even though irrational things were happening. Experiences like this truly identify how you respond to things like confusion and pressure. I did my best to keep my cool and approach all things objectively. I made sure I wasn't neglecting my responsibilities in my work and home life, and just kept studying and praying.

I sought answers to so many questions. I wondered if there was some way that all these differing faiths made sense if they're all happening in the same story of the earth. What are the rules for Christians, and how do I know I'm being a good person? I prayed every single day for truth, the ability to understand it, and the wisdom to know how to use it. I prayed constantly for sharper discernment so I could sort through all this information with accuracy instead of believing everything I read and getting confused by conflicting opinions. I tried to be scientifically thorough, isolating variables.

I realized the easiest way to do this was to rebuild myself from scratch. I decided to ditch the notion that I had ever known anything about anything at all and worked from the ground up with Christ in my heart. I toppled the tower of self I had built and put him in the new foundation. This means for me to feel authentic, I had to mirror it in my physical life too. As an outward reflection of an inner desire to love my true self the way God made me, I stopped wearing makeup, jewelry, and nail polish. I was tired of feeling like I had to change how I looked to meet society's standards or to be happy with myself. It's my heart that counts, and that's what I wanted to pour all of my attention into developing. I do wear a bracelet now, but it is related to the depth I feel in my faith.

I stopped dying my hair and committed to letting it grow out it's natural color no matter what it looked like or how long it took. I was bright blonde as a child, but around college I started dying my hair an auburn color. With a light complexion and hazel eyes, I thought it made my face pop more. I had always felt like a wallflower when I was blonde. It turns out that now my natural color is a bit of a dishwater blonde with a few white/grey strands already coming through. It doesn't bother me, and I'm certain a summer of sunlight will lighten it up.

I also stopped eating meat. This is obviously a bit more controversial, but after that fast, meat no longer looked like food. All I saw when I looked at it was dead flesh, and it didn't taste good anymore. At first, I was just scaling back. I cut back to only eating it in two meals a day, then one meal a day, then once every other day. I also started saying a small thanks for the animal for giving its life to nourish our bodies, and I prayed for it to find peace. Eventually in my Biblical study, I became convicted about being vegetarian which will be touched on again later. If I can survive without eating an animal, then the death felt gratuitous and unnecessary. I love animals and see life in them.

Fortunately, we live in a time with some incredibly delicious plant based meat substitutes, and it didn't really feel like my taste buds gave up anything. I did lose some weight, even though I wasn't getting much free time for exercise. Over time I just felt so much lighter, happier and healthier. As of writing this I am back down in the 250's and getting more time for exercise, so the number is steadily declining again.

I started cracking down on what goes in my body, because the Bible says our body is a temple (*1 Corinthians 6:19*). We started buying gallons of reverse osmosis drinking water, non-fluoride toothpaste, less toxic hypoallergenic detergent and other household products, and as many organic and non-gmo whole foods as we could afford. Suddenly I had to make a weekly trip to the grocery store instead of monthly, because we were eating so much more fresh produce instead of processed stuff. These changes made me feel honestly healthier than I have ever felt! Unfortunately, the numerous previous years of abusing my body still occasionally take their toll, but overall these changes have been very positive.

I have heard some prominent Christians condemn these same actions, suggesting all they are is legalism. However, these things were done because I chose to do them. It was what I personally needed, and the Bible and Spirit convicted me that I was on the right track. Don't allow people who are significantly further along in their growth journey of faith to lead you into skipping the steps necessary for you to process and accept the gospel on a deeper level. Of course we need love, peace, joy, and laughter! We just have a mess to sort through as well, personal accountability to accept, and trials to face before that can be our daily nature.

My brethren, count it all joy when ye fall into divers temptations; knowing this, that the trying of your faith worketh patience. But let patience have her perfect work, that ye may be perfect and entire, wanting nothing (James 1:2-4). The good fruit produced from trials, patience, and perseverance is what gives us the joy that carries us through the struggle, but that doesn't mean we can skip the hard stuff. God helps us through it. We pray for endurance and grace, not omission from trials.

While I was continuing my study, I started being more vocal in my faith. I would only share basic absolutes supported by scripture that I knew had wisdom but couldn't reasonably be argued with. I began focusing into my desire to feel purified of my past. Physical things that represented this spiritual process for me included starting a prayer journal and utilizing frankincense and other oils. I also wanted to be baptized again as an adult by choice. I didn't want to compromise on how I wanted to be fully submerged as Christ was, but it took time to find people who do that.

On the morning of September 30th, 2017, I woke up in severe abdominal pain. I questioned if I had a hernia, because it wouldn't go away. I have birthed one child back in 2008, and that was a c-section because she turned breech a few days after her due date. I never went into labor to know what that pain feels like. What I do know is this sharp pain is what I imagined it would feel like. I laid in bed for hours, watching tv close to tears. After about three hours of this, my friend invited me to go to the local fitness center not knowing about my pain. She called it the spa, because it was super high tech and had a dry room, a sauna, a jacuzzi, a therapy pool, and a track pool plus amenities like massages and classes. I had no intention of spending money on the Sabbath, especially since I didn't have any, but she offered to let me use one of her punches on her card and go free. I was all in! What could be more restful than that?

We were some of the only people there at the time. I ended up in the therapy pool all by myself. I decided to take a moment and pray. During this prayer I realized this was maybe as close as I would get to baptism for awhile, so I grabbed the bar on the side of the pool and held myself under for a few moments, praying in my heart. I asked God to allow it to count as a baptism by choice and the Holy Spirit until I could find a place I wanted to do it where all could see as we are asked. It was a private moment between me and God, and it felt like He accepted my pure intent.

Afterwards, I just floated around for a bit, being thankful as I felt my pain finally start to dissipate. By the time we left, the pain was almost entirely gone. I could sit in the seat of my friend's van without squirming in discomfort like I had on the way there. Not long after that day, I stumbled into a video explaining the differences between *baptism* and the *mikvah*, a Jewish ritual cleansing bath. It seemed I was led to doing both by the Spirit, so I started returning roughly once a month and repeating the cleansing action.

It felt like I was washing off all the struggles I had worked through repenting of since the last time I had come. I would work out hard for roughly an hour, then go down in the steam room and sweat some more. Then I would relax in the jacuzzi and purify in the therapy pool. It felt like burning away what I wanted to release from the inside out then washing it off in a prayerful way. I also began buying products that heal the skin instead of covering blemishes, and the work I was doing on the inside started showing on the outside. I was really starting to like my authentic self the way God made me. That was the whole point.

Forgiveness

During that year, I started working my way through each of those twelve commandments I shared about earlier. I studied each in detail and shifted my life to be in line with them. The first step was personal accountability. Every time I could recall a situation where I wasn't in line with the command I was focusing on, I did my best to repent and atone. If possible, I asked those I had hurt to forgive me. I hoped those who hurt me would ask for my forgiveness, but even if they didn't I made sure to accept that and forgive them for how I too had been hurt.

In my effort to be right with God, I asked Him to forgive me through Christ, and in truth it felt like he was erasing those sins from memory as I went through each one. (*Hebrews 8:12*) It also reflected a feeling of accounting for the ripple effect. My negative actions toward someone could cause them to treat the next person differently, and that next person may be impacted by that in a way that changed their behavior, etc. You don't truly know how far your moment of anger or weakness will spread in ways you will never likely see. Asking for divine forgiveness also felt like asking those strangers to forgive me who I didn't know my actions touched. We should never forget that our words and actions echo and alter realities as they travel.

When all my bases were covered, I finally forgave myself, something I just couldn't be comfortable doing until I knew I had done everything I could to make amends. I let go of the emotional distress but kept the lessons. Due to this experience, I like to tell people **time does not heal wounds, it just turns our pain into wisdom**.

It's important to identify that until we complete all these steps to forgive, the people who hurt us can still hold power over us. They have the ability to hit emotional buttons and triggers connected to the unresolved feelings, causing them to pull us away from the love, peace, strength, and protection of God and towards sadness, anger, feelings of weakness, confusion, and frustration. Their ability to do this is powerful at diminishing our trust in God, because we are choosing to focus on our pain instead of embracing His love, healing, and safety.

That's why we take each of these steps - to release the darkness in our lives properly on a soul level so it can no longer resurface. If we are intended to grow from a seed of faith (*Matthew 13:31-32, Mark 4:30-32, Luke 13:18-19*) into a tree that bears good fruit (*Matthew 7:17-20*), part of tending the garden is pulling the weeds out by the roots so your harvest has free and clear room to grow without the weeds claiming all the water and nutrients in the soil. Don't let negative feelings become weeds that drain the life from you.

Forgiveness is *NOT* easy. Not only is it a benchmark of the teachings of Christ that we must understand, but it hurts! Accepting forgiveness from Christ is just about as easy as believing you have been forgiven, but forgiving someone who hurt you is not easy. We need to humble ourselves in order to utilize this gift and face the mirror honestly. That alone I find most people are unwilling to do. *Then* we have to engage in an attempt to interact with others regarding it, because to forgive is a verb, an action. Very few people have ever been able to explain to me *how* to do it.

Shouldn't this be something we are taught in school? It's a pretty useful life skill to know how to forgive! People can explain its value at length, they know they want to do it, but rarely can they outline a process for something so feelings based. I guess it can be hard to verbalize feelings after such a long history where we have been taught to suppress and ignore them.

During my coaching certification (*Transformation Services, Inc, Joeel and Natalie Rivera*), I was provided an eight step process I would like to share with you in my own words. It is thorough but simple and concise. Hopefully this will be a helpful perspective as you work through forgiveness for yourself. Once we have addressed *how* to forgive, we will come back to evaluating what needs forgiven. It's only fair to equip you before sending you to the trials.

*Take as much time as you need on each step when you find yourself following this process. It will only work if the words are honest and the feelings behind the actions are authentic. It will be impossible to forgive until you **want** to do it. Embrace your patience, call on God's grace, and take each step at the pace He moves you. Prayer should be infused at every level.*

1 - IDENTIFY The first step is to run through your *who/what/where/when/why* list. Who needs forgiven? If we are being honest with ourselves, all parties hold some level of responsibility in the majority of situations, whether it be what we did or how we reacted. This does not exclude ourselves. *Be honest*. What happened? Are you confident you have collected all the facts? Are the wounds old or fresh? Lay it all out, preferably on paper. Journaling can be very helpful in this process.

2 - REFLECT *Ask yourself how this lack of forgiveness is impacting you.* Wisdom is knowing that harboring unforgiveness is like drinking poison and expecting someone else to die. Forgiveness is unlocking the door to set someone free and realizing you were the prisoner. We see so many TV shows these days about people who want vengeance. They plot and plan, losing friends and themselves along the way. When they finally get that revenge, they feel hollow and alone, realizing it didn't solve anything, only destroyed their own happiness. Then they turn around and *still* have to go through this same process. I believe that is ultimately where it leads when someone cannot forgive. They would have been better off skipping the vengeance, forgiving, and keeping love in their hearts. Evaluate what damage holding on to this pain has done to you, is currently doing, and has the potential to do in the future. How does it affect your relationships? Your job? Your mood? This will be your motivation to take the next step. Also, realize that the other parties don't know you feel this way, and likely aren't hurting like you are.

It is often the case that the person who hurt us doesn't see it as having hurt us, and they simply don't care. They might feel wronged or slighted by your response or have already let it go. We have a tendency to believe that if we hold on to our resentment and don't forgive the other person, that it is somehow hurting the other party to hold this against them. The truth is, holding on to it is only sure to be hurting ourselves. It will ultimately hold us back.

3 - APOLOGIZE *Identify what parts of the situation were your responsibility, and say that you're sorry.* You need to mean it, though. Perhaps the words *to express sincere remorse* more accurately reflects a genuine apology. Words are hollow without heart and integrity behind them. Sometimes you can't do this face to face. Maybe the person you are apologizing to has passed away, moved away, or is too angry to be able to have that discussion. If that's the case, writing a letter can be a positive step to help you release the apology in a tangible way. It could be that you took some bad news negatively, and you need to apologize for your behavior.
(*Matthew 5:38-39*) It's possible you did something with pure positive intentions, but the execution was poor or misguided and it caused someone pain. We all have what we felt at the time were good reasons behind our actions, so there can easily be innocent reasons behind bad outcomes. Just offer your apology knowing you did it with truth in your heart. Do **NOT** give an apology expecting a certain outcome! What you would like to see happen and what happens may not line up, and that will be what it will be. You are focusing on cleaning your own slate, not someone else's. The other person might not accept your apology. They might be angry it was brought up. They might just say thank you without reciprocating the act like you think they should, leaving you with a hanging feeling. *Let it be*. Maybe it will resolve how you envisioned down the road when they reach the same point in their growth journey as you, but there are no guarantees. If you attach yourself to a perfect resolution, you may experience a letdown. It is better not to set yourself up for that possibility. Then if it *does* resolve the way you wanted, it can be an added blessing. Pray for those who cannot forgive.

4 - EXPRESS GRIEVANCES *Make sure you feel you've been clearly heard and understood.* Again, do not attach yourself to an outcome. It is important to clear the air on how you feel a situation played out, and it is valuable to let another person know how their actions affect you and others. They may need time to process this information. It could take years or even a lifetime for someone to truly feel the weight of their personal responsibility on their heart enough to apologize or forgive. Speak calmly, rationally, and sincerely. Breathe deep, slow, and controlled, and do not allow anger or anxiety to guide your words into escalating the situation further.

Composure is an effective communication tool, so if you believe this will be a difficult task for you, try practicing in front of a mirror first.

5 - LEARN THE LESSONS *The silver lining of all pain is what it taught us.* Pain exists as an indicator that something is wrong. For example, you might get migraines if you are dehydrated or sleep deprived or starving or sick. You don't just get them for no reason. Even if you can't find the reason, that doesn't mean there isn't one. Emotional pain is the same in the sense that it is alerting us to unresolved issues. The stronger the feeling is, the more important it is for your own wellbeing to address it. Think of feelings like energy. The law of the conservation of energy says that energy cannot be created or destroyed, only transferred. Emotions build strength inside you to force their way out when they are suppressed, because you are not expelling the constant flow of energy. Instead you are trapping it inside you. Our feelings know that the caged bird sings for freedom. Once you've done all this challenging work to release that energy in healthy ways, it is likely not an experience you would like to repeat. You need to step back from the situation and evaluate what it taught you about yourself and others. This is the step where the feelings of pain get to change into wisdom. Did your experience bring to light that you struggle to keep your calm in tense situations? Then you learned that it's something you need to work on so you can do better next time. Did you get burned by someone and learn that trust is meant to be earned? Did you learn that someone in your life is toxic to you? There will *always* be at least one lesson, if not many layers of them. Truly learning them means implementing the new information into your life so mistakes don't repeat going forward.

6 - LET GO *Release your expectations.* Forgiving doesn't mean accepting unacceptable behaviors or that you're letting people off the hook. You may have changes to make in your life as you emerge from this process. You can forgive someone for the purpose of healing without readmitting them into your life or accepting their bad behaviors going forward. It is up to you to decide if more chances are given or if it is time to walk away. Sometimes letting go is about releasing someone from your life. But *STOP* placing expectations on the behaviors of others. The only thing you can control in any situation is yourself, and that is enough to worry about. Don't carry the stress of the behaviors of others. Decide the best way for *YOU* to proceed and **accept** that success as enough.

7 - REPROGRAM *Rewire your triggers.* It is often the case that certain words, places, or things can trigger flashbacks and emotional responses. It can sometimes be difficult to fully complete the process of forgiveness because something inconsequential will set us off and knock us back to step one. Work with loved ones and professionals if need be to break the power of a trigger, and of course, pray over it. For example, certain songs used to bring up sad feelings in me about the friend I went to California with after he ended his own life. Hearing them would stir up my completely normal feelings of guilt and hurt for not being able to prevent it. I had to work to reclaim a positive feeling when I heard those songs so I wouldn't tailspin back into grieving. I went through the process of forgiving myself, him, the other people involved, and making peace with the concept of death. I apologized to those I felt needed an apology from me. I prayed over it all and learned an endless multitude of lessons. Eventually I became able to hear the songs without crying and reattached fond memories to them instead of sad ones. This took a long time, so don't expect any change of worth to happen overnight.

8 - LIVE AND BE FREE *The best revenge is a life well lived!* Once you have done all this work, don't come back to struggling over the same things you've resolved! This process is meant to loose the chains of oppression that we place on ourselves with our own emotions. Forgiveness is *freedom*. This is a process of healing and liberation. *Don't put the chains back on*. Instead take that freedom and put it to good use. Be happy, live love, and shine God's peace into the world through your own peace.

Now that you have an outline you can follow, we are about to exit the belly of the whale onto dry land and use what we have learned. This is the part about honest accountability and getting in line with God. While societal standards will certainly be acknowledged in this journey, it is about putting God's authority higher and figuring out how to live that way in society. It's the conundrum of being in the world of man but not of it (*1 John 2:15-17*), because you are of the kingdom of heaven as a child of God. We are going to sift through that and find the gold Christ uses to repair our broken parts. In the belly of the whale, you realized the importance of listening to God and doing as He asks. So now you will dig into the words he left on this earth to guide you and give it the old college try to get it right as best you can.

There are people who will argue that stopping here is fine. Your soul is your decision, and I cannot make those choices for you. Nobody can force sincerity in your walk. All I can do is offer to help by sharing what helped me. I remember being in that place at one point, and I sincerely appreciate what this process has done for me in my life. I'm trying to fish from the right side of the boat right now by letting you know that once you get through it you will be glad you did, and until you try you'll always wonder. You are reading this book for a reason.

Write the prayer you would have said to God after being in the whale for three days, ready to come out and try to get it right the second time around. Write how you feel this applies in your life right now. What did you learn about forgiveness? Churn around the thought of how valuable Christ's lessons are, not only to you but to others. Realize that to be able to teach something later on is to prove that you have learned it well now, so this will be the part where we learn before leading in faith. The best lessons are from experience, not just books. Can we really share a gospel we don't understand enough to let it guide our actions? Remember, this is a hero's journey. Hero's save the day in their shining armor and spend lots of their downtime training.

6. The Road of Trials

*Shall the earth be made to bring forth in one day,
or shall a nation be born at once?
For as soon as Zion travailed, she brought forth her children.
Shall I bring to the birth, and not cause to bring forth?
saith the Lord.
Shall I cause to bring forth and shut the womb? saith thy God.*
Isaiah 66:8-9

Welcome to being in the womb of growth in faith. This is not about changing to please others, though these changes will certainly have a side effect of pleasing those around you. This is about choosing to change for yourself because you understand the value in not just setting goals to walk more like Christ, but in raising baseline standards which our fear of God urges us to do. It's about knowing that you've done this in a way that pleases God, so you can feel light as a feather with a clean conscience and His love in your heart.

Christ is the Word (*John 1:1*), and the gospel - meaning *good news* - is the message the Word formed. When he fasted in the wilderness for forty days, one of the ways the devil tried to tempt Christ is by telling him to turn the stones into bread and eat. (*Matthew 4:1-11*) Christ replied *Man shall not live on bread alone, but by every word that proceedeth out of the mouth of God.* In another passage, as one of the seven *I am* statements, Christ identifies himself as the bread of life (*John 6:35*). This is indicative of the fact that Christ's words came from God and they are our soul food that will provide us all necessary spiritual nourishment. The scripture shares the essence of those words so they can be heard and studied throughout the generations.

We all desire deep down to be the best version of ourselves. Working through these behavioral points in study of the gospel creates strength for success in life and will help make getting through tough times easier. This is just as much about the healthy act of accepting our personal responsibility as it is about loving ourselves and others. *Galatians 5:22-23* tells us *But the fruit of the Spirit is love, joy, peace, longsuffering, gentleness, goodness, faith, meekness, temperance: against such there is no law.* It's good to know that all of these positive traits will be the result of this journey, the fruit of your trials.

I learned the hard way that when you stand for nothing, you can fall for anything, and you can still fall for quite a bit even when you do stand for something. Doing this soul work to establish a moral code from God will help eliminate variable possible solutions in a crunch, because you've already prepared yourself for how you would prefer to respond to conflict ahead of time like a good boy/girl scout. It will *reduce* the stress of on-the-spot decision making and the possibility of hypocritical responses to problems as well. So it's time to grow in a much less confrontational and high stress manner than I experienced. Let's get through this. (*1 Timothy 6:12, 2 Corinthians 2:10-11, 1 John 3:8, Revelation 20:10... Be sure to look up all of these!*)

The soul work is your job and *yours alone*. All I can do is give you prompts in developmental sections that will hopefully benefit you and deepen your experience. This is like training, battling your wits from a distance, but you decide who wins. The closest word I can think of to describe this is *sparring*. There's no actual confrontation with me here. The Spirit will wield the rod of iron in your heart as your mind works through the information, helping you grow stronger in faith and prepare for any real battle you may face down the road (*Proverbs 27:17, Jeremiah 17:1, Psalm 2:9, Revelation 2:27, etc.*).

I am not putting a stumbling block in front of you. I will be sharing mistakes I have made in the past, but this is only for the purpose of identifying what they were as well as how and why I repented. This is intended to help you be more capable of identifying when a stumbling block *has* been put in your path so you can walk around it without tripping, or maybe even pick it up so nobody else trips on it (*1 Corinthians 8:9-11, Romans 14:13, etc.*). This keeps me level with you as well. I'm not talking down at you, just relating to the struggle.

I will help you confront yourself in a captain's call to battle for self-awareness. We are going to be like heroes in a role playing game and claim a tower. The tower is *you*. Right now there are twelve floors to conquer in order to claim total victory, but every floor has enemies to battle. It's a good thing you brought the armor of God! You are a paladin!

Where did this idea come from? There are many theories about Mary Magdalene floating around. I'm not going to stray into that, but at one point in time I was studying the subject for myself. Some say Magdalene is signifying where she was from, a city called Magdala. Others believe she was being called *Mary the Tower*. I figured if that had any Biblical truth, then maybe the Old Testament had mention of a tower as a person somewhere since patterns with God repeat themselves. I couldn't help but wonder what that could possibly mean. It's pretty broadly open for interpretation. I thought I had seen it somewhere before but couldn't pin it down in my mind, so I searched Strong's Concordance for words that meant *tower*.

H4026 - migdal or migdalah means *tower* and is found forty-nine times in the Old Testament. However, I also found *H969 - bachown'*. This word that means *tower* is found only one time in one verse. That is *Jeremiah 6:27* which says *I have set thee for a tower and a fortress among my people, that thou mayest know and try their way*. Most translations omit the word *tower* here and replace it by saying something like *I have made you a tester or assayer of metals.* (*1 Peter 1:7*) God was speaking to Jeremiah here. While I couldn't possibly say whether that has anything to do with Mary Magdalene, it is a discovery that inspired the format chosen for how we will journey through the trials of the commandments. Let's look at the difference between a bad tower and a good tower before we start off.

In *Genesis 11:1-9* we see the story of the tower of Babel. The word *Babel* breaks down into two parts - *Bab* meant *gate* and *el* meant *God*. They wanted to build a tower to God, I think to reopen the gate that was shut behind Adam and Eve after the fall. Instead of using proper quality materials, they used bricks with slime for mortar. It was poorly constructed, and God tore it down. He then divided the languages to prevent them from trying again.

They didn't understand what they were doing or how to do it. They built on inferior quality with false principles. This process I'm sharing with you is how I came out of metaphorical Babylon, though like all of us, she tried to claim me (*Jeremiah 51:45, Revelation 18*). I believe this is how we wash our robes and make them white (*Revelation 22:14*). Think of it like replacing Vashti with Esther (*Book of Esther*).

Before I started digging for truth, I saw the world through that lens. I was in the metaphorical thick of Babylon, and how could I have known? What we are born into doesn't feel out of the ordinary to us. It just feels typical. You have to exit your comfort zone to realize it. Most of us don't do that. Yet as I said, that tower of self was toppled and rebuilt with Christ in the foundations. He is the way, the truth, and the life. His unleavened gospel message provides the true and correct building materials, which is why he said the only way to the Father is through him. His message contains the instructions on how to be a person built for God, so here is where we gain that understanding. In Babylon we are God's enemies, but we are reconciled through Christ (*Romans 5:10*).

Luke 6:46-49 is a perfect statement from Christ on this subject which is an echo of the ending of the sermon on the mount in *Matthew 7:24-27*. *And why call ye me Lord, Lord, and do not the things which I say? Whosoever cometh to me, and heareth my sayings, and doeth them, I will shew you to whom he is like: He is like a man which built a house, and digged deep, and laid the foundation on a rock, and when the flood arose, the stream beat vehemently upon that house, and could not shake it for it was founded upon a rock. But he that heareth, and doeth not, is like a man that without a foundation built a house upon the earth against which the stream did beat vehemently, and immediately it fell, and the ruin of that house was great.*

Christ was the cornerstone the builders rejected, but he has now become a tried and precious stone for a foundation (*Isaiah 28:16, Psalm 118:22, Matthew 21:42, Acts 4:11, Proverbs 18:10*). So let's study what Christ commanded us to do and the life he lived as a man who perfectly followed God's will (*John 14:12-16*). Let us work through the process to make him our foundation!

If you'd like a refresher, the ten commandments are found in *Exodus 20:1-17* and the two highest commandments given by Christ are in *Matthew 22:36-40*. All Christ did was intended to preserve the spirit of the intention of these statements. At the foundation of this tower will be the first commandment. The two highest floors of this building will cover the two highest commandments given by Christ and tie them all together. One by one we will reclaim each floor from the enemy, from the bottom going up. Be certain you are praying as you go so that every floor can be filled with peace and blessing, like the all clear to continue forward.

For each command, we will look at how the Old Testament viewed the subject, then also how this message echoes in the New Testament, highlighting why they are good rules we should want to follow. We will try to confront deceptions and challenges of following these rules in the modern world as I share my personal experience doing this same process. Then we will tie it all together with questions for you to evaluate how you feel this applies to your own life. We will identify what form of dual behavioral traits we are trying to conquer through this command. Then in the space at the end, you will be guided to repent, atone, ask for forgiveness, and sum up your thoughts.

Hopefully this will help you garner a realistic and actionable understanding of each concept and feel a strengthening of your relationship with God and Christ. This doesn't just happen because you follow the rules more closely. It happens because you finally start to understand and respect divine nature. *"How does one become a butterfly?" she asked. "You must want to fly so much that you are willing to give up being a caterpillar." ~ Trina Paulus*

Keep in mind the trials are a dramatically longer section of the hero's journey since there are so many concepts to battle through. That is just part of the design. *1 Peter 1* is a great passage to read anytime you need a pep talk to keep going. You will feel so much lighter when you come out on the other side of this!

Since you are reading, there is no time clock forcing you along. Focus on the thorough quality of completion. It is not a race or competition of any kind. Take a moment to regroup between each of these twelve subsections so you don't get overwhelmed. Refresh and prepare yourself for the next challenge in joyful ways so this process is uplifting instead of depressing (*Philippians 2:14-16*). It's all about the attitude you bring to the table.

Sin is a word that has such a deep tone of judgment. Just saying the word can feel like the swing of an axe and push us from the desire to pursue personal growth. If it bothers you that much, try temporarily substituting the word sin by saying you made misguided choices before, but you *want* to make better choices with God's guidance now.

That's a safe, accurate phrase with more of a life coaching tone to it as you are working through this transition until the word sin can be used again without so much weight behind it. People hire life coaches all the time, but the second someone suggests using the Bible for personal growth they get attacked for being a legalist or judgmental or shoving faith down peoples' throats. That's silly, because as a life coach myself, I think Christ is the best coach I have ever seen. We *want* to grow! Know also that we are capable of feeling God's sorrow over our sins without feeling condemned thanks to grace (*2 Corinthians 7:10*). You will be ok. *For God hath not given us the spirit of fear, but of power, and of love, and of a sound mind* (*2 Timothy 1:7*). Now get on your armor, and *let's go!* (*Luke 5:32*)

1 - I am the Lord thy God, which have brought thee out of the land of Egypt, out of the house of bondage. Thou shalt have no other gods before me.

First let's briefly address the debate about the name of God objectively. It is worth highlighting that names can be important to a degree. It's healthy to know what to legitimately call someone, and I can't imagine that anyone wants to call out the wrong name in prayer. There have been many debates about the true divine names, so I'm not going to pick a dog in that fight. I feel that due to the Tower of Babel incident, God has a hand in all languages, so it's a difficult discussion to tackle unless an angel literally visits you and instructs you otherwise. That doesn't mean I can't help you narrow it down.

According to Strong's Concordance, the original word translated to *Lord* here is *H3068 - Jehovah*. This is based on the Hebrew tetragrammaton YHVH. In translation different people have added vowels in different ways, so some people will instead say Yahweh (*Exodus 6:3*). Also, *H430 - Elohim* is the original word that was translated to both *God* and *gods*. When studying the word *Elohim*, it is a word often translated to *God* in the Bible, but it is also often identified as being plural. In the New Testament, the only thing resembling a name for God is *G5 - Abba* (*Mark 14:36, Romans 8:15, Galatians 4:6*), though many believe that to be a word for *papa*. The trinitarian principle identifies Christ as God (*Acts 4:12*). As you can see, there are many perspectives.

There are long lists of all the divine names for God that are fascinating to study. The other options tend to be descriptors of His character though, not actual names. That concept is not unsupported by scripture. He is often referred to as eternal, immortal, and invisible (*Exodus 33:20, Deuteronomy 4:12, Job 9:11, 1 Timothy 1:17 & 6:16, Romans 1:20, etc*). In this book, I utilize the most universally acknowledged word ***God*** in reference to God the Father.

When we look at Christ, in the original Greek of the gospel he is *Iesous Christos*. In Hebrew he is called *Yeshua Ha Mashiach* (*Jesus the Anointed One/Messiah*). Others will call him *Yahushua/Joshua*. In America, *Jesus Christ* or *Jesus the Christ* is the most common. Keep in mind the letter *J* didn't exist until the 1600s when it was differentiated from the letter *I*. In Islam they call him *Isa*. I chose to say **Christ** in this book because it felt like it would offend and distract the least number of people. If it does bother you, I humbly suggest that your frustrations are misplaced.

The Holy Spirit also tends to cause a bit of contention. Some people will argue that it is simply a concoction of the ancient church that was added to the Bible, while others will declare that it is real and argue about whether it's gender is male or female. Originally in Hebrew the spirit of God was called *Ruach ha'Kodesh* which translates to *set apart Spirit/breath/wind*. This is a title, not a name, that is feminine in origin. It was definitely present, even in *Genesis 1*. In the Greek it was referred to as *Pneuma* which is gender neutral. In Latin it was translated to *Sanctus Spiritus* which is masculine.

I have seen people adamantly argue for all three potential gender identities with what they feel is scriptural support. Our society tends to divide up certain behavioral traits as being more masculine or feminine, but God encompasses all things, all behaviors, all traits. We were made in His image, and the things we consider feminine are a part of that in some way. I'm not really worried about the gender of the Spirit.

If you are arguing over it, you are likely missing the message. I do acknowledge this set apart spirit as being real, and I will say **Spirit** or **Holy Spirit** since it's a fairly universal identifier. It is healthy to be aware, though, that there are other spirits out there besides just the Holy Spirit, and differentiating them can be important. For that reason, I typically refer to it by *Ruach ha'Kodesh*.

I wanted you to be aware this is a real discussion people have and to acknowledge the question since the subject is at the heart of this command. I shared what I have seen others say and what I say in this book. You can do all the private study you'd like to decide how you will proceed for yourself. I saw someone comment online once claiming that people who call him *Yeshua* are not talking about *Jesus*. That is an absurd notion, so let's just be clear that there is a legitimate basis for people to have been confused.

Moving on. Earlier I mentioned one way the devil tried to tempt Christ in the wilderness. In another one of his ploys during those forty days, the devil tried offering him all the kingdoms of the whole world if he would but fall down and worship (*Matthew 4:8-11*). Christ turns this offer down telling the devil to be gone, because it is written that we shall worship God and are only to serve Him. At this point, Christ clearly acknowledges through his actions that we are intended to follow this command.

Just because there is only one God (*James 2:19*) doesn't mean there are no other beings of high power and stature below Him (*Deuteronomy 8:19 & 30:17, Jeremiah 5:19, 2 Kings 17:35, Psalm 81:9, etc.*). With how much work the angels (*messengers*) do on behalf of God, it would be easy for us to think we should worship them. They fly and are often involved in miracles. It's ok to admit they're impressive! Fallen angels like the devil even seek this kind of attention out, hoping you will worship them instead.

Even in *Revelation*, John himself makes the mistake of bowing to worship at the feet of the angel that showed him these things, and he was told *don't do that, I'm a fellow servant* (*Revelation 22:8-9*). Christ himself says of John that there has been nobody born of a woman greater than him, though he would be lowest in the ranks of heaven. (*Matthew 11:11*) That sounds like setting the balance of a scale to me. Perhaps as a scribe, his life was the measure of a man. (*Zechariah 2:1-5, Matthew 5:20, Revelation 11:1 & 21:15-17*). For this great man, John, to still make this mistake must identify it as a pretty fundamental problem God is battling to get us to overcome. No wonder it is the very first rule He wrote down! If you don't know this at the foundation, the rest of this journey will get confusing.

We have been questioning lately if we are alone in the universe. Don't be that person who bows down to some advanced life form just because they look impressive (*Colossians 2:18*). Take a second and put yourself in a future hypothetical situation. Ask yourself, if aliens landed and claimed to be gods, would you just believe them? The world *alien* just means *foreign*. It doesn't have to mean monster looking creatures. What if they were advanced humanoids of some kind? Could aliens really just be crafty demons? Angels used to be called gods, princes, and sons of God (*Genesis 6:2*), but the lower case *g* reflected their lower status.

If a story sounded believable and they could do some fancy tricks, would you just believe, or would you be skeptical enough to question what you are told? *Revelation* warns that the antichrist will cause fire to fall from the sky. Don't we have satellites and planes that could potentially replicate that kind of thing in modern times?

What if artificial intelligence advanced past the human race?

I see so much danger in the way scientists are playing God with technology. Would you be subservient to robots? We are told the antichrist will come before Christ, and reign forty-two months (*Revelation 13:5*), and that people will follow (*Revelation 13:11-18*). I could go on and on with these kinds of questions, and I think we should all contemplate them at least once in life. It seems our number one sin is not being able to identify who God is and what it looks like to truly represent Him.

When you study the scripture on this deeper level, it will begin to sharpen that discernment meter. Every Christian agrees that the Bible is the true Word of God that you can come to when you want to determine who is being true or false, even if we must sort through some things in study. You are meant to be able to trust it. If you had your own vision of a being of light, would you assume it was a good guy without considering if it was a fallen angel? Again, recall that Satan transforms into a being of light, and we are warned false prophets will be very good at deception. They will know scripture well enough to sound legitimate as they twist it.

That's why it's so important to actually be reading the book with your own two eyes, not just listening to people talk about it. If I am being misled, I want to know and correct it! Don't you? There are so many dystopian television shows in the modern world who try to paint God and the Bible in a negative light by taking real things in it and twisting them out of context, often removing the message of love. We must be aware.

This command also obligates me to make a few things ***crystal clear*** about who I am and what I am doing by writing this book. I beg of you, do ***NOT*** twist my words. If you are inspired by them, then my prayers will have been answered and you should thank God for moving in your life. Please do NOT try to elevate my status in some ridiculous fashion. I am a person just like you. I was born into sin, just like you. I feel everything you can feel. I may have had uncommon experiences, but I'm still me.

I poured my heart out into this book with the purest intention to share the light God put into my life from a relatable perspective. I have seen this world struggle long enough, and in all my deep thoughts and prayers, the only solution I see to start lifting us out of the chaos is to increase our baseline standard of emotional intelligence in each heart. We are only as strong as our weakest link, right? I can admit that my love may be strong, but it was chaos before Christ. My study of the gospel refined it to be fruitful and healthy. I finally stopped feeling like I had to look for more answers elsewhere and grew to love God.

I would like to be an artist that adds a brushstroke or two to painting a world where politicians have integrity, and our tax dollars can go to improving society instead of war because we have peace in our hearts. It would be amazing if we didn't have to fight about gun laws because we eradicated the desire to kill. I see us heading in an authoritative, controlling, manipulative, divisive direction, and I don't like it. Kids should be able to play outside anywhere without parents fearing for their safety. Those children should be able to go to school not fearing a shooting. I want them to grow up having parents who worked to leave them a better world instead of one drained of it's resources and in shambles. They shouldn't have to spend their adult lives paying for our mistakes and cleaning up our messes. If we are going to teach them to play nice with others, we should be able to demonstrate it too.

I'm sick of the perpetual feeling of fear people have, because there is always someone threatening war. This book is about what I believe each of us is completely capable of contributing as humans to heal the larger problems through Christ who strengthens us. Personal responsibility should be in unison with compassion! We've all been a little right, and we've all been a little wrong. Every Abrahamic religion has prophecies of how their teaching will become twisted over time and people will stray towards false beliefs. Clearly conflict and aggression haven't solved anything, only made it worse. It's time for us to all acknowledge God in our personal lives and try things the way He wanted it all along, where people all have human decency infused with divine grace.

Unfortunately, I must be this thoroughly wordy, because stepping back from this book, I can foresee certain possible outcomes if I don't clarify my intentions. History is a shining example of how these things can evolve into being, so… distorted. I do not want to see any new religions or ladder cults created based on this book. I don't want spiritual groupies. I don't want to see people shove this down peoples' throats as a justification for extreme legalism or antinomianism or to strong arm people into agreeing with their perspective.

Without love, you are just making noise at people (*1 Corinthians 13:1-3*). Don't regard me as a guru or attempt to deify the messenger. Remember my previous statement that I wish to spark your deeper thought processes, but Christ is your teacher. I'm not Martin Luther (*Protestant*) or Ellen White (*Seventh Day Adventist*) or an Absalom spirit (*2 Samuel 13-19*) or anyone attempting to put another split in the church. I'm also not advocating a one world religion, because that will inevitably turn into a force and control mechanism where those who are not yet convicted in their heart get persecuted.

When it comes to man, absolute power corrupts absolutely. Only God and Christ have the true ability to carry that responsibility, so if men try to do it you know it will go south. That's essentially what prophecy says will happen though. We will fall into a beast system, turn on each other for lack of agreement, and kill the outcasts. People will die for the name of Christ. I would like to think we are all better than that. If someone is truly an atheist or alternate religion and wants to disprove the Bible, the very first thing they should do is *not* fulfill its prophecy about their behavior through killing those who believe.

Your faith was *designed by God* to be chosen by your free will. We can all choose to agree if we'd like and that would be lovely, but we should never *enforce* the agreement. That goes against everything we were instructed to do. When God wants to do that part, He will, at a day and hour no man knows (*Matthew 24:36*). All of these possible outcomes I wish to avoid stem from a lack of true understanding of this first commandment. Please don't create new doctrine.

However, I do see various doctrines being supported these days that I do not believe are scripturally sound. If this book encourages you to reevaluate your previously held doctrine so that you can work through the cognitive dissonance of now being aware of a contradictory perspective, well then I pray it creates a healthy shift for you in your relationship with God to sort through those feelings. This book has been successful ***IF*** the reader treats it as a personal and private growth experience to strengthen and enrich the authenticity of their relationship with God, then lets it echo into their daily lives. I would also find this book acceptable for Bible study groups so that discussion, fellowship, and prayer can be involved.

That being said, it would be my humble honor to be invited as a guest speaker at an event. I would be thrilled to participate in an evening with your Bible study group. I will be downright joyful if you choose to participate in the forum on my website or interact with me on my social media accounts. I will treat you as a friend whether we are friends or not. I will listen and do my best to offer support as your sister in faith. I'm not pushing you away with these requests, only trying to draw the outline of what *realism* looks like. So, the last time and way I will say it is this - ***please***, do not *ever* make me feel like writing this book has caused me or anyone else to violate this foundational truth. I don't want the weight of that on my soul.

This commandment also exists to put our ego in check. Pride comes before the fall (*Proverbs 11:2 & 16:18, James 4:6, Psalms 138:6, etc*), and no matter how proud we become (*Ecclesiastes 3:22*) we should know God will always be the highest authority and can strike us down. If you ask me, that's not a burden I would wish on anyone. Making this statement honestly takes a burden of responsibility off my shoulders. When you accept Christ, it kick starts this deeper realm of feelings in your heart. You start to be more aware of the ocean of suffering in the world and you want to be able to just fix it all. It immediately becomes clear that an army of one cannot save the world. Yet when many come together in faith and prayer, it is a force to be reckoned with.

When we do this, we are supposed to be aware that judgment will not be our job. God renders judgment not just by his authority, but by his mercy so that we may be able to walk more fully in love and compassion on this earth leaving the hardest decisions to Him. Yet somehow, we choose to judge each other anyway, the much more aggressive and stressful path. Don't be a stickler, obviously I am not taking a jab at our judicial system which we do need *(Deuteronomy 16:18-20, Isaiah 10:1-4)*. I'm referring to our personal interactions with others.

Look at how critical people are of God in the modern world, how harshly people talk about Him like the chance to exist at all isn't enough to be joyful about. People refuse to believe in Him on the premise that their life isn't perfect, and He isn't parting the clouds to give them whatever they ask for. We are meant to worship God. He is not meant to worship us. It is a joyful gift to have a relationship with Him, and it works best on mutual respect. That means He respects us most when we act respectable.

Acknowledging one true God is the foundation of the characteristic of humility - *humbleness*. It exists to clarify that point, because there will be attempts to deceive you into thinking otherwise. Plus, apparently it is human nature to glorify the messenger or the self. The angels all know better, and they live by the heavenly standard. This is our wake-up call to stop glorifying the messengers everywhere and focus on the message. God loves you, and He is asking us to be loving in return.

Ask yourself, does anyone really like *that guy*? You know the one. We all know someone who is just plain arrogant, egotistical, and thinks they know everything. They believe they are God's gift to humanity, so they are condescending and completely incapable of ever acknowledging they could be wrong about something. I truly can't stand people who get that *holier than thou* mentality. They make the worst leaders, yet they are often ones who become leaders when pride and ambition meet charisma.

There is value in confidence and pride when people look up to you, but I prefer a leader who will come down to my level and meet me rather than look down at me. These people who see themselves like the world revolves around them *need God* to put them in their place when nobody else can. Isn't that the essence of what made Christ so special? He was humble (*Philippians 2*), came to the people, healed the sick that others would not dare approach, and was willing to die for the people in his charge instead of focusing on self-preservation. He never used his gifts for personal gain, and he even turned the other cheek when provoked instead of biting back. No matter how many times he was tested, he always gave credit back to God, because he knew to give credit where it is due, to He who is the source of all blessings (*John 17*). He was the true picture of a leader who walked in God's divine nature.

Look back on your life. Can you think of any time that you verbalized disbelief in God to others? Do you believe that your moment of doubt being shared with another person hurt their view of God? How frequently have you heard people deny God in social or media-based settings? These questions are *not* condemning questions. When I went through this process, I recalled a couple times where the topic of religion had come up in a social setting, and I was surrounded by people who valued science higher. At the time, I thought like they did, and we were all discussing our two cents on the matter. It really didn't feel like a big deal in the moment, but validation only reinforces what you believe, even if your belief was false.

Admittedly most of my life I kept my moments of disbelief

to myself, but I still struggled over the thought of it in my heart and mind. I couldn't commit to what I thought was true for a long time. I ended up letting my circumstances determine my ethics, situation by situation, instead of establishing a standard I wanted to live by at all times. These are not just laws to me. They became my moral code.

The ten commandments were a covenant with God, an agreement of behavior. The problem is that Moses didn't explain to the people why the law was good. He just showed them what would happen if they broke the rules. That changed the structure of the covenant. It was no longer an agreement. They were *commandments*. Moses was supposed to speak to our hearts and compel the people to love and appreciate what the law would do for them.

Why give people a Promised Land without a guide map for building the perfect society? Should Moses have just called them building plans instead of commandments so people didn't feel oppressed? If he had, would people have taken them seriously? These laws were supposed to be the key to heaven on earth! Moses was supposed to help them understand why they were a great idea and bring them closer to God, with the law being followed in the hearts of every person through their own choice to do so. If we can identify God as the one true and living God, then shouldn't His authority, wisdom, love, and divine instructions matter more to us, or do we really think He just gave us rules because He likes to punish?

In the space provided, tell God that you are sorry for the times in the past where you denied Him as the one true God, ask for forgiveness, and thank Him for carrying the responsibility and burden of judgment so that we can live in love more completely. ***Identify where you fall on the spectrum of being meek, humble, and reverent versus proud, narcissistic, and arrogant.*** Describe what a healthy middle is regarding these behaviors. Share specific examples of events if they stand out to you as extra important to learn from. Explain what you understand about it now and how you could have handled the situation differently for next time.

_____
_____
_____
_____
_____
_____

2 - *Thou shall not make unto thee any graven image, or any likeness of any thing that is in heaven above, or that is in the earth beneath, or that is in the water under the earth. Thou shalt not bow down thyself to them, nor serve them, for I the Lord they God am a jealous God, visiting the iniquity of the fathers upon the children unto the third and fourth generation of them that hate me; and shewing mercy unto thousands of them that love me and keep my commandments.*

This is one that is going to be a little gritty to get through. I have seen some churches ignore this commandment entirely by removing it from the list of ten then breaking one other law into two to fill in the slot so they still have ten. That's some tricky stuff right there, but I assure you it's right there in your Bible. Go ahead and check it out (*Exodus 20:4-6*).

This commandment is one of the wordiest, most specific requests God made of us. It was a point being made even before the commandments were given. (*Genesis 35:2-4*) It is again stated in the New Testament in places like *1 Corinthians 6:9-10 & 10:1-8* and *Acts 17*. Why? What makes God jealous? What's the big deal? For starters, this certainly reiterates the point made in the previous section about not bowing to anyone other than God. Now we are adding to that instruction not to bow to any graven image. These aren't living beings. These are statues, sculptures, and idols. They often were associated with pagan deities, but not always.

This immediately brings some tough questions to mind in the modern age, doesn't it? How does God really feel about television binges, artificial intelligence, art, toy action figures, or even crosses and sculptures of saints? I'm more scared of not having the right answer than of asking the question. We are surrounded by imagery everywhere we turn. It's part of being in a capitalist society that is highly visual. You will be bombarded daily by ads glorifying products, money, guns, cars, food, and lavish lifestyles. You can have the latest and greatest distractions delivered to your doorstep, and God gets left behind in a sea of our carnal desires.

What idols do you have in your life? Idols aren't always the golden calf (*Exodus 32:1-6*), my friends. Idols can be in your heart. (*Ezekiel 14:3*) What things hold a higher importance in your life than God? It's a legitimately tough question and tends to be a brutal wakeup call for people who didn't realize they obsessively cared about drugs or money or fame or finding a spouse to an unhealthy or unbalanced capacity. Bare minimum, to be following this command, God needs at least 51% controlling shares over your heart in any situation. Does He? Is your cup half empty or half full? The good news is that as we clarify this command, we will find that it's not as condemning as it sounds.

Let's begin this talk with money. Christ is clear in the sermon on the mount that you cannot serve both God and Mammon, which is often translated to money (*Matthew 6:24*). Mammon is generally associated with a demon of greed. Christ said not to store up treasures on earth, but instead store up our treasures in heaven because where your treasures are is where your heart will be (*Matthew 6:19-23*). On yet another occasion the Pharisees were trying to *entangle him in his talk.* They were trying to put a stumbling block in front of Christ hoping he would trip on it and out himself as not actually being sent by God. They asked if it was right to give tribute to Caesar, and he told them *Render therefore unto Caesar the things which are Caesar's, and unto God the things that are God's* (*Matthew 22:15-22*).

It is commonly stated that money is the root of all evil. That stems from *1 Timothy 6:10* which says the *love* of money is the root of evil. This concept is echoed in *Hebrews 13:5.* Here is my take on it. Money at its roots is representative of contribution to society. You earn money through doing work, then are allowed to spend it in exchange for goods and services. It's more versatile than only being able to trade goods with someone when you have something they need in return. Everyone accepts money. In a world where you can have your paycheck electronically deposited into your bank account then swipe a card in a machine to spend it, it is clearer than ever that money is an idea. At least when it was all cash and checks it felt like a physical thing, but the truth is that money is and always has been a symbolic note.

Consider that money is a form of energy. It only holds value because we give it value through our actions. An item that costs a dollar is relatively easy to throw away, but the house we live in and computers we type on are highly valuable since we worked so hard to earn enough money to buy them. Therefore, money itself is neutral energy. We create its value based on the effort we put behind acquiring it. Neutral energy is not good or bad until someone influences it one way or the other. Money is only the root of all evil if used for evil purposes, and in turn it is a force of good when used with positive intentions. ***This means the person holding the dollar is more important than the dollar itself.***

    Blaming lack of financial abundance on life's hurdles seems like a simple place to point our fingers, but that is deflection. We need to accept that our perception of it is the true source of our struggle. *Maslow's Hierarchy of Needs* suggests food, water, air, sleep, shelter, and clothing are base necessities for physical survival in the world. A step above that is safety and security through health, employment, prosperity, family, and social stability. Everything above that ties to love in some way, either of the self or for others. This book covers how God tells us to address all of those needs.

    Of course we have assigned a monetary value to food, shelter, clothing, and water. This allows for equal and fair access to basic necessities in a world of finite resources while urging every person to be a contributor to society. It sounds pretty straight forward and logical that doing your part earns you these necessities so we don't face anarchy and dangerous competition over those limited resources. Teamwork makes the dream work! If our population weren't so massive it might not be necessary, but it is.

    The problem then presents itself that somehow we have a society where people's base needs are not being met. It's the top 1% versus the lower 99%, and the gap between them keeps growing and growing. There's *always* a reason. There aren't enough jobs, taxes are too high, jobs we do have don't pay enough, racism and sexism reduce opportunities, and so on and so forth. This is where we find a great deal of contention in politics - defining the role of government regarding these issues.

    While that is all fair discussion for another time and place, what about *our* role regarding these issues? All of this consumes our lives. It draws all our attention to materialism instead of focusing on a relationship with God. So yes, money is an idol if it consumes all your focus. It's not impossible to exist without it. In fact, people did that for a very long time! If we experienced a severe financial disaster where our economy collapsed and suddenly the dollar held no value, couldn't we still get up and go to work like we have every day and keep society functioning? Was that dollar, which is now practically invisible, the glue that holds together society and keeps us from abandoning our rational minds? I certainly hope not! In that specific emergency instance couldn't we just set a rule to take what you need without hoarding, and contribute what you can? Or would it really turn into martial law, looting, and anarchy like you see in the movies because people start to panic?

I'm *not* saying you must transition to a life without money or that communism is going to solve all our problems. Being required to earn money to live is unfortunately the main motivator not to be lazy in our time. Competition also drives innovation. It serves its purpose *as long as* you don't glorify it. If God calls you to it and convicts you in your heart of minimalism, you should certainly listen though. He definitely placed on my heart a need to reduce my stuff to necessities and increase my focus on heart-based matters.

It is also important to consider what Revelation says about money. When the mark of the beast comes, you will not be able to buy or sell without it (*Revelation 13:15-17*). This means the mark will either be currency, a financial system, identification, or a means by which you access your money. Are you prepared to reject the mark of the beast in order to follow God?

That is not a reason to become a doomsday prepper. I'm making you aware of an uncomfortable truth that you may possibly have to make this choice someday. We are dependent on things that could be yanked out from under us too easily. Money isn't the only one. I recall enduring a twenty-four hour power outage once on a particularly sweltering summer day and felt so handicapped. When is the last time you did math without a calculator? Could you feed yourself without an electric stove or microwave? What if you no longer had working plumbing? Could you purify your own drinking water? Is it possible that we idolize technology?

Clearly it is important to be aware and have plans in place for emergencies. In all reality if your faith prohibits you from taking such a mark, then the government should not be able to force your hand, literally your right hand according to scripture. They cannot overrule freedom of religion as that would Constitutionally be tyranny. However, the Bible suggests that most people will be deceived and probably accept it willingly, and those who don't will be killed.

To remove an idol from your heart, you must be able to see it from a clearer perspective and detach yourself from obsessing over it. This doesn't mean you have to be crazy fan-girl obsessive about God, but you could be aware of how much time you devote to money and give more of that time to God in prayer. You could put a little less money in your savings account and donate it to those in need, because it's only money. Your needs being met is important. The extra stuff really isn't. Don't get me wrong, you can want things and go shopping. I don't think all consumerism is sin. However, if it is all your life is about, that probably means God has not been a priority.

In an effort to correct this error in myself, I started taking breaks from social media and television, trying to get outside more. It led me to start doing volunteer projects so my hands were being used for more constructive things than holding a remote or smartphone. I started spending more time praying, reading my Bible, and even listening to audio lectures at work to keep my mind focused on God more. I also went around my home and removed items from my time in the new age movement that I now felt might be offensive to God. I worked a day at a time to declutter my home and life so I wasn't holding on to unnecessary things.

After some detox time from distracting idols, I didn't miss it all that much. I still have moments where watching some tv while relaxing is nice. I simply decided to let the list pile up of shows I wanted to watch. I didn't worry about staying caught up, just enjoyed it when I had time. I stopped allowing it to dictate my free time and reclaimed my control. I enjoy all the incredible games and movies and creative content we have access to in this world. It's truly fascinating! It just isn't what gets me through the day anymore. *God does that now*.

We should be able to spend time with our friends and family without checking our phones. We should be able to eat without always taking a picture of our food and sharing it on social media. Admittedly I do that sometimes if I think others will appreciate the recipe or an anecdote, but some people can really go overboard. Yet if you're a chef or a health coach, it's just advertising, so when and how much do you feel it is appropriate, and where is the line that crosses into excess? We don't need to stand in line for days so we can be the first to get the latest tech upgrade when we won't even spend five minutes sitting down to read the Bible. What are our priorities?

Ask yourself, at what point do too many selfies turn into worshipping yourself as an idol? Can you accept the first shot without taking ten more to get it perfect because you want others to shower it with likes? That's not where your self-esteem should be rooted. Do you take a selfie daily or just on occasion to mark special moments in your life? This ties together how vanity can be an aspect of idolatry when taken to unhealthy levels.

Let's call our egos swollen or inflamed, because inflammation is a cause for many health issues in the modern day. You should definitely love yourself and appreciate your reflection. I told you that I quit wearing makeup and other things that altered my appearance to practice exactly that. Self love and care is healthy! Vanity and narcissism are not healthy expressions of self love. We all know what happened to Narcissus, and that is not far from the story of Satan. Pride and vanity were his downfall.

What about art? Honestly, I don't think creative expression in and of itself is sin, especially in the abstract form where it doesn't resemble anything in particular. It can be a great therapeutic tool when we struggle to put our feelings into words and let them out. One of the volunteer projects I worked on was with an art therapy program for recovering drug addicts. Not only was it cathartic for them, but God was freely welcomed to the table. Many people painted expressions of how faith was helping them heal.

There was also a long portion of history where illiteracy was the norm, so art was used to share the gospel in visual format. Pictures were a universal language. I imagine if people had not been able to see things like the Sistine Chapel, the faith may not have survived as strongly as it did. I can't imagine any of these things making God angry if they brought people towards Him and His will for them.

The line at which art becomes idolatry is when we care more about it than God, or the imagery being portrayed pushes people away from faith and towards sin. This doesn't mean money doesn't again come back into that equation. If you are willing to spend thousands, even millions of dollars to own a piece of art, couldn't that money have fed someone who is starving instead of just feeding your eyeballs? I know some people who collect expensive art, but they also make pretty much equal if not greater contributions to charitable causes. It is up to you to sort through whether you feel art is something that has become an idol in your own heart and life, and I hope you will allow God to guide you through it. Proceed through the modern world with caution and awareness at what message imagery is trying to convey to you and discern for yourself if it is appropriate to have in your life.

It also seems to me there was a particular focus on carved images, basically sculptures and statues. People bowed and prayed to these objects in the time these were written (*Isaiah 44:17-20, Daniel 3:5-7, Psalm 106:38, Acts 7:41, etc.*). We are *definitely* not supposed to bow down or worship any inanimate object. We are also not supposed to sacrifice or offer things to them. Looking at something is one thing, worshiping it is another. It doesn't matter what it represents, where it is located, or who/what you think may be inside it. We worship the God of life, and he finds it offensive when we devote our praise to items that have no life in them.

When I started to explore these complicated questions, I spent some time detaching from all symbolism. I identified that symbols can be representative of concepts and thusly helpful for teaching purposes, but I didn't really need them for anything. They were turning into a crutch for me. What they mean to others is not always the same as what they mean to me. A swastika for instance used to represent good fortune before Hitler utilized it, but I would never wear one now. As I studied, I found that every single symbol I ever thought was positive had a negative interpretation to someone somewhere. It was an emotionally draining study.

I realized I don't need to see a cross sitting on my nightstand to be able to cherish the sacrifice made on it in my heart. It can be a lovely daily reminder to see it there, absolutely, especially early on in the journey! *But* pushing myself to be *stronger* in my faith meant to embrace that feeling of appreciating the gift and sacrifice of Christ without the need for a physical object to remind me. It was creating a spiritual laziness in me where I didn't have to carry feelings about things when I could always see reminders, when in truth God cares most about what is in our hearts, not what stuff we own.

That being said, I own a shirt with a cross on it and have no problem wearing it sometimes. I'm not ashamed or afraid of the cross. Once I detached myself from symbols after studying their worldly meanings for awhile, that space allowed me to reclaim what one means to me personally. If this is an area of concern in your life, pray over it and allow God to place in your heart the true meaning

He wants you to take from these things.

Let's come back around to that jealousy issue. Why would God be jealous? The Bible tells us we are made in His image, so what are some things that would make you feel jealous? Maybe your spouse cheated on you and you are jealous of the attention the other person was getting (*Isaiah 62:5*). How about when someone gets credit and positive affirmation for your idea (*Psalm 146:6*)? What about when you see your brother, sister, or coworker get unequally more attention than you (*John 12:31, 2 Corinthians 4:4*)? Does God perhaps have a reason to feel jealous sometimes?

Yet even after how we have treated God by ignoring, disobeying, and rejecting Him, He still opened His arms in love and sent His son, Christ, instead of abandoning us. We are offered forgiveness and a choice. How magnanimous! That is real love.

We have a serious arrogance problem in society. Divine nature does not reflect that same arrogance, so it is up to us to put it in check. How does God help with that? God shows us we are all equal, because we are not Him. Christ shows us that His superiority over us doesn't mean we are not loved. The Holy Spirit shows us how special we all are by moving in each and every individual to convict them personally and help them grow in divine nature. God used the Bible to show us that everyone is equal, and everyone is special, all at the same time - balanced yet again. None of these things require items or images to be understood or appreciated, so make sure that the true lessons are being learned and proper credit is being given to God where it is due. Pray over the rest, and let Him help you through the sea of imagery we are submerged in.

In the space provided, tell God you are sorry for the idols you have allowed to be in your life, both in the physical world and in your heart. Ask Him to forgive you for these things you didn't realize you were doing, and make a commitment to do better going forward. Write down where you intend to start. Are you going to go through your closet and donate clothes you don't need to charity? Will your children be asked to give away toys they don't play with anymore? Will you go through your jewelry box and remove what items you no longer feel are appropriate? Will you be spending less time on electronics? Make a realistic commitment about what you feel the Spirit is convicting you to do regarding idols in your life. ***Identify where you think you fall on the spectrum of materialism versus all***

things spiritual. What do you feel is a healthy balance? Let God know that you intend to trust Him more and more each day.

3. Thou shalt not take the name of the Lord thy God in vain, for the Lord will not hold him guiltless that taketh his name in vain.

It seems that many people struggle over what this command really meant. Obviously modern slang didn't exist all those years ago. To suggest it only means not to combine swear words with holy names sounds like a copout to me, so let's dig deeper.

In Strong's Concordance, the word translated to vain is *H7723 - shav*. This word is used in the contextual sense as meaning desolating, evil, destruction, ruining something, falsehood, lying, and worthlessness. If you ask me, this sounds like God's plea for us not to throw His name in the mud and walk all over it. He asked us not to ruin His reputation as a good guy and to make sure that when we speak of Him, we do it in truth. He commanded **respect**.

All false prophets are thusly breaking this command. The New Testament warns us against them a great deal, as previously mentioned. This will tie in again later when we cover the command about not lying as well as when we dig deeper into leadership levels of discernment. The number of times and ways the Bible addresses *honesty* should make it *very* clear that it holds a pivotal role in living with integrity and that it is a key piece of divine nature. Christ is the personification of truth, so spend some time contemplating what that means about following him.

Remember when I talked about what it meant to do something in Christ's name in the section about prayer? It meant do as I do, in my character, the same way I would. When God asks us not to take His name in vain and defile it, that requires us to clearly understand His true character. Where we see God telling us not to take His name in vain, Christ lived a perfect sinless life following all of these laws and said do things in my name. He demonstrated God's character like a color-by-number painting! God commanded it, Christ lived it, and we follow in the Spirit!

God's nature is divine. The further we go through this, you will continue to see verse after verse emphasize the point that God is GOOD. He is life and love and joy and peace! There just need to be boundaries, there's no way around that. Just like you as a person need boundaries when it comes to others so they don't walk all over you and repeatedly break your heart, God needs those boundaries with us. The Bible does a good job of compartmentalizing each aspect of God's character in a way we can try to study and understand. This command asks us to pull those various aspects of character together and understand them, remembering that God is all light and no darkness is in Him at all (*1 John 1:5*).

Let's explore who God is as a whole. Consider this. We are told that before the fall, Lucifer was God's favorite angel (*Ezekiel 28*). Then he rebelled, betrayed God, and took a bunch of the angels with him. Have you ever thought about how much that must have broken God's heart? I read an article once that explained it like this. God created Lucifer to be perfect, but he perverted his perfection through his pride. He started to think too highly of himself and rebelled, because he wanted to be greater than God. Lucifer sounds like an angry high school student who is pissed because his parents won't trust him to drive the car and go to a party, so he stomps out and threatens to go live on his own.

I think we all go through a moment in life where we just feel like we know better than others. It's that arrogance thing again. It evolves from pride, which can be a good thing in small doses. It's good to appreciate your accomplishments and feel that they are good and righteous. It's healthy to be able to identify when we have done a good job as parents, employees, and friends.

Unfortunately, some people feed that moment and blow it *way* out of proportion. They turn what started as a warm moment of being proud of their work into a raging fire of better-than-thou mentality. They forget to humble themselves to God, and the ego starts inflating like a balloon, ever so gradually over time, as they start to receive compliments and praise. It sounds to me like there came a point where God had to put His foot down about it, and Lucifer made the wrong choice by being combative instead of understanding. The devil put himself in his heart above God.

Clearly it's a good thing God put his foot down about it. It was obviously God who had the superior wisdom regarding our need for humility. He has the true wisdom, foresight, and power. There's a reason we hold respect for His authority! Even when he was betrayed and heartbroken, He offered us a way back to Him. This is why God is called steadfast in His ways (*Exodus 34:6, Psalm 25:10 & 136, 2 Thessalonians 3:5, etc.*). He is consistent. If you truly want to understand something about God, know that both His love for us and His desire for us to be loving has never changed. He is a true leader, who understands the weight and responsibility of His place as the one true God as well as the value of love and forgiveness. The things He knows and understands are beyond us, but He gave us plenty of benchmarks of character to be able to appreciate Him.

Once we do start to wrap our heads around who He is, two things will simultaneously happen. Not only will it be clearer what words and actions would take His name in vain, but we will respect Him with a reverence that makes us want to speak carefully regarding Him. I see people defend the name of politicians they support with vigor. They don't want to think the person they voted for and supported could be wrong, because that's like saying they too were wrong. Yet these same people will not defend the integrity behind God's name.

In fact, I have heard very many Christians express that they don't believe faith is meant to be talked about. It's supposed to be personal and private. Faith should not be considered a taboo topic! Silence in prayer and reflection is where we hear God, but amongst our friends and family, silence is where faith goes to die. I will not stifle my love for God by not sharing it openly when I feel compelled to do so.

If you're asked if you are a Christian and deny it, thusly denying the son He sent to die for us, you are taking God's name in vain by not being honest as would be in His character. If you say to people that you love God, but you turn around to do and teach sinful ways, then you are taking His name in vain. If you utter the name of God in a way that defiles His character, then you are violating this request. This command was like a call to speak and live in line with God's will, because that is the only way that you will not take His name in vain.

We are also asked in the Bible not to swear (*Matthew 5:34, James 5:12, Joshua 23:7, Hebrews 7:21*). Unfortunately some people take that out of its context, though it does still fall under the blanket of taking God's name in vain if you do it. This is about making oaths. This is telling us not to say things like *I swear by this or that to do this or that, so help me God*. The concept here is that only God has the authority to swear anything.

This is one commandment I didn't feel I had as much issue with working through. I do have a tendency to call out to Christ if I injure myself. I will say *God bless it* in place of swearing sometimes. However, my intention in doing so is to avoid speaking ill and to instead legitimately call on God when I'm having a difficult moment. There have been times in my past where I did take God's name in vain, but through this process I worked to address each situation as it arose. Following this request starts to come naturally as you grow in your faith.

What my study of this concept gave me was an awareness. It drove home the point that words are delicate. Jeff Brown put it nicely -*Words. So powerful. They can crush a heart or heal it. They can shame a soul or liberate it. They can shatter dreams or energize them. They can obstruct connection or invite it. They can create defenses or melt them. We have to use words wisely.*

Think for a moment - in a time where science is commonly regarded higher than faith, how difficult can it be to follow this command? It's so easy to deny God's hand in things. Equally we can feel so overzealous to preach *our* truth that we speak out for God before we are secure in *His* truth. It is a mildly embarrassing admission that I did this when I wrote the book that I pulled from publication. I thought in my pride that I understood many things, and I'm sure there are points I made with the best of intentions that were not in line with God's character.

Honestly I don't remember too much anymore, because once I felt I was forgiven for this error I erased it from my list of worries just like I erased it from publication and Christ erases our sins from memory. I was able to salvage a couple pieces. It certainly wasn't all bad, but even those pieces were modified to properly reflect God. We don't always get a chance to retract something before the damage is done, so I feel blessed that I caught myself and course corrected with the help God placed in my life. I couldn't have done it without Him. *Proverbs 13:10* tells us *Where there is strife, there is pride, but wisdom is found in those who take advice.*

In the space provided, tell God you are sorry for the times you took His name in vain. Provide examples if one stands out in your mind as carrying a strong lesson with it. Identify that it makes total sense why He doesn't want His good name tarnished, especially by His own children. Declare your intention to study His character so that you can be better at following His will. **Where do you feel you fall on the spectrum of pride versus respect? Do you feel you understand God's character?** Identify what you feel a healthy balance of these concepts would look like in your life that still matches the divine nature. Do you feel there are certain habits you will have to break? Do you need more strength and support in your walk to be able to meet God's hopes for us? Write down benchmark characteristics of God that you believe He wants you to respect. Pray and ask God how he feels, because we care about the feelings of those we love.

4 - Remember the Sabbath day to keep it holy. Six days shalt thou labour and do all thy work, but the seventh day is the Sabbath of the Lord thy God, in it thou shalt not do any work thou, nor thy son, nor thy daughter, thy manservant nor thy maidservant, nor thy cattle, nor thy stranger that is within thy gates. For in six days the Lord made heaven and earth, the sea, and all that in them is, and rested the seventh day; wherefore the Lord blessed the Sabbath day and hallowed it.

  This one sure tends to spark a lot of heated debate! It is clear that the Sabbath was instituted at creation. For six days God labored to create the world, and on the seventh He rested. He consecrated the day to be holy (*Genesis 2:2-3*). Again, God's own hand wrote for us to honor this day and keep it holy in the ten commandments. Christ set the example of honoring the Sabbath when he and his apostles attended synagogue as was customary (*Luke 4:16 & 23:56, John 15:10*). We are even told to pray that our flight to safety in the end times does not fall on a Sabbath, so it will clearly still matter (*Matthew 24:20*). The cherry on this cake is in *Mark 2:27-28* where we are told that Christ is the Lord of the Sabbath, indicating it is in him that we find rest. It sounds pretty uncontested.

  God just wants us to take a rest day? Sure ok! Piece of cake! Honoring it is considered a clear sign that you follow Him (*Isaiah 58, Ezekiel 20:20*). It is a sign of the Israelites that follow Him *forever* (*Exodus 31:17*). The first question to ask yourself is when is the Sabbath? *Ahhhhhh...* That's where the problem starts. Throughout the Bible it is regarded as the seventh day (*Matthew 28:1*) and doesn't really identify names like Saturday or Sunday. We do all identify Sunday as the first day of the week though, and by doing so identify Saturday as the seventh. Traditionally speaking the Sabbath has always been sundown Friday until sundown Saturday. There is not a single verse to the contrary in the whole of the Bible. This is when the Jewish people have always honored it.

  There are some who claim that historically all Christians have followed Sunday Sabbath. This seems to not be factual-*ish*.

About 100 years before Christianity, Egyptians introduced a sun worship festival on Sunday in the Roman empire. Some Christian churches began to adopt it in an attempt to differentiate themselves from the Jews who had rejected the Savior. Eventually Constantine named himself Bishop of the Catholic church and enacted a civil law about Sunday rest in 321AD. Pope Sylvester officially named Sunday the Lord's Day in 338AD. There were many discussions hashing out the details of what constituted rest during this period of time. It evolved in stages. This is how changes snowball through time.

Some Catholic doctrine attributes this to the Council of Laodicea in 336AD where they claimed to transfer the solemnity of Saturday to Sunday. Their reason given is that Christ ascended on a Sunday and appeared to the apostles on a Sunday. I would imagine that is probably because the previous day - the Sabbath - was considered a day of rest even for Christ, but I suppose I could be wrong there. Others say the church made this choice, but the official documented doctrine states Sunday is the Lord's day which follows the Sabbath. It doesn't actually deny the Sabbath still exists. They just moved the place of emphasis.

The Seventh Day Adventist church follows the belief of Ellen White, who claimed the pope has no authority to change God's law. This particular statement I fully agree with. Not even Christ himself changed it, and we are warned of those who would try to change times and laws (*Daniel 7:25*). Christ only infused love and compassion into our understanding of it through his example to clarify the most appropriate way to follow the law in word and deed. Not even the pope should be able to change God's commands, just like a president should not be able to change the Constitution.

However, Ellen White believed from her visions that the mark of the beast would be the forcing of people to regard Sunday as the Sabbath. I really don't know that I agree with that based on the scripture, but it isn't ruled out. To think that anyone would be capable of forcing me to worship a certain way seems foreign to me in a country where religious freedom is an essential part of the foundations. Yet even if you shoved me in a box or put a gun to my head, you couldn't change my heart. Force will accomplish nothing but conflict.

Some people claim that *Colossians 2:16-17* abolished the Sabbath, but I certainly beg to differ. It says to let no man judge you for your practices. It is about freedom from man's traditions, not God's rules. This passage goes on to warn you to be wary of those with self-imposed worship, false humility, and harsh treatment of their body claiming it may seem wise but it's not worth denying the flesh. This is true, though if you take a statement like this to extremes into gluttony and hedonism that will certainly make it against Christ's commands. Balance strikes again!

    I do things like fasting as a choice, because I appreciate the practice. It's not something imposed on me, and I do it for positive reasons like improving my health, *not* to be harsh on myself. I enjoy doing it and appreciate who it is helping me become. If any of the things you do to follow God are equivalent to basically spiritually flogging yourself every day, it's definitely not being done in the spirit of Christ.

    I feel *Colossians 2* may be the most adequate passage that reflects the concept of being under grace. You shouldn't be judging and beating yourself into submission to God, nor should you be judging others. This journey is about developing your love and appreciation for God and His ways. Sure, some of it will be hard, but the Band-aid has to come off whether you rip it fast or pull it slowly.

    We are being woken up to what we didn't see before. That can be disorienting, but once we have repented, atoned, and worked through forgiveness, the hardest stuff is over. After that it's just about remembering to respond to conflict in the appropriate ways despite the temptation to give in to old habits. It might seem like a dark wilderness some days, but it's really just a phase of growth from a seed in the ground that cracks open to becoming a plant that produces good fruit. Trials will happen, but those who are wise and able to learn from them will eventually see them cease, even if it's just a state of mind they carry with them that all experiences carry value.

    If you wish to further study when the Sabbath is, you will find a multitude of resources available to you online from various perspectives. Practice discernment against scripture, and be certain you check factual sources for historical information. There are some out there who like to flub the details, hence the reason I just presented you different opinions on the subject.

    What do I do? Saturday used to be the day I got *everything* done since I had the day off work. It was a high traffic day. After my study on this commandment, I began doing my best to honor the

Sabbath from sundown Friday until sundown Saturday. As is suggested in scripture, I do not work to earn any wages, buy, or sell during this time unless I am cornered into having no choice. For example, I get paid around lunch time on Fridays, and sometimes my rent is due on that or the next day. It has to be paid when my landlord is able come pick it up, and there is nothing I can do about that. However, I pay every bill I can on my lunch break Friday or after sundown Saturday. I try to do grocery shopping Thursday nights or Sundays. Yet again, if I'm out of food and ran out of time, I will not starve my family for the sake of waiting. That isn't restful at all.

As a working mom, it can be hard for me to get time during the week for much house cleaning. If the thought of a neglected mess is truly keeping me from being able to be restful, I will do some cleaning. I do my best to try and avoid this scenario during the week, but it's just not always feasible. It seems fine since cleaning is a stress relieving activity for me right next to hiking and a hot shower. Otherwise I take the time to unwind. It is also a day I will devote to writing in my prayer journal, reading scripture, blogging about faith, and family time. I keep it holy by using it for some devoted time with and for God.

I have encountered situations where it was in my heart to participate in a specific charitable cause or an event that happens to be scheduled during the Sabbath time. Obviously not everyone holds the same belief or practices that I do. I will often pray about it and have always felt that as long as it is done in the spirit of Christ, that it has been acceptable. That is still keeping it holy in my book.

This is supported in scripture. Christ explains that it is lawful to do good on the Sabbath. Man was not created to honor this day. Rather, this day was created for the benefit of man (*Mark 2:27*). The Pharisees accused Christ of breaking the Sabbath when he performed a miracle on that day (*Matthew 12:10-13, Mark 3:1-5, John 9*), and on another occasion when he and the disciples walked through a field plucking and eating grains (*Luke 6:1-5*).

This emphasized the point that the Pharisees were being too focused on tiny details to the point of not just losing the spirit of the law, but actually violating the law in their nitpicking. There were even specifications about how far you could walk on the Sabbath. They built a hedge around God's law which violated *Deuteronomy 4:2*. These actions created a burden and stumbling block to the people rather than fulfilling the spirit of liberation through following the law. Christ's example in one of these passages was if a sheep fell into a pit on the Sabbath, wouldn't you pull it out rather than waiting until the next day?

Bless their hearts. I know their intention was to follow God's law to the letter in purity, but in focusing too much on the details they seemed to lose sight of the big picture. *Halakhah* was supposed to be about clarifications in your walk, but in that time it turned into overly oppressive laws taught by those who were hypocritical (*Matthew 23*). Some don't carry that spirit in the modern world, but many do. In turn, today most Christians see the big picture of love but have abandoned the details that God used to define it. Some don't, but many do.

In *Revelation 12:10* it says the dragon is cast down for accusing our brethren day and night unceasing. I think digging *too* deep to be perfect opens the door to that feeling of constant criticism that pulls us from love. That's why this book studies major principles. They are the main truths against which we discern what steps to take in our walk. Understanding them unlocks everything.

Rest is basic self care 101! Take a day off once in awhile! God just specified to do it once every seven days. I find it hard to argue with that logic, mostly because I just don't want to. I think all people on this planet - working parents especially - benefit from downtime.

Does this mean I am opposed to attending a church service on a Sunday? No, of course not! Just because I honor the Sabbath on Saturday doesn't mean I wish to neglect God the rest of the week. Plus, the selection of churches who offer Saturday service is very small. As long as it is honored in spirit and truth, then you are following the command. It's not regulating how you spend the other six days of the week.

To me, every day is holy, and every breath is precious and worth gratitude. When you feel that way all the time, holidays or special days don't seem like a big deal. As I said previously, they are more about being reminded of certain lessons, so I honor them in that capacity. I must say, though, that it was honoring this command in particular that really signified a shift for me in my relationship with God. I felt a difference, almost an increase of presence, when I got in line with this change. I have heard testimonies from others who suggest the same thing. Many are becoming convicted to at least understand the Sabbath if not honor it.

As a last point of discussion, this command states that not even your manservant or maidservant are to work on the Sabbath. A secular man once argued to me that he could write a better version of the Bible for the purposes of morality. His claim was based on the immoral practice of slavery that was allowed. While I find it absurd to think that anyone could claim to write the Bible better, there is certainly merit to the discussion of slavery. Let's just go ahead and take this window of opportunity.

I do *not* consider it to be moral to own slaves. Obviously it is something we have abolished, though it took way too long if you ask me. Yes, the Old Testament makes it clear that owning slaves was normal in those times. What I would like to point out is that was a decision of men, not God. What I see in scripture is that God said *if* you have slaves, you must treat them fairly. If you do the study for yourself, you'll find many laws that say as much. He never said we *must* have slaves.

In the New Testament, if you recall the verse I told you was my favorite in the beginning of this book, *Colossians 3:11* tells us *Where there is neither Greek nor Jew, circumcision nor uncircumcision, Barbarian, Scythian, bond nor free: but Christ is all, and is in all.* The word *bond* here means *slave* or *servant* and is translated that way in other texts. Yes, there may have been slaves in existence when Christ came and before, but it is clear when you study the gospel that he did not support that notion. We are all one in Christ. Recall that I also shared previously how he says he will no longer call us servants. Instead he will call us friends. That very clearly identifies to me that slavery is not in the divine nature. Christ sets us free from the chains of the devil. He does not enslave us to him. It is the devil who supports slavery.

Last, the issue of slavery requires us to identify our place in the financial system. As was touched on earlier, money has become a required thing. Even off grid living costs money to buy land and materials, pay annual taxes, and other expenses. You would have to live like a nomadic cave man to completely avoid money, foraging and hunting to survive. You would have to make clothes out of what materials you could find. Even if you wanted to do this outside of the country, it would cost even more money to be able to leave.

Ultimately, we are all enslaved to the dollar to a degree. It serves its purpose, but this is certainly a valid perspective to evaluate. Sure, we get to pick our jobs and homes and spend the money left after bills however we choose, but we still have to work to earn it and follow the wishes of our employer and government regulations. We have capitalism, but there are still *haves* and *have nots*. An employer can't beat people with whips like they used to, but we can certainly be written up, reprimanded, have hours cut, or be fired on the whim of the boss. Our need for money serves as a societal leash. All I ask you to remember is that it is a device of man, not God. There was no money in Eden, and there will be none in heaven.

In the space below, tell God you are sorry if you have not been honoring the Sabbath in a way that you feel is appropriate. Ask him to forgive you. Identify what you have been doing before, then state what you intend to do going forward. Perhaps that means you will be doing some more study and prayer first, and if so then state that. **Where do you feel you fall on the spectrum of being rested and calm versus overwhelmed, stressed, or anxious?** Do you feel like you are working too hard in a way that neglects your self care? Does this feeling of stress, anxiety, or exhaustion impact your strength, willpower, or general success in life? Do you think that's what God wants for you, or do you think He wants you to be able to face each day refreshed and joyful? Are you going to have to rearrange how you handle your weekly schedule to accommodate God's request? Do you serve money as your master, or do you trust in God? Lay it all out, and pray for the Holy Spirit to help you embrace your day of rest more fully.

_____
_____
_____
_____
_____
_____
_____
_____
_____
_____
_____
_____
_____
_____

5. *Honour thy father and thy mother that thy days may be long upon the land which the Lord thy God giveth thee.*

Ephesians 6:2-3 tells us this is the first commandment with promise. Starting with this command and continuing through the rest are specific instructions Christ listed as requirements to receive eternal life when he was asked (*Matthew 19:16-22, Mark 10:17-22, Luke 18:18-23*). They mirror what is said in *Proverbs 6:16-19* about things that God hates. Many of them are short, and all of them are behavioral. These statements being included in the New Testament gospels are a prime example of how they are still relevant principles, so we will give them their due focus. If they merit eternal life, they must be pretty important!

The word honor means to show high respect or esteem. The word translated to *honour* is H3513 - *kabed*. It's more general meaning is not just honor, but also to make heavy/dense and glory. This suggests to me that honoring our parents is not just about what we do to respect them and prosper the family name, but also what we do to help lift the heaviness of their burdens. It should go without saying that Christ absolutely followed this command with the entirety of his life, and God acknowledged that this was His son in whom He was well pleased (*Matthew 3:17 & 17:5, Mark 1:11, Luke 3:22, 2 Peter 1:17*). There are also plenty of New Testament scriptures that reiterate the point, such as *Colossians 3:20* or *Luke 1:17*.

Let's talk about the word *father*. The word it is translated from is *H1 - ab*. It does mean father, appearing in scripture 1,212 times, but it appears to have a dual application of both earthly and heavenly nature. In *Matthew 23:9* Christ instructs us *Call no man your father upon the earth: for one is your Father, which is in heaven.* Feel free to let that soak in a little bit. This verse, when taken in context with its surrounding verses, is about not calling someone father in a sense of religious superiority. In the previous verse Christ told them to call nobody but him teacher (*Rabbi*), but then he also later instructs the disciples to go teach others about the gospel. The clarification necessary here is that we are not to elevate ourselves as though we are the top of the spiritual food chain.

The word translated to mother is *H517 - em*. This word

appears 220 times in scripture and has a wide range of applications from a literal biological mother to a queen mother to Eve as mother of a race. It is even used in application to Deborah. As a leader of her people, she fulfilled a sort of motherly role.

Do you notice how on a chessboard it is the queen who protects the king? Women may be a helpmeet, but their unique strengths become apparent in the way they mold society, both raising children and providing support and wise counsel to their husbands (*or in some cases foolish counsel*). To me, this hints to why society has always painted the divine feminine aspect as the throne and the one that bestows a crown. A mother can mold her son to have the qualities of a king. She is often the heart and moral compass of a family. The role of women is vital to the shaping of society, even if it has traditionally been more of a behind the scenes kind of influence.

As far as a heavenly mother, I'm not going to get into the heated debate about the gender of the Holy Spirit or if God really had a wife. I will say there is some scriptural indication of a heavenly mother (*Proverbs 1:5-9, Galatians 4*). Study it for yourself if you are moved to do so. What I will comment on is that the Holy Spirit definitely serves the function of a mother type when you think about how it quietly gets to work tending our spiritual house on an internal and intimate level. A *Proverbs 31* woman gets to work taking care of the family! The conviction of the Spirit towards morality through gentle nudges guiding us in growth is a very motherly role.

The parents who raised us, whether they be biological, adopted, or otherwise, are supposed to be leaders of the household. If they are walking in God's will, then children simply need to follow suit. If these commands are the foundation of heavenly nature and God's character, then certainly He intended for all parents to be upstanding citizens and follow them, setting an excellent example to pass to the next generation.

Obviously that is not always what happens today. In modern times we battle high divorce rates, and there are plenty of people who fall victim to things like alcohol, drugs, laziness, violence and more. Honoring someone whose opinions and actions we don't agree with or respect is a difficult thing to ask of anyone. We have to do our best. I can only pray that every child is either in a loving home or put in one. Children with abusive parents for example can't just run away. They are scared, innocent, and are far from capable of surviving in the real world on their own. Some even learn to feel as though they deserve such cruelty.

This brings us back to the importance of being aware of those around us and encouraging honesty. Every child needs to know that if they are in a dangerous situation, they have somewhere to turn. This can be a sticky situation though, because sometimes the information you report to authorities is not enough to have the child removed from the home, but it is enough to involve human services or other authorities. This can potentially make things worse for the child after the problem is confronted, because the parent blames them for bringing trouble in their laps, then puts on a different face when they are visited. If you ever feel a child is in danger, approach the situation delicately and safely as best you can.

If we feel that our earthly parents are not people we should model ourselves after when we want to be right with God, then how do we follow this command? I suggest at this point we look to the next layer and remember that in Christ, we are all God's children. God is our heavenly Father! He sets the standard and is the most truly good anyone can possibly be (*Luke 18:19, Mark 10:18*). He is a Father everyone can honor in word and deed, just like Christ did with the entirety of his life. He makes it clear that doing the things we are talking about in this book and living in love are exactly how to honor Him.

Really, even if you had amazing birth parents, I feel this point is an important layer to this commandment. This again goes back to preserving the integrity behind the goodness of His name. Isn't it neat how these concepts build upon each other? I am certain that was by design.

I think following this command sort of just bloomed for me as I did. When I was young, I was a bit of a brat at first. I vaguely recall having a few tantrums when I couldn't get the toy I wanted at the store. It was just my mom and I during the school year growing up. My parents lived a thousand miles apart, and my siblings were in high school when I was born. In fact, my mom was thirty-six when she found out she was pregnant with me. In the 1980s that meant the doctors offered abortion out of fear of birth defects. I was a surprise! This means my mother, who worked third shift as I was growing up, was in the thick of menopause when I hit my hormonal teen years. Needless to say, we had some disputes.

My dad legally immigrated with his family from Holland when he was young (*my two cents on immigration is in Leviticus 19:33-34 & Matthew 7:12*). As an adult, he had a strong sense of patriotism and appreciation for the blessings of American citizenship. He served in the air force for many years. After he retired as a Master Sergeant he became a police officer, and eventually even taught for homeland security. He loved to joke around with everyone he met and put smiles on faces, but he could also be a drill sergeant on occasion. I loved spending summers with my dad, but of course work like that demands a lot of your time and attention. We didn't get as much quality time together as I would have liked, but I certainly appreciate all his hard work.

Growing up, I received good grades and was active in plenty of school activities, so my parents both expressed their pride in me. However, that cocktail of hormones, sleep deprivation, and exhaustion on all our parts had plenty of chances to cause clashes. Dad used to joke about how the copper wire was invented when two Dutch men were fighting over a penny, so I guess there's a bit of stubbornness in our blood too.

As an adult, I became pregnant right before turning twenty-one with a man I wasn't married to, and I was still in college. There was nothing that broke my heart more than hearing my mom say *I'm not mad, I'm just disappointed.* Come on, we all know disappointed is worse! When it became clear to me that I could not remain in a relationship with my daughter's dad, we ended up living with my mom for awhile. I felt terrible for putting a strain on her, and for many years she was a lifeline of support we wouldn't have survived without. However, I was now also a mom, so again our differences about how to handle parenting and life in general left plenty of room for us to clash.

Eventually when I moved in 2013, I slowly worked my way towards starting to be able to stand on my own two feet. That is when our relationship finally started to heal. It was one of my main motivators to move (*among others, of course*) to remove my burden from her lap and get to a place where I could repay her someday. While I haven't been able to pay her all of it back yet, I have been able to do some things for her as life has improved. We started talking and having visits together without a single dispute. She could see that she didn't have to worry so hard about me anymore, because that is what moms do best.

My dad's side of the family was never good about staying in contact much, though in recent years that has also changed thanks to social media. There have been some wonderful reunions! Disputes with dad always seemed to happen when we discussed politics. I have always leaned more towards democratic views, and he leaned towards republican. As an independent now, I do my best to hear all sides to a story, but I didn't always put that much effort towards seeing beyond my own perspective, so we had clashes there too.

Ultimately, what I noticed is that when I started being open in my faith in God in places like social media, that is when I started getting the feeling that I was truly honoring them. We stopped having conflict pretty much entirely. I made several apologies to mom as I realized the errors of my past ways, asking her to forgive me. She shed some tears of joy every time and reminded me she prays for me daily. Dad started going out of his way to say that the things he saw me posting really touched his heart and that he was so proud of me. There is just that something extra that shines through when you embrace the love of God. It echoes into every area of your life, even your relationship with your parents. Honoring my heavenly Father was the thing my earthly parents seemed to appreciate most.

If I'm being raw and real with you, the thought of this is making my eyes water right now. I knew the way my parents saw me mattered to me. I just didn't know how much it mattered until I came to Christ. They are the only constant, the only people who have known me for my entire life. There is so much I didn't understand when I was younger, and I know that is par for the course. I am just so grateful that it is healed and forgiven. I'm so deeply gladdened that we are in a good place in our relationships that are improving each day. I feel an extra level of fulfillment in my life knowing that is at peace.

This may be a very difficult topic for some people. I will not be foolish enough to think that everyone shares the same experience as I did. We may have had conflict, but I always knew my parents loved me, and I can see how hard they worked to give me a good life. That has not been the same experience others have had. However, I do feel that in order to follow God's will, it is an area we must address.

If you are able, I hope that you will visit or call your parents now. *Right now.* Put down the book and do it. You can finish this later. Create a positive memory with them, or have a necessary discussion. If they are no longer with us or you've never met them or if there is any other reason you can't connect with them, write them a letter working through the stages of forgiveness that were previously outlined.

I cannot say this strongly enough to anyone who is not in a good place with their parents. Set aside your pride. Stop holding on to grudges. *Just heal this.* Invite God to help you through it in prayer, asking for whatever extra strength and wisdom you need. More times than I would like to recall, I have seen what it looks like for the parent/child connection to be separated by death before the issues are resolved. We always think we will have more time, but we just never do. It doesn't matter whether it's the parent or the child that survives the matter, but the unresolved conflicts will haunt them for the rest of their life. It leaves scars. Take advantage of the time you have. Don't set yourself up to regret not getting a chance at what could have been.

As a parent myself now, I feel it is just as necessary to look at the responsibilities of a good child as it is to identify good parenting. I'm not going to call myself a perfect parent by any means. There is no manual that can prepare you for what it's like to be responsible for someone 24/7, a little person you get from scratch who can't even speak at first. They have free will just like adults do. It just isn't reinforced with tons of experience and wisdom yet. That is our job as parents. It is essential that we instill values in our children through the example we set in front of them and how we teach them to resolve conflict.

The fact that modern society pressures our children to all be the most beautiful, top performers that are prepared for the workplace is too much sometimes. Further, we aren't equipping them with coping skills and ways to process their emotions/stress/anxiety. Many parents today want to *give* their children the world. When all these things pile up, it can be a huge disservice to them which I feel is producing the opposite of the result anyone wanted from it. We set the younger generations up for failure instead of success when we teach them that mom and dad will do everything for them, but they still need to be the best and just figure out how to deal with it on their own. The second they enter the real world and have to clean their own room or get turned down for a job, they feel lost.

Being aware of the things I see people suffering over, I have tried my best to implement a balanced approach in my home. For starters, I have insisted on manners at all times. When my daughter was a toddler, we had an outing day with grandma. There was an hour drive home, so we bought fast food to eat on the way. She had been acting a little bratty that day, so I refused to hand her the kid's meal until she asked me to in a complete sentence with the word *please*. I then wouldn't let her open it until she said *thank you*.

Almost forty minutes later, she caved. It may have sounded a little cruel, but ultimately I asserted my authority and that she cannot demand things from me with tantrums. From that day going forward, she has never had a problem with manners. Occasionally I have to remind her to use them, but there's not even a moment of fight from her. If a child is asked to use manners but is unwilling to speak one or two little words out of simple respect in order to get what they wanted, that defiance is a strong indicator that they may have no respect for you at all.

I apply a lot of my conflict resolution skills as well, insisting that all parties involved own their part and identify what could be done differently the next time. I make sure that I honor my word, whether it be making good on a promise or following through on a consequence. My daughter gets free time and friend time, but we also have family time. I hug her and tell her I love her daily, but I also stand firm about following rules and having some order in our home. We divide up responsibilities fairly, and the two rooms she plays in are always her job to clean. If they are clean and homework is done, then she gets free time. Responsibilities come first.

Overall, the more focus I have given to balancing out my parenting, the more successful and healthy my daughter has grown to be. I get better and better reports from school every time we have conferences, both regarding behavior and performance in the classroom. In turn, she has become a child who reaches out to other kids who need a friend, and I know she will lead with the example I am setting for her.

It can be so incredibly easy as busy working parents to let kids do pretty much whatever they want and just chime in when we need to correct or reprimand a bad behavior. I see it *a lot*. That's just so unbalanced. If the only thing a parent ever shows their child is that we are supposed to work hard, do as we are told, sit down and shut-up, then they will ultimately rebel. If we always clean up their messes, they never learn how to clean them up themselves. Parenting is a very difficult experience, but it is also meant to be incredibly joyful! Children are our mirrors, and the adults they become will mold the future.

We must make sure that we teach our children the lessons we learned from our mistakes in life rather than teaching them to repeat our mistakes. This is the core reason that personal development will change the world. What changes inside us echoes loudly, especially as parents. My friend likes to say if you want to change the world, start in your own home, and I couldn't agree more. One of my favorite quotes of all time was from Lao Tzu. *If you want to awaken all of humanity, then awaken all of yourself. If you want to eliminate the suffering in the world, then eliminate all that is dark and negative in yourself. Truly, the greatest gift you have to give is that of your own self-transformation.*

In the space below, tell God you are sorry for the times where you dishonored your earthly parents He gave you as well as Him. Ask Him to forgive these transgressions, whether they be mistakes of youth or difficult choices we had to make. Be honest with God about your experiences with your parents and how it affected you. Do you feel that if things had been different with them that your life would be as it is now? Would it be better, worse, or are you satisfied with your childhood? What did you learn? **Where do you feel you fall on the spectrum of being honorable versus dishonorable? What do you think is a healthy balance of obedience versus independence?** As a parent, what would you do the same as yours did, and what would you do differently? If you are already a parent, is there anything you would like to change now that you are trying to make God a higher priority in your life? What behaviors do you not like about yourself that you see your children mirror, and how can you work to heal it together? What do you think it means to be a child of God in Christ and how should you act accordingly? These are all feelings that can run deep, so take as much time as you need.

_____
_____
_____
_____
_____
_____
_____

6. Thou shalt not kill.

This command and the rest that follow are quite short and to the point. They aren't wordy, and there are no other details given. It becomes important to derive context for the details in whatever way we can. I intend to evaluate this topic extra thoroughly to acknowledge many points I feel we must consider if we aim to truly wrap our heads around the weight of this specific command. This level of detailed analysis is intended to inspire a deeper value of life as a whole and encourage us to be more cognizant of the behaviors that lead to death so we can change them.

The original Hebrew word that is translated to *kill* here is *H7523 - ratsach*. Other translations choose to instead use the word *murder*. Many people will get technical here and argue that murder is intentional, so this commandment isn't saying all killing is wrong, just murder. They claim accidental death or war in order to defend your people from danger is not the same as murder.

The thing about that is *ratsach* is used in forty-seven other verses in the Old Testament. I'm not going to list every single one. If you want to fact check me, I absolutely invite you to do so! In fact, I encourage it! This word is used to describe both intentional *and* accidental deaths. It appears it can be used accurately in either situation. The true translation really is *kill.*

This is a command that on the surface sounds easy to follow, doesn't it? Should I even have to discuss the value of not killing each other? Shouldn't we inherently know that killing = bad? I searched online once to see how many years of peace we have actually had as a whole. The answer I found was that out of 3,400 years of recorded history, less than 300 of them were peaceful with no war. What qualified as war reflected more than 1,000 lives lost, so there may have been smaller skirmishes in those 300 years.

To be fair, people are capable of being destructive in the name of God. The Crusades happened. The Ku Klux Clan happened. Millions of Jews were killed for their faith in the Holocaust. We cannot be ignorant that violent extremists have existed. You'll find extremists in every faith. I guess we then come back to the need for love no matter what angle you look at our problems from.

While most people would say killing is wrong if asked what they thought point blank, it is unbelievable how many people are up in arms to defend their right to kill, *especially* professing Christians!

I'm sorry if it is an uncomfortable truth to face, but killing is not righteous. If every single person followed this one command, there would be no war or school shootings or terrorism. I would much rather see people standing up for their right to not be killed and speaking up for God's instruction not to kill than fighting for their right to own guns.

In the sermon on the mount (*Matthew 5:21-22*), Christ said *Ye have heard that it was said of them of old time, Thou shalt not kill; and whosoever shall kill shall be in danger of the judgment: But I say unto you, that whosoever is angry with his brother without a cause shall be in danger of the judgment: and whosoever shall say to his brother, Raca, shall be in danger of the council: but whosoever shall say, thou fool, shall be in danger of hell fire.* Christ declared that conflict should never get so far as murder and that we are to control our temper. He increased our liability to the command not to kill by instructing us to get to the heart of the matter and deal with it before it escalates. If you continue through the next few verses, he talks about handling disputes quickly and fairly. He also later addresses that instead of an eye for an eye as you had previously heard, that we should turn the other cheek to an aggressor.

Let's look to the apostles for some extra guidance. One of them was named Paul, and a decent portion of the New Testament was written by him. Before accepting Christ, he helped persecute many Christians who were arrested and killed. He had sworn to wipe out the whole church. The high priest authorized him to arrest the followers of Christ in Damascus. On the road to get there, he was struck down by a bright light. It is uncertain whether he saw the resurrected Christ at this point or just heard him speaking, but it was identified as Christ who appeared to him. Christ asked Paul why he was persecuting him and the church so strongly. Paul was then made blind and led to the apostle Judas in the city where he stayed for several days. Christ then sent Ananias to lay hands on him and restore his sight. This led to Paul being baptized into the church.

Paul provides a solid example of how someone's actions change to line up with the divine nature after they come to Christ. He became aware that he was wrong in his prior actions and *stopped* doing them. He replaced his efforts against the church with efforts for the church. That is the kind of works that matter. When we are told faith without works is dead, the point is *not* that you have some checklist of charitable contributions and good deeds to complete to go to heaven. The point is to line up your thoughts, words, and actions in the spirit of Christ. Nobody likes a hypocrite, so when we accept Christ, we need to accept his character and follow that example as best we can.

The book of *James* also states in *1:27* that *Pure religion and undefiled before God and the Father is this, to visit the fatherless and widows in their affliction, and to keep himself unspotted from the world.* This says to me that God values life so much that one of the purest acts you can do is to comfort those who are grieving a loss. Staying unspotted from the world means to keep the blood off your hands. Comfort those in pain rather than causing their suffering.

If we are going to look at how to follow a statement as vague as *don't kill*, we will have to address it in layers. Don't panic, though, because we will hit way more angles than you might expect, so don't get riled up. Just read.

On the surface, I think we all agree intentional murder is wrong, hence the reason we have so many laws surrounding it in our judicial system. Of course we would all prefer to avoid war as well, right? Look at the billions of dollars annually that go to fund it. Look at the lives lost and families that are separated for years at a time while their spouse is on deployment, worrying that whole time for them to come home safely. I certainly deeply respect anyone willing to put their life on the line to defend our safety and freedom. Deep down the willingness to go to war comes from that same love that Christ had for us when he was willing to die on the cross. There is no greater love than to give your life for your friends (*John 15:13*).

I just keep asking myself why we have been in perpetual warfare for the majority of recorded history, and why sending people to war has been a large part of every major dynasty. Haven't we learned yet that events are defined by how we respond to them? Haven't we seen enough examples of how responding to darkness with more darkness only makes us dark ourselves? Martin Luther King Jr. hit the nail on the head when he said *Dark cannot drive out dark, only light can do that. Hate cannot drive out hate, only love can do that.*

Spoiler alert: In the movie *Arrival,* an alien species lands in various places around the world. Eventually their means of communication is derived, and the more the main character studies it, the more she starts to see reality like they do. She begins to see time in a non-linear fashion. Not everyone else in the world sees what she does, and it comes down to her to try and prevent a world war. She is on the phone with the leader of China, trying to convince him not to lead people into this catastrophe. She has no clue what to say, only that she saw a vision of the future where she had said the right thing.

Suddenly she gets a glimpse of a future point in time where he finally meets her and whispers in her ear exactly what she had said to him on the phone, which she then repeats in the present time. She basically saw a memory of a future she had not yet lived. It is spoken in Mandarin so that you must seek out the translation. Do you know what she said? *There are no winners in war, only widows.* They were the last words spoken to the Chinese leader by his dying wife, and this simple, profound proverb touched his heart so deeply that he called off the war. Why can't we always carry that level of understanding with us? What must happen to make those words matter?

There are a few questions you must ask yourself to truly know how you feel about murder. First of all, would you kill one person to save many? Pretend you could have killed Hitler before World War II. Would you stick to your conviction not to murder and try to lock him in prison or find some creative solution, or would you kill him hoping nobody would rise up in his place? What about an attacker? If someone broke into your home and threatened to kill you and your family for one reason or another, how would you respond? These are not meant to be easy or offensive questions. They are intended to help you define the boundaries of your conviction. How far would you go to honor God's command, and what would your limit be?

Another layer down, can we all agree to be more self aware and careful so we can prevent as many accidental deaths as possible? The example that comes to mind is to restrict yourself from ever driving drunk or using your cell phone while driving. Another way it applies is that if it is your job to build things like cars or planes, always use the highest integrity. Don't cut corners to save a buck if it will cause a safety hazard. Focus on ***quality*** over quantity. Pay attention to the work you are doing and be aware of how it will impact others. Does this layer have any application in your life?

On the next layer, let's tackle that pesky conversation about abortion. My personal opinion is that life starts at conception. We are all completely informed about what pregnancy is and how it works. You know what it will become if left alone, so whether you end that life at the first cells or full development seems to be an irrelevant point to me. You are still ending what would have without question been a life, even if it doesn't have a heartbeat instantaneously.

When I became pregnant out of wedlock, I was asked more than once if I was going to have the child. My response was emphatically *of course I am*, because I could not ever bring myself to have an abortion under any circumstance. The second that life is being carried inside me, it's life becomes more important than my own. End of story for me.

That being said, it is a difficult subject to discuss. I might even go so far as to say it is one of the single most controversial topics even more than politics, so bear with me as I try my best to address something so delicate. I know people who have been raped and became pregnant, and the whole situation was incredibly traumatic. There are cases where contraception failed and someone wasn't in a position to be capable of raising a child. There are emergency cases where the mother could die if something isn't addressed. While I know how I would handle each of these situations personally given the strength of my faith, I can understand what leads people to make their decision regarding the subject and am sympathetic to the struggle.

Instead of condemning those faced with hard choices, I would like to address it from a more positive angle. There are three things I believe we can do as a society to dramatically reduce the abortion rate. The first is tackling the concept of promiscuity. We need to help people develop the emotional intelligence that reflects will power against temptations and not being driven by lust. It would certainly help if the media took a stance of modesty more often rather than trying to constantly intentionally appeal to our sex drive. It would probably also benefit people to have a better understanding of the effects of overpopulation so they can appreciate what a growing family means to the world around us.

The second thing is improving our health. That may sound roundabout, but physical health is intimately connected to our emotional state and ability to pass sound judgment in a situation. Plus, if I can't stop people from making the free will choice to have sex when they aren't prepared for the possibility of a child, it is necessary that access to contraception is free and easy. The best way to stop abortion is to prevent unwanted pregnancy. Prevention can mean a million different things, so effort in each area will do vast amounts of good.

When someone is going to have a baby, be certain their expenses can be covered. If I hadn't had access to Medicaid and WIC when I became pregnant, I would not have been able to afford a single doctor's visit, the cesarean section that was required when she turned breech, or the formula when we couldn't get her to take to breastfeeding. Make sure programs like this are protected and supported. There are also women who will have abortions if they are told their child will have a birth defect, so making sure the children born would have appropriate access to medical care, extra assistance, and necessary treatments is crucial to their decision making process.

The third and final thing is to dramatically improve the foster care/adoption/orphanage situation. When someone discovers they are pregnant with an unwanted child, they are more likely to carry it to term if they know the child will go somewhere loving and safe. We hear so many horror stories about kids who get stuck in a system that doesn't really care about them. We hear about kids who weren't adopted by a certain age, so they just bounce around from family to family until they are old enough to be emancipated. The reputation of the low quality of this system has led people to have abortions, because they don't want to put a child through that ordeal.

That may sound harsh, but it is logic I have heard people use to justify the action on numerous occasions. If you are truly convicted about being against abortion, then fill that space in your heart by being *for* the care of children that result from unplanned pregnancies. Invest in the children who are born and turned over to the system so that people can trust the child will be loved and have stability.

The sad truth is that once someone becomes pregnant unexpectedly, many who have chosen abortion have divulged that they felt it was the more loving choice. It makes me want to cry to think that some consider death more merciful than a chance at life. If someone truly believes bringing someone into the world would be cruel and unusual punishment given their circumstances, then that leaves society just as much to blame for the abortion rate as the person who made the choice to have one. Personal responsibility in this world falls on everyone. If you are against abortion but you are also against contraceptives and want to cut Medicaid, are you more concerned about the life or the dollar?

As a side note here, if you are pro-life regarding abortion and also walk around fighting for your *God given right* to own a gun, you are contradicting yourself. Either all life matters or no life matters. It's all life. God didn't give you the right to own a gun. He insisted that we respect life and not kill. The purpose of a gun is to kill, that's it. Your God given right is to *live*. All three of the people I lost to suicide shot themselves, and all three of them used a gun that was registered in someone else's name. The friend I talked out of killing himself intended to use a gun. Needless to say, my disgust with guns is not unfounded. You might say guns are for hunting, so that will be the segue way that takes us to the next level deeper on the discussion of life versus death.

The next layer is still treated as controversial. Do you feel this rule applies beyond not killing humans? What about animals? Do you identify them as conscious life that shouldn't be killed? I can't decide the answer to that for you. It is a topic you'll have to discern your feelings about for yourself. What I can tell you is that my Biblical study convicted me about becoming vegetarian. Due to that experience, I feel I have an obligation to present the information that convicted me so that you can properly evaluate all angles of the discussion for yourself.

I'm not a murderer. Heck, I'm rarely even truly angry. When I'm stressed I will sometimes raise my voice as a passionate person. It's something I work on daily, but overall I'm pretty peaceful, fair, and level headed regarding conflict. People tend to seek me out for help with conflict resolution. *However*, I used to be a hardcore carnivore. I was raised on delicious home cooked meals where the plate typically had one meat item, one serving of vegetables, and one starchy carb like mashed potatoes or pasta, the same formula for most school lunches.

When I was in junior high and they obligated us to take agriculture class, I was forced to watch a video of a cow being slaughtered. I was so disgusted I stopped eating meat for a month. I only came back to it when my mom made my most irresistibly favorite teriyaki wings. Let's face it, at that age conviction just wasn't in me yet. I loved meat and taste buds prevailed! As an adult, when I was focused on following a low carb eating plan for weight loss, I would eat meat in every meal and often as a snack due to the high protein.

After I did that first three day fast, meat just didn't look good anymore. It was like waking up from being hypnotized or drunk. I looked back on how much meat I had eaten in my life and just felt *gross*, so I began scaling back on my own. When I started studying this commandment shortly afterwards, that is when I started to apply a spiritual meaning to it. I asked myself just as I have asked you if eating animals counted as killing.

I've had many pets throughout my life, and every one of them had their own personality. They were like members of the family. If I couldn't eat my dog or cat for that reason, why could I eat a different animal just because I hadn't bonded with it? I decided to commit to being vegetarian. This was partly to account for my gluttonous meat consumption previously, but I also wanted to do something that demonstrated to God that if I believed animals count regarding this concept *in my heart*, I would not be hypocritical and eat them anymore.

I literally went through what almost felt like a withdrawal period as I transitioned out of eating meat. It was quite the wakeup call to realize how many sections of the grocery store I could no longer shop in, or how many restaurants I couldn't eat at anymore. I did, however, experience fantastic improvements in my health, mood, and energy levels once I got the initial cravings of withdrawal under control. I have friends with fibromyalgia and others that battle anxiety who all experienced improvements in their condition when they quit eating meat as well.

There is of course scripture that both supports and goes against this when you seek to understand it further. One thing which spoke to me was that before Adam and Eve fell, there was no death. In *Genesis 1:29-31* it says *And God said, Behold, I have given you every herb bearing seed which is upon the face of all the earth and every tree in the which is the fruit of a tree yielding seed, to you it shall be for meat. And to every beast of the earth, and to every fowl of the air, and to every thing that creepeth upon the earth, wherein there is life I have given, every green herb for meat, and it was so. And God saw every thing that he had made, and behold, it was very good.*

Both times the word *meat* is used here, it was translated from H402 - *oklah*. This word actually means *food*, not meat. That means that in the beginning when everything was exactly as God wanted things, before Adam and Eve fell, we ate a plant diet. We were intended to be caretakers for the animals of the garden. This passage clearly expresses that animals were given the same breath of life that we were, even if we have dominion over them.

After the fall, it brought death into the world. There was a sacrificial system in place, but it was considered a sin to eat the meat that was sacrificed. It was after the great flood when vegetation was wiped out that Noah and his family were permitted to eat clean meats (*Genesis 9:1-5*). I truly believe the restrictions about unclean meats given by Moses were for our health, not just to narrow our selection. When we look at the meat available to us today, there are plenty of documentaries and studies available suggesting no meat is truly clean anymore due to the chemicals that get into the animal's bloodstream while alive. Carcinogens found in meat (*as well as other foods, alcohol, etc.*) are even considered one of the leading causes of cancer.

I have seen studies that suggest blood types are good indicators of whether your health will be optimal as an herbivore or omnivore. Plus, you've probably been hearing about the health benefits of a plant-based diet in the news and on social media. There are foreign countries who incorporate it into their healing practices for treating things like cancer. It certainly seems our bodies have a positive response to it if handled appropriately and our balanced nutritional needs are not neglected. If you have a desire to make this change for yourself but are concerned about any negative impact it might have on you, especially if you have a preexisting health condition, please consult a doctor or dietician.

Coming back to scripture, *1 Corinthians 10:31* says *Whether therefore ye eat, or drink, or whatsoever ye do, do all to the glory of God.* This justified for me that as long as my motives behind not eating meat were to honor God's command not to kill on a deeper level and to cherish His creation, then I am not in the wrong for making that choice. I wasn't following a trend. I was following God. *Isaiah 66:3* also states *He that killeth an ox is as if he slew a man. He that sacrificeth a lamb, as if he cut off a dog's neck. He that offered an oblation, as if he offered swine's blood. He that burneth incense, as if he blessed an idol. Yea, they have chosen their own ways, and their soul delighted in their abominations.*

There are also external texts such as *Demonstrato Evangelica* by Father Eusebius, the man called the Father of Church History for his journalistic style of record keeping. This text claims all the apostles refrained from meat and wine and participated in fasting. St. Clemens of Alexandria was also a vegetarian, and he wrote about the apostle Matthew saying *It is far better to be happy than to have your bodies act as graveyards for animals. Accordingly the apostle Matthew partook of seeds, nuts and vegetables, without flesh.* St. Clements in his *Clementine Homilies* quotes St. Peter as having said *I live on olives and bread, to which I rarely only add vegetables.*

That being said, there is scripture to the contrary of this point. The most direct would be *Timothy 4:1-5*. What I would say to that is I'm not rejecting anything, because in the modern world I choose the groceries I buy. People know my decision and don't offer it to me. He also warns against people who teach you not to eat these things, but I am not doing that. I am simply identifying a subject that has become complicated in modern context and presenting you both sides of the discussion to identify what your personal choice will be about it.

Romans 14 is clear that we shouldn't dispute with someone who makes this choice, though for me it is not about weak faith. I made the choice out of strength of faith and have held onto it to be a better leader. Apostle Paul wrote *Romans*. He also wrote *1 Corinthians 8* saying he would not eat meat for the purpose of not being a stumbling block to those of weak faith regarding the issue of things sacrificed to idols.

As a quick aside about things sacrificed to idols, in the modern day this is not just about meat. Some branding (*not all*) is built around idol worship, and I have heard stories of restaurant owners who offer up the plate to their gods before serving it. We are not to eat these things, so be cautious.

I have never prohibited my family from eating meat, but as the grocery shopper and cook I will only buy and prepare meats that are deemed Biblically clean. Given what we have access to, they get beef, chicken, turkey, and fish. I feel that what God deemed clean has been defiled by toxins and man, so through Christ I have the right to refuse it. If you love and respect me as the Bible commands, you will not present me meat to refuse as a test, and in turn I will not judge you for eating it.

The Bible also says Christ did feed a crowd of people fish (*Matthew 14:13-21, Mark 6:30-44*), even though there's nothing that says he partook of that for himself. There is indication that there was a Passover lamb eaten at the last supper as that was customary

(*Matthew 26:17-30, Luke 22:7-38, Mark 14:18-26, etc.*). The only place in scripture that *directly* says Christ ate meat in front of anyone is *Luke 24:41-43*, everywhere else it is only implied. You can also find people who contest all of these points and others quite thoroughly based on translation disputes. If you want to know more, you should do a study for yourself. It is a fascinating journey to undertake.

    This isn't a point I wanted to shove down your throat or force on anyone, but I certainly am not doing my job if you do not have this scriptural perspective available to consider for yourself. Evaluate the information, pray about it, and proceed accordingly. *Just don't be hypocritical to what you believe is the truth.* When I studied for myself, it boiled down to this. We have the freedom *to* eat clean meats as long as they have not been sacrificed to idols. We are also free *from* eating meat. The swing vote was that God has shown me love, mercy, and given me life. He is a life giver! It is the thief who comes to steal, kill, and destroy (*John 10:10*). I made the choice to show the same mercy to animals as God has shown me. *Blessed are the merciful, for they shall obtain mercy* (*Matthew 5:7*).

    After becoming vegetarian, I became aware I struggle with mild lactose intolerance. Pretty much the only animal byproducts I still consume are occasional eggs and cheese which I am slowly scaling back on over time. Mass production needs have created situations where many animals are caged and borderline abused. The practices that put food on your table are not something I would wish on anyone, not even an animal. Again, do the research for yourself and decide where your ethical boundaries lie and how God would feel about what you have seen. I'm someone who sheds tears over road kill. You can decide if that means I'm hyper sensitive or that I sincerely value life in the spirit of divine nature.

    If you do decide to continue eating meat, I would like to encourage you to be mindful about not wasting any of the animal. I know that if I were killed for food, I certainly wouldn't want to see pieces of me wasted in a garbage can. At a bare minimum, respecting that a life has been taken in order to nourish you means acknowledging it. Take a moment to say a thanks for that sacrifice so that you never forget the value of life.

    Let's move on and peel back another layer. Do insects count, and to what degree if they do? I certainly am not going to tolerate something parasitic like scabies or lice or bed bugs just to allow them to live. That's a hard line for me. One of the names used for Satan is Beelzebub which means lord of the flies. So good news, there is some scriptural precedent for disregarding insects! At the same time, I have on occasion wondered what the world looks like through the eyes of a spider. We are like colossal giants to them! Just because we have dominion over life below us on the food chain, does that mean they deserve to be smooshed just because it is more convenient for us?

  I certainly wouldn't want God to look at us through that perspective. If we ourselves are merely tiny specks compared to God but by his mercy are not expendable and He loves us all, then perhaps we should reflect that divine nature towards things much smaller than us. Next time you find a spider, could you let it outside instead of smashing it? Again, these are all points intended to make you consider the value of life. This is not about me forcing you to make my same decisions. Reflect on your perspective and why you hold it.

  I think the last layer loops back around to how Christ identified the core of the problem by instructing us not to rise to anger. To clarify, that doesn't mean we are not allowed to feel a wide range of emotions. If Christ was the perfect example, what did he do? There was a time he was so disgusted by the actions of the money changers and the people buying and selling things in the temple that he flipped tables (*Matthew 21:12-13, Mark 11:15-18*). The shortest sentence in the whole Bible simply says *Jesus wept* regarding when Lazarus died (*John 11:35*). Christ resurrected him and knew he could, yet he still shed tears. Obviously even Christ experienced many feelings beyond just love and peace. That is normal.

  What isn't normal or acceptable is allowing emotions to spiral out of control to more destructive behaviors. Even the Old Testament tells us it is wise to avoid befriending people who are angry all the time (*Proverbs 22:24*). That is so you don't adopt their behaviors for yourself. That doesn't mean you can't be a support and try to help them, but boundaries or walls keep unsavory things from entering your temple.

  Maybe you've heard people say your vibe attracts your tribe or that the five people you spend the most time with are the ones who shape your personality. We are all saying the same thing here. Your external environment impacts your inner self, and what exits your inner self through word and deed impacts those in your external environment (*Matthew 15:11-20*). Existence holds a responsibility to be aware of ourselves, our environment, and how one impacts the other.

What are some suggestions we are given about handling this? Let's start with *Matthew 18:15-17.* It says *Moreover if thy brother shall trespass against thee, go and tell him his fault between thee and him alone. If he shall hear thee, thou hast gained thy brother. But if he will not hear thee, then take with thee one or two more, that in the mouth of two or three witnesses every word may be established. And if he shall neglect to hear them, tell it unto the church, but if he neglect to hear the church, let him be unto thee as an heathen man and a publican.*

In laymen's terms, confront your conflict alone. If it doesn't work, bring in some help. Maybe that means a counselor or coach, or perhaps a friend can help mediate objectively. I personally like to cite Bible verses, especially words directly from Christ, as a witness in dispute so it's like he is fighting my battles for me. If that doesn't work, consult with your church. If you've tried all these things and can't find resolution, then walk away and pray for everyone involved. Know when it is appropriate to disengage.

When something happens once, it can be chalked up to chance. When it happens a second time, it could still potentially be coincidence. However, when something happens three times a pattern has officially been established enough to determine how to proceed. Chance becomes choice. If you approach a problem three times and ways and are still faced with conflict, it's time to agree to disagree and proceed accordingly. That's when we can say we made a fair effort to try resolving it but it's their choice. Larger more complex problems may need more chances and effort than this. Just keep it in mind as good parameters to work from.

In *Titus 3:9* we are instructed to avoid foolish questions, genealogies, contentions, and bickering over the law, because this is worthless. If we are all one in Christ, it doesn't matter if we are descended from a certain bloodline. If love is the fulfillment of the law, then we have no need to get into quarrels over nitpicking the details. If we are embracing wisdom, we will learn to ask questions of value, seek answers in God, and not waste our time trying to set a date for the return of Christ. We will be more concerned with being ready whenever that date comes. In other words, to avoid rising to anger, be cautious of where you place your focus.

Another great instruction is found in *Romans 16:17. Now I beseech you, brethren, mark them which cause divisions and offences contrary to the doctrine which ye have learned; and avoid them.* Don't let people try to sway your faith away from what God has shown you to be true. There are plenty of people who will march into a discussion prepared to battle, and it is up to us to turn the other cheek to attacks, especially when it is clear their goal is to be divisive. Know the difference between someone who is engaging in genuine discussion with you about contrary opinions and someone who is just trying to be right and push buttons.

1 Peter 3:8-9 says *Finally be ye all of one mind, having compassion one of another, love as brethren, be pitiful, be courteous: Not rendering evil for evil, or railing for railing, but contrariwise blessing; knowing that ye are thereunto called, that ye should inherit a blessing.* In short, don't follow the doctrine of an eye for eye. That will make the whole world blind, one poked out eye at a time. Instead, repay evil with blessing. Christ says the same thing in the sermon on the mount (*Matthew 5:38-42*) when we are instructed to instead turn the other cheek. *...And if anyone wants to sue you and take your shirt, hand over your coat as well. If anyone forces you to go one mile, go with them two miles...*

In a moment where you are faced with conflict, you have three choices. You can choose to escalate the situation by meeting anger in kind. You could choose to walk away and ignore it, even though we all know that doesn't really eliminate problems. The third option is to bless it. If someone is angry, pray for them. Clearly they need it. If they are hurt, try hearing them out and being there for them. That is the only choice that both confronts the problem and helps to heal it.

There are plenty more verses you can reference for Christian conflict resolution. While I will not - and frankly could not - possibly dig through every one of them, some verses you could start with on your own would be:

Matthew - 5:25, 5:34-45, 7:1-2, 7:12, 22:36-40
Mark - 9:38-40, 11:25-26
Luke - 6:36, 10:30-37
John 15:12

You will find in all these verses and many others that we have a clear arrow pointing to peaceful interaction. We must remember that all parties in a conversation have their own perspective, their own life experiences, and their own feelings. We cannot force people into peaceful resolution, but we can choose not to engage in anger, violence, or hurtful conflict just because a situation escalates. These things can be challenging to implement, but Christ offers forgiveness when we repent. Guidance in how we live our lives more peacefully going forward is exactly why I think Christ is like the ultimate life coach. I'll say it again - he is the way, the truth, and the life!

If you struggle in this area, an excellent book to dig into after this one is *Bait of Satan* by John Bevere. He so eloquently works through how the spirit of being offended by everything is the bait Satan uses to control and manipulate us. I could hardly put this book down! It is clear there was an anointing on his message, because it just filled me with so much peace to read.

Before we wrap up this discussion, let's touch on the subject of the gun debate. I have no desire to own one. As I've made clear, their only purpose is to kill. I don't know anyone who enjoys living in a perpetual state of mourning over tragedy after tragedy. It does appear that we are past a point where completely eliminating them would even be possible, and handing them all over to government control is the recipe for a military dictatorship. Keeping gun violence under control is going to take many approaches working together in unison.

We must pray *and* change policies *and* enforce what is already in place. We must help people work through their struggles in healthy ways. We must improve the quality of living in a myriad of ways to reduce the motivation to commit crimes. The mental health care system needs a significant increase in support and services need to be covered on insurance. *If* we all came together as a whole to tackle *all* of the valid concerns relating to guns, we might actually accomplish something. Instead we bicker about which one answer is right. Get over your need to be right and get busy saving lives.

Rules to Defeat Death

If you've ever seen the movie *Zombieland*, the main character had a list of rules he followed to survive the apocalypse. I like the idea of having guidelines for difficult subjects. One day it occurred to me that in a similar way, maybe we could have rules for defeating death by choosing life. I'm not saying that doing these things are some required part of earning eternal life, but this may be a way to get ourselves into the *mindset* of the eternal life we will receive in the kingdom. If death was personified in a boss fight on this level of the tower, this would be how we would win, just like Christ will return and defeat death (*1 Corinthians 15:24-26*).

1 - Accept Christ into your heart. Pick up your cross and follow him!
2 - Don't kill anything - not even animals for food or spiders that are creepy.
3 - Remember that blood represents life, not death. - Leviticus 17:11-14
4 - No longer fear death. This takes away its power and control over your actions. Revelation 12:11
5 - Don't let clocks be in charge. Time is a construct of man that places focus on aging and increases stress. It is only a tool.
6 - Avoid things meant to hurt or kill like poisons, toxins, guns, etc.
7 - Speak more life into the world with loving words and actions!

    Overcoming your fear of death can be difficult. This is not a process meant to turn you into someone who charges head first into battle or dangerous situations. Faith shouldn't make you a maniac. Fear of death is a safety mechanism. It just isn't meant to *control* us. Conquering my own fear of death came down to this. If it is my time to die, then I will die. Nothing will change that. If it is not yet my time to die, then God will protect me from death just like He did when I almost crashed my car. If you truly trust that fearlessly in your heart without needing to test it, then you can walk in each moment as though you are invincible even though you know you are not. It creates a safe barrier that allows confidence to shine through your words and actions, to know that you are safe to speak your truth and do what is right. It allows you to focus on just being good and doing your best in each moment.

    You will feel bolder once you accept that death will come for everyone and that you are no exception. Through faith in Christ, death will simply be a transition to an immortal life in heaven. I'm just not afraid of that anymore. My faith is solid, and I believe in where I will go when I die my physical death. I can only hope that it will be an honorable death that held purpose. I will not squander my short life on earth doing things that will just kill me faster. I will utilize my time as best I can to do things that matter.

It's simple. If I'm afraid of death, it controls me. If I accept it, I overcome it. We are born again in Christ. The old self dies its spiritual death. Being reborn in Christ is the transition to choosing love and life! You are born into his immortal spirit. It's almost like the human body is just a vessel in which our soul is tested and transitioned. It allows the experiences that determine what path each unique soul really chooses once it is given free will. The body will amplify whatever the soul's true self is and develop the potential of that path. We get the chance to become aware of our misguided ways and change towards divine nature. We decide how committed we are to that, choosing every step. Who we are as a person and how we got there is the culmination of those choices.

If bravery can be taught, it is in this way, developing strength of character at our core. To be brave is to see the positive value in your actions as being higher than your fear of the consequences enough to see them through. We have to dive into how deeply we mean that and how far we would go to do what's right. We also need to know how far is too deep to go. When we are convicted in our moral compass set by God, we start implementing it into our lives through how we act. Bravery is a byproduct of understanding such a major topic as life and death that when addressed gives that whole armor of God a super pro level upgrade. Developing this in ourselves is like polishing that armor to be blindingly shiny.

I simply have faith that a best way exists, and we can find it if we work together with the greatest good in mind and God in our hearts. If God commanded us not to kill, then I believe there are ways to solve these problems without turning to killing. Nobody will convince me otherwise. It will all come down to personal responsibility. Even freedom has a price. I just don't want to see any more lives be used to pay it.

As mentioned earlier, Christ warns us that we may be hated for his name's sake (*Matthew 5:11-12 & 10:22, Mark 13:13. John 15:18-19*). There are so many reasons this will happen. Some people will not like the false perceptions of the faith they have been taught, and they'll judge the behavior presented by false leaders without digging to understand scripture for themselves. In the modern era, many are atheists based on science, so they will express anger at anything they cannot study in a lab or write an equation to explain.

Some people will feel like your mention of Christ is you judging them, because he lived a perfect life and when they compare it to their own lives they just see how they don't measure up. Some people get lost about how to study scripture and give up when it doesn't make sense. Others will be mad at you just because of a poor experience with another Christian or church.

Anger is an easy way to deflect when we experience cognitive dissonance attached to deep rooted, personal issues. If we don't want to *go there*, we tend to instinctually take a stance of being either defensive or offensive. It feels like an attack! Nobody likes to be told they are wrong, especially about something they feel made them happy. They are still living with a lack of understanding that there is something more or different than their current reality. If we feed into their anger by mirroring it back, we cause a pattern of escalation that is the foundation of violence. Our example then also teaches the opposite of the message.

That is another reason to walk in the love of God. If you are a loving person, people will be attracted to your demeanor and want to know the source of your peace and joy. I imagine that walking with the Holy Spirit gives you a sort of soul level glow that can be seen and felt by those looking for light. They will ask questions, and when they accept Christ, the Holy Spirit will convict them. Sure, we need to have confrontation for people to know change is necessary. It's just not a particularly effective method to lead with. We will talk more about the subtlety of sharing the gospel later. Just know that while open discussion is great and adults should be able to embrace healthy communication about difficult subjects, we just aren't there yet! If we lean into love instead of anger, we will get there faster.

As a last note, *Ecclesiastes 3:1-8* does state that there is a season for everything, even to kill. There are plenty of Old Testament stories of combat that celebrate the victor. However, that does not negate the commands of God. We must do our best to follow His will for us. If a time to kill comes, it will not be by my hands. That is my conviction. What is yours?

In the section below, tell God you are sorry for anytime you have violated this command in any of its many facets. Ask Him to forgive you for your trespasses. Identify for yourself how you now view life.

Do you value it more than you previously did? Do you understand that God is life giving and deems it as precious? Who do you believe has the right/authority to kill? *__What are your boundaries going forward regarding life and death?__* Have you ever experienced a loss that deepened your understanding? If so, share about your experience. *__Where do you feel you fall on the spectrum of anger/rage versus calm composure when facing conflict?__* Does Christ help you feel brave in a healthy way? Take time to pray about God's intentions for you regarding this difficult subject.

7. Thou shalt not commit adultery.

Most little girls grow up wanting a fairy tale wedding where the knight in shining armor carries her away and loves his princess forever. We watch movies and tv shows that rarely neglect portraying romantic tension, let alone being entirely about romantic relationships. We see beautiful movie stars in perfect lighting act so wildly in love that the passion is like fire. Then we come back to the real world and fantasize about the perfect mate for ourselves. As we go looking and start dating, we don't get the same perfect experiences, and learn that life is not a movie. Relationships are work.

We live in a society that for the most part has lofty expectations and low standards when it comes to romantic love. Too many people go into marriage knowing divorce is a possibility they can fall back on if things don't work out. Even though I knew the ten commandments as a kid, adultery in my mind was about not cheating on the person you married. I figured as long as I took my time on finding the right marriage and didn't rush into anything, then I wasn't violating this command. However, the root of following it is about developing healthy relationships that don't lead to wanting to cheat in the first place.

Christ knew this. He addressed it at the sermon on the mount (*Matthew 5:27-32*), giving us his instruction. *Ye have heard that it was said by them of old time, Thou shalt not commit adultery: But I say unto you that whosoever looketh on a woman to lust after her hath committed adultery with her already in his heart. And if thy right eye offend thee, pluck it out, and cast it from thee, for it is profitable for thee that one of thy members should perish and not that thy whole body should be cast into hell. And if thy right hand offend thee, cut it off, and cast it from thee, for it is profitable that one of thy members should perish, and not that thy whole body should be cast into hell. It hath been said, Whosoever shall put away his wife, let him give her a writing of divorcement, but I say unto you that whosoever shall put away his wife, saving for the cause of fornication, causeth her to commit adultery, and whosoever shall marry her that is divorced committeth adultery.*

In a country where roughly half of all first marriages end in divorce, and it is common to remarry a second and third time, that can be a jarring passage to read. (*Hebrews 13:4*) We are pulling the divine essence of these commands while still breaking free from the law of sin and death. Rather than focusing on severity and punishment, I would instead like to focus on the concept of building stronger relationships that are more capable of standing the test of time. That is the real purpose of a command like this. We all know the value that can be found in honoring our commitments, and in the modern day I think the real problem is more about the way we rush into them with unrealistic expectations and a weak understanding of love that devalues it.

My grandparents on my mother's side were married for sixty-six years until my grandpa passed away. She was sixteen and he was twenty-one when they married in 1948. I certainly had the chance to see what a lifelong love looks like. It's no surprise to share that God was present in their relationship, and they cherished their faith.

My parents were both each other's second marriage, and my dad remarried a third time after their divorce. My mom did not remarry. So, I have also lived through the hardship of separated parents. I have two older half sisters, a half brother, step-brothers and step-sisters, but no siblings that are full blooded or anywhere near my age. Despite my large family, I grew up living with my mom during the school year and dad during the summer as though I was an only child. I'm not blaming my parents for anything. I understand what happened between them. It just resulted in me not being aware that I didn't know how to interact with men.

Since my mom worked third shift in a factory, I spent a good bit of my time alone so she could rest. No dad or siblings were around to develop my social skills with, and mom was understandably exhausted a large amount of the time. When I watched those romantic comedies, they taught me that if you get along well with a guy it meant you should be in a relationship, and all romantic relationships are sexual. What a hormonal time in life to learn that! It wasn't until my last years of high school that I was popular enough for it to matter, though.

It took me until I turned somewhere between twenty-eight and thirty to really start realizing the impact these things had on my life. Living in a society that promoted sex before marriage as a natural part of the dating experience and attending churches too scared to talk about this kind of intimacy left a gap in my understanding that I didn't know was there. By the time I began to truly understand, the damage had already been done. There's a difference between reasons and excuses. I'm not making up any excuses for my behavior, but to change I had to understand where the behaviors came from. I had to rip out the weeds by the roots, not just mow the lawn.

As stated previously, I have never personally been married, but I have been proposed to by four different men and been in several long term relationships. My first long term relationship lasted three years during high school. He lived in Georgia near my dad, so it was long distance most of the time. Once I entered college and he went to military boot camp, we eventually drifted apart. When I had completed three years in college for vocal music performance and acting, that following summer I hit a bit of a party phase. Life had hit me hard financially the previous year and I wanted to lighten up and have some fun.

Near the end of that summer, a couple weeks before turning twenty-one, I became pregnant by a man that I had only been seeing for about a month. Before I realized I was pregnant, I had become aware that I couldn't possibly continue the way I had been when school resumed in the fall. I was trying to figure out if I wanted to break up with him and how. When I found out, I spent about a week in shock. At the time I wasn't sure I wanted kids. One night I was nauseated by some pizza and he came to check on me, so I told him. He was remarkably calm and composed about it. He didn't panic and run. He stayed, so I committed to see it through with him no matter what.

As a child of divorced parents, it was important to me not to repeat that for my own child. Over the course of the two and a half years of our relationship, that feeling was challenged. I experienced things that made me deeply question my belief about staying with him no matter what. My limits were tested to extremes. I do not wish to dive into the details, but eventually I left with our daughter. It was for the best.

The next guy I was with lived with me for about a year in an untitled relationship. The next after him lived with me for a winter in an open relationship. The next lived about three hours away still sharing an apartment with his ex, because he couldn't afford to move out. After him I threw my hands in the air and quit dating. I kept getting hurt, and it was draining. I didn't want my desire for partnership to interfere with my parenting. It was that summer of

2012 when I met the man I went to California with. That was the real pivot point when I started to see more clearly, and he and I never even dated. It was just a really deep friendship. My year of abstinence and newly elevated awareness of self started pulling me out of this dilemma.

The friend I moved with in 2013 was the guy I had previously dated that had lived three hours away with his ex. He had two children from two past relationships and wanted to be closer to them. They lived roughly a five hour drive away from where I was. Given time apart, he and I had become friends again. I had been nonchalantly chatting with him about maybe moving to Georgia since an old friend had asked me to earlier that week.

I told him I wanted to move somewhere for a fresh start but not be too far away from my daughter's dad. That friend said *how about move with me instead*. I found work and we moved. As roommates we could both afford that fresh start that we otherwise wouldn't have been able to pay for. After six months as roommates, the kids were asking when we were getting married even though we weren't dating. We took a chance on a relationship, and it lasted four years.

We blended into a family, and I knew I wanted marriage from the start. In the beginning, he had a personal policy about not marrying someone he hadn't lived with for two years. It was a reasonable precaution from his own experiences of seeing marriages fail. I found that to be acceptable enough. We were approaching that two year mark for us when his mother ended her own life. Her husband, who cheated on her for seventeen years with various women, filed for divorce to marry another woman. He was engaged to the new woman before he had even told his wife he wanted a divorce. Some of her last words to her son were to not do to me what her husband had done to her. Naturally trauma caused scars about the subject of marriage, which I sincerely understood. I decided to remain patient as best I could until he was ready to get married.

However, after our three year anniversary is when I committed to Christ. As I was evaluating my life against the Bible, I became convicted that I should no longer be living in sin by being sexually active outside of marriage. I didn't want to put him on the spot, though, so when it was clear he wasn't ready, I asked him to give the issue sincere focus and said I needed to know his position on the subject by the end of the year. That didn't mean we had to be married by then, but ideally engaged if I was who he really wanted. I needed to know he was coming to the same page as I was, and that our love was stronger than his fears. I wanted him to find comfort and healing from his trauma in the positive experience of our relationship.

That gave me roughly eight months from that point going forward to work on correcting my other behaviors. I wasn't a bad person, but I wanted to be certain I lined up with the real Christ and not some false persona of him. I wanted to be completely authentic in my faith. I would come back to our relationship last. I made it clear that eventually marriage would be a deal breaker and tried to just be supportive during that time.

The year ended, and nothing had changed. If he had truly understood the importance marriage had to me at that point, he would have sought counseling or had difficult discussions with me about his concerns, but the time passed like he had no desire to work through it. I waited into January before putting my foot down that I was losing my ability to be patient and close to leaving. He already knew it though. Our friends had been pushing the subject too.

It was becoming ridiculous, because I was the one taking his daughter to her appointments like a step-mom but having to get his permission every time since I had no legal rights. He had health insurance through his job, but I couldn't be on it since we weren't married, even though his child support obligations forced me to be responsible for paying the majority of the bills. It became complicated, and marriage stopped being able to be about love like I wanted it to be. It started having to be about our obligations to each other. We cleaned up the small bit of damage on my credit and were talking about wanting to buy some land to build a forever home, but he still wasn't committing to a forever relationship.

I waited another month, and still saw nothing change. We stopped being intimate in this time. I was so convicted that I was displeasing God that I felt guilt at the thought of it. To me, marriage was a simple, easy solution after four years together. To him, it wasn't. We had other smaller problems to work through which I'm certain we could have resolved, but marriage was the one issue I couldn't budge on.

I ended that relationship as I started writing this book. It was like my final step, and I didn't want to be a hypocrite about anything I shared. I may have gone out of order, but I was attempting to accommodate for his genuine emotional struggle with compassion. It really didn't hit me how serious the issue of marriage was to me until I realized I couldn't get ordained unless I was single or married. That's when God led me out of it one step at a time.

We were monogamous and loved each other, don't get me wrong, but the church and scripture both viewed the way we were living together and being sexually active as a sin. Seeing those words felt like judgment, and it hurt deep. I didn't even know if I even wanted to be ordained, but seeing that I couldn't was eye opening. Until that point, my heart had grown to feel comfortable like we were already married, so my inner self didn't feel out of line. I had to see something outside of my awareness that reminded me we really weren't married, and he wasn't ready.

Eventually, my inner conflict became too much, and I couldn't wait anymore. If he didn't know after four years, I felt he would never know. We were not in line with God's will and that had to change. It was time to put God first, because I trusted His will for us and that marriage was the right thing to do. I would have accepted a quarter machine ring and a courthouse wedding, but he had to want it too.

Even after ending the relationship, a hope arose in me that maybe the reality of losing me would push him over the edge to commit, but by that point he ended up just seeing the expression of those feelings as me trying to manipulate or force him. I had no such intention. It just broke my heart that it came to this. We could both acknowledge that we would always love each other. He told me he believed in God and was a Christian. He just wouldn't move forward with me.

When I ended things, I made a personal commitment not to have sex again until it was with a man committed to marrying me, even if that meant I never will again. I committed to only engage in relationships with people who have similar values as I do. The way I feel, though, I have no desire to seek a relationship again. It would take God planting someone in front of me and practically parting the clouds with flashing arrows to be interested in someone right now. My focus is being placed in Christ. I learned that there are some things I can compromise about, and there are some things I can't when it comes to my life partner. If I had come into any of these relationships with the moral fortitude of Christ in my heart, it is likely none of my heartbreak would have happened.

I know now that I was incredibly ignorant, but that doesn't change what I learned from these experiences. They have all provided valuable lessons I could only truly learn through living them. I did the hard work of repentance, atonement, and forgiveness. My daughter may have been born out of wedlock, but God turned my poor choices into the biggest blessing in my life. Does that mean I would recommend following suit? *Not a chance.* Please learn from my mistakes, don't repeat them! I would have preferred to have children when I was ready and married.

I can only try to move forward in God's will having learned from my poor past choices. The backlash of pain I frequently experienced from making them was enough as it is. Now that I finally understand my mistakes, I can avoid repeating them. My baptism was a few weeks after the breakup. My born again self is a virgin in spirit, and she will maintain her purity.

This commandment is probably going to be the one that hits the most nerves to work through. What has become the societal norm is not even remotely close to God's design. In the historical perspective of the Bible, marriages were treated more like business contracts. They were typically arranged and came with a dowry. The bride would spend one year away from her future husband preparing, then he would come collect her at the end of that time. Men would sometimes marry many wives in those times as well. It seems to me that was allowed as a survival tactic in small populations. Procreation was a more serious matter when the population was still small. Again, large families also provided more labor for farming, like a commune. God makes it very clear in scripture, though, that His original intention for marriage was as a unification of two souls in one flesh, so it is not meant to be taken lightly (*Genesis 2:24, Mark 10:8, Ephesians 5:28-29, etc.*).

Today we have billions of people on this planet, and the majority of places allow you to choose your spouse. We don't really have a need to increase the population further. We have free will, infinite choices, and a culture that glorifies casual sex. That can be overwhelming in and of itself before we filter in what God wants us to do. When I was in college with more of a science focused mind, I thought of sex like fulfilling a biological impulse for creature comfort, a drive of our animalistic behavior and hormonal impulses. Today, having experienced long term monogamous relationships and having found faith, I see sex as an entirely spiritual experience. It is meant to be shared as a form of intimacy, and it invites a part of the other person's soul to join with yours.

Everything I did regarding men in my past had stemmed from my lack of deeper understanding about what I was doing. It was consensual, and I always thought I had real feelings for the people I was with. I didn't realize those feelings weren't real love, though I'm not sure that applies to the last one. The majority of them were an illusion of intimacy. What I ended up doing was cheapening my own life experience by not holding a high enough value on my body and my heart. As a loving person, I gave parts of myself away to each person that was willing to fulfill my desire for connection.

I can't get those parts of me back, only learn to live with who I am and move forward in Christ who makes me whole again. I see my errors now, and they will serve as a reminder of who I no longer wish to be. I have become someone whose heart cannot be bought with gifts, seduced with sex, lied to, or cheated on. I want a marriage where we fix things that break instead of throwing them out. I value real connection, joy, honesty, loyalty, partnership, and intimacy. I have boundaries and am capable of both giving and receiving love in a healthy way that reflects divine nature.

That is a standard I set for myself and will not drop below again. God loves me and has shown me that I am a woman of worth who should not settle for less than He intended for me. It honors Him when I respect that worth through my relationships. Being reborn in Christ allowed me to work through the healing process of forgiveness to all parties involved, including myself, and release that negative past.

A year ago, I would have been super embarrassed to publish something as raw and honest as this. Then I realize that my story of simple ignorance is far from the worst one out there. I assure you I have seen many horror stories. While I'm not comparing, we all grew up in this world together, seeing the same acceptance of sexual promiscuity in the culture developed by media and advertising. Cultural norms don't meet divine standards, so we need a wakeup call in order to change.

What sounds hard at first becomes easy when Christ is holding your hand through the growth process. I never imagined myself having the strength to take control of my impulses, but I did it! When I realized that I didn't want to let God down or lead by a poor example, I was blessed with the strength to make a better choice. This may mean that I am now a single mother, but a *Proverbs 31* woman gets to work, and that is what I do. I have faith now that if I am meant to marry, God will send the right man my way. I don't have to seek him out, and I can focus on being my best self in God's service until then.

    All relationships have love in them, but not all love is romantic. The nature and meaning of it from every angle is obviously the theme throughout this book and I assure you countless others. I could tell you the dictionary definition is *"an intense feeling of deep affection"*, but that doesn't even begin to describe its endless nuances. Still, you know it when you feel it, don't you? You know the love you have for your mother, father, siblings, and extended family. You know that despite Freudian theories, that is a different love than what you have for a life partner. Your friends, well they're family you choose, so of course you love them, too. People will even tell you how much they love a song or poem or food, so even inanimate objects get to share this label. It is the most universally applicable feeling with undoubtedly more words devoted to describing it than anything else in existence, with good reason.

    I think a major modern problem is that people confuse different aspects of love, and it ends up leaving them hurt. What makes love shared with your partner extra special? Not only do we choose the person we romantically love unlike our family, but we make a lifetime commitment to them unlike with our friends. This bond becomes the foundation of a new family, so if it is strong and healthy, the family bond will reap the benefits. It holds a higher place of importance than an acquaintance or your favorite toaster pastry, so let's give it due focus.

    A truly functional marriage relationship will not be made of two halves forming a whole, but two whole people who complement each other as a new unified whole. Sometimes we are drawn to the way our partner is different than us, and others will prefer someone who is similar to them. No matter what the case may be, it is important that self care comes first so that both partners are bringing their best selves to the table. *The greatest gift you can give to somebody is your own personal development. I used to say 'If you will take care of me, I will take care of you.' Now I say, 'I will take care of me for you, if you will take care of you for me.'* ~ Jim Rohn

    The Bible says to let nothing sever what God has joined (*Mark 10:9*). Let's break down some of the most important traits of a successful marriage relationship to honor and strengthen that joining of souls. It should go without saying *love* is the most essential element! Our ability to marry for love is a gift, even if picking one person for life can be challenging. The way love feels may evolve over time to be less about passion and more about comfort and security, but it should always be present or both parties lose. I have noticed over time that couples who genuinely have God in the foundation of their relationship typically never lose love for one another.

Of course *communication skills* and total *honesty/trust* are a must. I highly recommend if you'd like to learn how to communicate better with your romantic partner to read *"The 5 Love Languages"* by Gary Chapman. Different people are more responsive to different methods of communication. Some people see giving or receiving gifts as a sign of love, while others may find helpful contributions around the house to be a demonstration of your feelings. This book breaks it down into five categories, helps you and your partner identify which suits each of you, then gives tips on how to communicate better through your respective love languages. Keep in mind that just like there are five fingers on one hand, all five categories may apply to you in some way. You will likely lean into one or two more strongly than the others, and they will help you communicate more effectively. If you cannot have truth with your partner, you have nothing, so put it in your foundation.

Loyalty and *respect* are near the top of the list. As I stated earlier, the divorce rate in this country is alarming. Growing old with someone means you fix what breaks. Too many people jump to throw things out these days just because they hit a hard spot. It seems like it's all about controlling impulsive responses. Don't rush into marriage, and don't try to rush out of it once you have it. There is absolutely no excuse for cheating. Any person who commits to a relationship should honor that first whether dating or married, and only move on from it if both parties have identified the problems cannot be solved and the relationship has been *officially* ended.

Sex is also a part of this equation. While I'm not going to get racy here, I will state that every person has sexual impulses. Our bodies are just built that way. It is not fair to either person in the marriage for that to be neglected (*1 Corinthians 7:1-7*). When we stop paying attention to our partner and their needs, that is when eyes inevitably tend to wander, so in order to avoid breaking a command of no adultery, I think it is fair to address meeting this need for our spouse.

Sex is not wrong in a marriage between people who love each other, so don't be that couple who is afraid to talk about it. However, we should not just accept the Jezebel spirit either. If we want to overcome, the only option is to take personal responsibility and not make bad choices. Keep in mind when it comes to any discussion about sex that the Bible says our body is like a temple for the Holy Spirit. That means that everything that enters or interacts with it matters. Never forget your value as a person and that you deserve respect from your partner as well as yourself. You should never cross a line that makes you uncomfortable, and even when dating, never give yourself away. Honor the gift of your life and body (*1 Corinthians 6:18-20*).

Creature comfort through touch is also beneficial, so don't be shy about occasional kisses, holding hands, or daily hugs. They are good for your health and affirm your commitment to your partner. There's also no need to overdo the PDA either. One of the things I miss most from my last relationship was the way he would give me a long, warm hug every day. It was the kind of hug where he stayed until I was ready to let go, and it was seriously like therapy.

Equal effort and *appreciation* are next on the list, and I feel they go hand in hand. Conflict will be around the corner without fail every time someone feels their partner is not pulling their weight. Finding that balance is one of the biggest tests of living together. Just as each person needs to be doing their part, they also deserve acknowledgement that their efforts are appreciated. Sometimes it can be easy to get caught up in the busy day to day workings of life and forget things like *thank you*, but taking the extra second to say it now and then will save you from frustration and fights later. A study about what it *actually* means to be a virtuous man/woman can help build strong foundations. The Bible makes it clear that both parties should get to work, not just leave everything to their spouse (*Ephesians 5:22-23, Colossian 3:18-19*).

This leads right into the next necessity which is the virtue of *patience*. Nobody is perfect, and you will spend a large amount of time together. You will depend on each other, and expectations will likely be set and occasionally not met. While I typically try to avoid setting expectations of people, it is fair when two people commit their lives to each other to expect the basics I'm listing here. That doesn't mean to constantly be applying pressure. With solid communication, it should become clear whether two people will meet each other's needs or not. There is no need for drama. Take it easy on each other.

Sensitivity is something I feel is crucial. They say the only people who can truly hurt you are the ones you love, because their opinions matter most to you. We need to be aware when interacting with our partners that as a spouse our words and actions hold a heavy weight in the heart of the other. We often make the mistake in modern society of regarding being sensitive as being weak. However, when we apply scripture to our lives, someone who is sensitive becomes an even better form of strong than we ever knew was possible. Balancing our feelings with the knowledge of our rational minds and reinforcing it with God creates a trifecta of beauty. Make sure that is present in not only this, but in every relationship. It is a fundamental piece of compassion.

The last part of a successful relationship I would like to touch on is *fun*! Romance may involve plenty of serious moments, but it is meant to be enjoyed! Love is supposed to feel good and help you see the beauty in the world! If it doesn't, you are likely out of balance by being more focused on responsibility and the material world. Your souls are partners, not just your bodies. Allow them to meet and light up a room. Joy is infectious! Laugh together!

There is a verse you will hear read at pretty much every wedding you ever attend. This passage identifies characteristics of love. While I would normally share from the KJV translation, I can't bring myself to do it here. They translated the word love to charity many times in it, so I will share the NIV translation that everyone is familiar with. Don't just barrel through reading it. Really contemplate each concept presented here. Each word holds depth, and can be applied to every kind of relationship, not just marriage. This passage is thick with wisdom. *1 Corinthians 13:4-8 Love is patient, love is kind. It does not envy, it does not boast, it is not proud. It does not dishonor others, it is not self-seeking, it is not easily angered, it keeps no record of wrongs. Love does not delight in evil but rejoices with the truth. It always protects, always trusts, always hopes, always perseveres. Love never fails...*

That, my friends, is real love - *humble*, forgiving, and pure. Overall, love may be complicated at times and there are many more intricate facets I'm not discussing here, but it's only as hard as we make it out to be. If we live in truth, the right people will stay, and the wrong people will go. Fear should never be allowed to dictate our lives and relationships or decrease our love.

It seems everyone has an opinion about marriage, but rarely do church leaders address life as a single Christian. We have an economy that makes it significantly easier financially to be married, which also carries with it heavy societal pressure to conform to this way of life. Our financial system is designed to have families as its backbone.

It's not like we can force someone to marry us just because we want marriage. Coming back to *1 Timothy 4:1-5*, it also warns against people who teach forbidding marriage. It's worth clarifying that I'm not teaching against marriage, only suggesting that we follow God's will presented in scripture and prayer and play the cards we are dealt as best we can. It is, however, noteworthy to read *Matthew 22:28-30* and *Mark 12:25.* There will be no marriage after the resurrection.

God also commanded us in the beginning to go forth, marry, and multiply. That doesn't mean being single is bad or wrong. In fact, in *1 Corinthians 7,* the apostle Paul tells us that he wished we could all be single like him. He depicts marriage almost like a solution to preventing sexual immorality. He says it would be better to be intimate with a husband or wife than to burn with lust and lack self-control. I see the benefit now of saving sex for marriage and intend to live that way going forward. If you feel called to a life of chastity, then follow the call that has been placed on your heart. Only you can determine what you feel He is leading you towards. Just make sure it is God doing the leading.

Furthermore, there are many times in scripture where God tells us He will be our husband. *For thy Maker is thine husband; the Lord of hosts is his name; and thy Redeemer the Holy One of Israel. The God of the whole earth shall he be called (Isaiah 54:5)*. Hosea 2 also paints a vivid picture of a woman who leaves God, her first love, in search of other lovers. He says she will return to Him, and at that time she will no longer call Him Lord. Instead she will call Him *Ishi* - husband.

To tie it all up with a bow, many of us in a modern world full of carnal desires will find ourselves asking why God created our bodies to receive pleasure from sex if He didn't want us to have it. Why do we marry and procreate if it is so divine to be chaste/abstinent? What's the point of all this?

    For starters, if sex did not feel good, would we have desired to procreate? I don't think so. If you don't believe me, go to the YouTube playlist and watch the True Facts video about ducks. It will really make you appreciate the anatomy God blessed us with. Be warned that visuals of duck anatomy are given for educational purposes and there is some mildly explicit language.

    More than that, perfect love as we have been exploring is defined by its balance. When one person as an individual is single, they are supposed to work to be balanced within themselves. They develop their personality traits to be healthy. When that person feels desire towards something outside of themselves, it creates a shift towards being uneven, pulling them out of balance. I believe that is at the heart of why coveting is a sin, too.

    When two people get married, God unifies them. That shifts the dynamic. No longer are these two individuals trying to just be in balance as themselves. Now they work to balance each other. These two whole and balanced people become one half of something. Sex then becomes an act which brings together what God joined as one. That is still balanced as long as both people desire each other. They are not just desiring a physical act of intercourse. They desire to be unified with their other half and balance out.

    In my humble opinion, this is why God prefers either chastity or marriage and none of the in between stuff. Balance equates to stability in this sense. To desire - whether it be a person, place, or thing - is to become an unstable element. It is like saying somewhere inside yourself, you are unsatisfied or unfulfilled without having this thing. When you desire something, you give it your focus, your attention. It averts your eyes and efforts away from God and gives away some of your personal power.

    Desire and passion are two different things. Desire most often pulls you away from balance. You want something you don't have. Passion most often amplifies your balance to be more useful, at least in its healthiest application. Are you passionate about God? Are you passionate about loving people? Are you passionate about helping people? That feeling creates a forward momentum towards action. Like fire, it just needs to be reigned in so it doesn't become all consuming.

    Unfortunately, I am obligated to clarify *Deuteronomy 22:28-29* and *Exodus 22:16-17*. People like to use these two passages as a way to invalidate the entire Bible and the concept of marriage entirely, and I don't find that acceptable. They both suggest that in the Torah law, you were obligated to marry your rapist.

In that time period, a woman was given into marriage in purity by her father with his permission and a *bride price*. Chastity wasn't just a virtue. It was family honor and part of her financial value. If this was violated and people found out, she would likely be cast off, damaged goods. It is possible she might never marry. That is why Joseph almost ended his engagement to Mary when he found out she was pregnant with Christ (*Matthew 1:18-25*). He would have been within his rights. An angel had to explain what was happening. Skipping over the father's permission would also have been a grave violation.

Not only was this law written to protect the woman from being publicly shamed for life and likely unable to wed, but it prevented the man from ever divorcing her, even on the basis of adultery. That was intended to be a punishment, sort of like a *you break it, you bought it* concept. It seems to me it was written as a *deterrent* for rape. Whether you were someone who interpreted it that way or as a way to mark your territory without following the proper channels decided whether you were a man or a beast. Being *that guy* would make the rest of your life rather difficult when you look at the context of the times. In those smaller populations, everyone knew everyone. Everyone needed everyone. Community was too important to throw away.

In the modern world, we have alternative punishments that don't force a rape victim to live in trauma. Today, asking a father's permission is a courtesy, your partner is your choice, and we are not obligated to provide a dowry or pay a bride price. We have social services to assist someone effected in this way, and in civilized circles at least, a rape victim is not publicly shamed or prevented from marriage down the road. All the reasons this law existed no longer apply as we have shifted towards love which the law hangs from.

I would be more concerned about it if it were one of the ten commandments written by God's hand, but this was one of the laws written as a clarification in the context of the times. Everyone clearly knew the consequences. Even if you are someone who chooses to adhere to all Torah law, I fully believe that the one who committed the rape is the one who is liable for having broken the command. I can't imagine a loving God punishing the victim or telling them they sinned when they didn't actually do anything wrong. That wouldn't be in line with the character of anyone identified as being fair.

God does obviously understand all of this as our maker and knows what He is asking of us. In creating us capable of desire, it's not all bad and serves a purpose, but when allowed to run rampant, we sacrifice our self-control to what we wanted. We start to seek more and more things to satiate ourselves instead of God.

He may call you to a life of chastity, and He may lead you to a life of marriage. It all depends on who He designed you to be. Trust that He knows what His plans for you will yield, and His promises always revolve around joy. Don't forget to pray about this! This world is designed to lead you into desiring anything and everything. In prayer, God will bring the peace that pulls you back to center.

In the following space, tell God you are sorry for any past sexual immorality or vows you have broken and ask for forgiveness. If you are moved to share examples, please do. **Where do you feel you fall on the spectrum of lust and promiscuity versus marriage, commitment, and purity?** Is there anybody you feel you need to apologize to or exchange forgiveness with? Identify how you saw romantic love in the past compared to how you see it now. What makes a marriage different when God is the head of the household? If you are in a relationship, what concerns would you like God to help you work through to strengthen it? Be sure to pray about your problems and *ask God to guide you*. Don't just tell Him what solution you want Him to agree with. What are some things you can do to strengthen your relationship that God would approve of? If you are single, do you feel you are trusting God to bring you the right spouse in His timing, or are you in a panic about hunting someone down? Are you prepared to wait for the right partner, or do you need to pray for the strength not to settle for less than God has planned for you? Do you feel stable as an individual or led by desire? There should be no judgment present regarding either option, just honor who God made you to be. Reflect on the way societal pressure and the media have impacted your feelings about romance.

_____
_____
_____

8. Thou shalt not steal.

There is *so* much scripture to supports this command. With little variation, it all pretty much says the same thing. Don't take what does not belong to you! For example, *Proverbs 29:24* tells us *Whoso is partner with a thief hateth his own soul. He heareth cursing, and bewrayeth it not.* In *Psalm 62:10* it says *Trust not in oppression, and become not vain in robbery. If riches increase, set not your heart upon them.* You can also look to *John 10:10, Leviticus 19:11, Ephesians 4:28, Mark 10:19, Matthew 6:19, Luke 18:20, Romans 13:9 & 2:21*, and so on.

Nobody wants their belongings stolen, so do not steal from others. This is the easiest application of the **golden rule**, though it certainly has applications well beyond theft. *Do unto others what you would have them do unto you* (*Matthew 7:12, Luke 6:31*) This is a relatively straightforward command. It's short, easy to understand, and even the laws of man are structured around it.

Maybe you've heard the saying that possession is 9/10 of the law? This basically means that verifiable ownership holds the strongest weight about how legal disputes regarding property or money are resolved. A command not to steal is about the closest thing to overlap you'll see between God's law and man's law. The difference is, close to 9/10 of God's law has nothing to do with physical possessions. It is all structured around spirit and behavior. That doesn't mean God doesn't understand that physical reality is full of physical possessions. He just insists that it not be where we place our focus in our hearts.

What is interesting about this command is where wisdom is applied. For starters, in *Ephesians 4:28*, Paul tells us that as Christians, instead of stealing we should be putting our hands to work for charity. He deters us away from our carnal nature by reminding us life is not just about us and our needs. We should be doing honest labor that aids others who are in need. When I accepted Christ, I started feeling the need to use my time for more volunteer work. One of my favorite ways to contribute is stocking shelves at the local food pantry. They always need assistance and have helped my family out in a pinch a few times.

Proverbs 6:30 says *Men do not despise a thief if he steal to satisfy his soul when he is hungry*. It does, however, continue to say that if he is caught he will have to pay it back sevenfold, so it's still not considered an appropriate course of action. What is our instruction in desperate circumstances?

Luke 12:22-31 is a perfect answer about turning to God, just like Christ did when he fasted in the wilderness. *And he said unto his disciples, Therefore I say unto you, take no thought for your life, what ye shall eat; neither for the body, what ye shall put on. The life is more than meat, and the body is more than raiment. Consider the ravens, for they neither sow nor reap; which neither have storehouse nor barn; and God feedeth them. How much more are ye better than the fowls? And which of you with taking thought can add to his stature one cubit? If ye then be not able to do that which is least, why take ye thought for the rest? Consider the lilies how they grow. They toil not, they spin not, and yet I say unto you, that Solomon in all his glory was not arrayed like one of these. If then God so clothe the grass, which is today in the field, and tomorrow is cast into the oven, how much more will he clothe you, O ye of little faith? And seek not ye what ye shall eat, or what ye shall drink, neither be ye of doubtful mind. For all these things do the nations of the world seek after, and your Father knoweth that ye have need of these things. But rather seek ye the kingdom of God, and all these things shall be added unto you.*

Luckily in modern times we have great resources like food pantries, government assistance programs, and non-profit charities. Dire circumstances that lead to stealing are much less common than they had the potential to be before advancements like industrialization. There is almost always a resource available for the necessities if you know where to look. Obviously we still have homeless people and ghettos. Not everyone gets access to health care or quality nutrition. The system is far from perfect, but I would like to think it's better than it could be.

Public services don't negate the power of prayer and faith, though. I recall a day where my cabinets were getting pretty bare, and I wasn't going to be able to get groceries until the following day. All I wanted to get us by was enough milk for one bowl of cereal, something to make everyone for lunch, and some snacks for later in the afternoon. As I was silently thinking of this list to myself and contemplating what to do, my daughter walked up and handed me a plastic shopping bag. In it was one eight ounce milk, some packages of easy mac, crackers, jerky, and some apples. She said they had given it to her at school. They had a backpack program through the local food pantry that sent these kinds of bags home once a week, but we had not been participating in the program at the time. She wasn't sure why she had gotten it.

It felt like God answered my prayer before I even prayed it, practically just downloading it into my hands. God knows what you need. *Trust that.* We won't always have food bags materialize when we need them. Often we must watch for the blessings, like better job opportunities emerging or sales/coupons that allow you to afford exactly everything you needed. Just kick that trust up a notch and see how God shows you His appreciation for your faith.

I find the book of Job to be relevant here as well. It is the oldest book in the Bible, so to me that suggests it may contain one of the most important points God wanted to share. Its message runs so deep with such vast application. The super short synopsis is that God sees Job as a good and faithful servant. Satan challenges that and claims he was only that way because God had blessed him. If he were to face true struggle he would change his tune.

God gave permission to Satan to test Job however he wanted as long as he didn't touch a hair on his head. Job's family was all killed. His income and animals were all wiped out. He was left with nothing. His friends even came and accuse him, saying surely he must have done something seriously offensive to God to receive such a severe punishment. Despite the fact that he didn't know why this was happening, Job kept his faith, even though eventually he just wished for death.

At that point God talked to Job then returned what he lost plus a good deal extra. To me, the most crucial point of this story was to give a detailed example of keeping faith no matter what challenges we face. This man had no idea why he was suffering. His entire world was shattered far beyond what we would expect the average person to face in the modern world, yet he didn't abandon God or speak ill of Him to those who confronted him. If he could do that, why can't we?

Whenever I feel a moment of weakness, I remind myself that maybe Job is our *job*. The Bible warns that we will face trials. If that weren't the case, we wouldn't have anything to overcome or endure as we are asked to do. A benchmark of God is that He is true to His word. He has shown us He will win against Satan. He has answered prayers and performed miracles and sent His son for our salvation to be possible. We can trust that He will provide, and if we just come to

Him for help, He will never put us in a position to need to steal.

In the space below, tell God you are sorry for any time in your past where you may have stolen something. Ask Him to forgive you. Do you feel like you have a debt to repay? If so, notate your intentions about how to handle it. ***Where do you feel you fall on the spectrum of taking personal control versus trusting God? Do you spend more time focusing on carnal needs and desires or on spiritual pursuits?*** Do you need to research financial assistance options or find extra work so that you are not tempted to steal? Do you ever put your hands to work helping others in need? If not, write down some ideas you'd be interested to participate in.

9. Thou shalt not bear false witness against thy neighbor.

Most English translations of this commandment simply say *do not lie*. Overall that is a fair assessment, though I think it was not originally being quite that broad. To bear false witness against your neighbor implies lying in a way that negatively impacts someone else or about something you saw them do. In those times punishments as severe as death could be doled out on the account of two or three witnesses who spoke against you, so your honesty could be life or death serious.

It probably should just say *don't lie*, though. As we previously stated, truth is one of the most benchmark characteristics of God, and Satan is referred to as the prince of lies. God keeps His promises, and Satan deceives and manipulates. Honesty is one of the most paramount important characteristics one can exhibit.

I could give a lengthy list of scripture to support this command in both the Old and New Testament. For those who enjoy seeing scripture on the page, a slew of example can be found in *Proverbs (10:31, 12:22, 13:5, 14:5, 16:6, 17:7)*. That is a book all about the wisdom of Solomon. It is made very clear that truth with grace is the benchmark of wisdom. Some New Testament examples would be *Ephesians 4:29, Colossians 3:9, 1 Timothy 4:2*, etc. Let us also not forget that Christ says he is the way, truth, and life. He literally declares that truth is something HE IS. It's a part of his makeup! If we are to follow after him in the Spirit, we need to refine ourselves to be honest. I repeat it over and over, because it is a crucial element of real and perfect love.

Truth is something I have always valued. I see it as a foundational part of living with integrity. Plus, lies never stand. I have never seen a single instance in my life where someone lied and the truth didn't eventually surface. As a kid I would joke that I was always completely openly honest so that if I ever did need to lie for some reason, nobody would question it. The truth is I just prefer being honest and transparent, and people were more accepting of hearing it with ulterior motives and humor attached. Without that statement I was just a goody-two-shoes. With it, I was seen as being alright and down to earth. Today I am not only honest, but I encourage it in others. I'm no longer afraid or ashamed to embrace honesty. I don't care if others don't like that I'm honest. I care that God respects that behavior in me.

Is there really anyone who is ok with lies? The only people who like them are the ones who tell them, but then they carry the weight of them so their appreciation of it doesn't usually last long. When you think about it, lying is almost a form of theft. When the truth is shared between two people, they are both on an equal playing field about how to handle it. When a lie is told from one person to another, the liar claims the advantage over the other person. A lie steals fairness. Nobody gets excited or joyful about being on the receiving end of falsehood.

Is there ever a time it is ok to lie? Biblically speaking, it appears white lies for good reasons are not expressly forbidden. For example, if you are trying to surprise someone, they can't know the truth until it's the right time. What if you end up in a life or death situation? What if a small white lie will avoid an explosive conflict? Sometimes the ability to lie holds value.

However, I feel if you are truly committed to honesty, truth should be in the core of your heart, spoken, and lived to the best of your ability. If your friend asks you what you think of their new haircut and color and you don't like it, you could choose to lie so you don't hurt their feelings. You could *also* choose to say something about it you honestly do like, even if you end up saying *if it makes you happy then I'm happy and what I think doesn't matter*. That is true. There's always a way to respond with something true if you choose your words carefully.

I have seen people try to justify lies as part of self care. True self care is about love and healthy behaviors. Self-preservation is about your fears or paranoia and feeling cornered into doing things you wouldn't normally do to protect yourself from a *perceived* threat. Lies, secrets, and manipulation are acts of self-preservation based in a false understanding of what is healthy in the grand scheme of things. Real self care is always honest. Do I think that if you tell a lie you should be cut out of your church or pay the penalty of death for sin that they used to face? No. I *do* believe you should be responsible for your words and actions, even if we are covered by grace and forgiven. Is there anyone who doesn't see that as common sense?

Honesty is a very important thing that I focus on with my daughter. We have many discussions about behavior. When someone comes to me to tattle, I always ask every person involved to share what they think happened. Then we identify the truth and discuss how each person could have handled it better. I insist that they have a level playing field of fair and equal treatment. She knows that if she is caught lying and trying to avoid the trouble she thinks she will get into, the punishment will be double what it would have been.

She used to try and fib her way through things with lies of omission or deflecting the blame to other people, but we have been working on understanding my role as a parent is to both love her and teach her. I step back and remind her this is my job to help her grow into a lovely young woman, and while I will always love her with my whole heart, I simply cannot allow certain behaviors. As I have grown in Christ, it has definitely trickled down into my parenting. She mirrors my growth in herself.

Without truth we cannot trust, a behavior that is crucial to any successful relationship whether it be friend, family member, co-worker, spouse, teacher, or any other interaction. I would like to take some time in this section to discuss communication. If we can approach a difficult discussion with a better grasp on effective communication skills, then we will not feel compelled to lie to avoid conflict. It will become easier to address things that hurt us and own up to our own mistakes.

Communication skills are used to project our reality outward which will garner responses from peers. It is essentially the building blocks that allow my perception of the world to meet yours. Eventually this builds relationships in many different capacities, and their complexity continues to grow with time. It is important to keep the communications from our mouths a true outward projection of our inner selves rather than being sucked into changing who we are at the core for each conversation to appease others. Yes, it can be helpful to adapt to a person's mood and communication style, but truly healthy communication requires the fortitude to be true to both God and yourself.

What does communication consist of? Recall when I stated that only 7% is the actual words used! 38% of it has to do with tone on voice, and a whopping 55% is all in your body language. That means full communication requires the active use of your mouth, ears, and eyes cohesively. I preach this statistic often regarding texting and social media, because all you have to work with in many instances is that 7% of typed words on a screen. It becomes painfully easy to escalate bad situations (*or sometimes even harmless ones*) simply because the person reading your words applied the vocal tone and body language they assumed was correct. This can often be impacted by their mood in the given moment, which you cannot see for yourself via text. We all know what they say about assumptions…

Please, pick up the phone and call people sometimes! At least you can use 45% of your communication skills that way! Even better yet, take advantage of advanced technology and video chat! My personal favorite choice, however, is to put the electronics down and interact with real people. Go ahead, *try it*. It will change your life!

A technique you might notice in very socially adaptable people is mirroring. It involves reflecting similar body language and tone of voice back to the person you're communicating with. It is possible to go too far with that, though. Don't be a creeper who literally replicates every move someone makes like a mime. However, I would wager that this is the key difference between sales people you find to be pushy and those you enjoy working with. The people who relate to you on your level of interaction will make you more comfortable, not the ones who are too stuck focusing on their own head and goals. It's the difference between someone asking if you will help them reach their goals or asking what they can do to help you reach *yours*.

This ability to understand how the other person in the conversation behaves and feels reflects one of the most powerful tools in the human arsenal - *empathy*. To communicate well, our viewpoint cannot be the only one that matters to the conversation. In turn, the same applies to the person you're speaking with. They too need to acknowledge your perspective and not just make everything about them. Each perspective brought to the table becomes a part of the whole. The truth is rarely one sided and will fall somewhere in the middle of all perspectives involved.

Grab a friend, and have them stand in front of you. Hold up a quarter in between you. What do you see? What does your friend see? One will see heads, and one will see tails, right? You both saw the same quarter, and what you both saw was true. You just saw it from different perspectives. Some truth is three dimensional like that. There can be many aspects from which to view the same thing.

Isn't it fascinating how with everything I've shared, finding a balance in the middle ground is the best choice? Remember that finding common ground is not about old labels opposing each other like male vs. female, black vs. white, young vs. old, and so on. It's also not about changing the truth to fit someone's needs. It's about forming a new and better label where both sides are honored. I would like to boldly suggest that label be *human* and encourage people to see everyone through that lens.

Empathy is what breeds the ability to respond with *compassion* which is defined as *a feeling of deep sympathy and sorrow for another who is stricken by misfortune accompanied by a strong desire to alleviate the suffering*. It is literally translated as *to suffer together*. Compassion is one of the most love based concepts to exist, and it can be broadly applied across every situation. However, for most people it is not instinctual, rather it is a learned behavior best reinforced in the given moment.

Please, grab those teachable moments with your children! Don't let your chance to teach them compassion slip by just because *that's just what kids do*. Explain the difference between their response to a situation and a compassionate response. For example, when I was in my four year relationship, we had an issue where one of the girls would see something on the ground that she wanted, pick it up, and take it. When it's a penny or shiny rock, nobody cares, but one day she came home from the after school program with a teddy bear that wasn't hers. When asked where it came from she said she just found it.

I had to explain that the compassionate and honest response would have been to put it in lost and found, because someone might be looking for it. They could be sad their bear was missing, just like she was sad when she lost her bag of Valentine's candy. I identified a relatable emotion, thusly explaining empathy, then told her how to apply it,. Last, I appropriately labeled it so she knew the definition of the word compassion when I used it later. She took it back and put it in the lost and found the following day.

Warning: As with everything, there is another side to compassion. While it is essential for success in this world, being compassionate also opens you up to be a witness of darkness. *Andrew Boyd* said it best. *Compassion hurts. When you feel connected to everything you also feel responsible for everything. Your destiny is bound to the destinies of others. You must either learn to carry the universe or be crushed by it. You must grow strong enough to love the world yet empty enough to sit down at the same* *table as some of its worst horrors.*

This is why self care and God need to come first. Stepping forward through the door of compassion is a responsibility, and it will require your personal strength and resilience. A balanced, healthy individual will hold compassion in high regard as one of the greatest blessings we can share, just like Christ did in the perfect example of his life. Someone who is not will see it as a curse.

What else is important to communication? While I honestly couldn't fit everything into one section, or probably even another book for that matter, I will share a few tips to get you started. First and foremost, engage in active listening! When it is someone else's turn to speak, let them! Don't interrupt, it's rude. Stop talking, make eye contact, hear them speak, then paraphrase what they said back to them to acknowledge that you understand. Most people really just want to be heard. You don't have to agree, but it will validate for them that their perspective exists and can be understood.

Another helpful tip is using "*I*" statements. This keeps the conversation focused on your feelings instead of the other person's behavior. Remember what we said earlier. People get defensive when they feel attacked, and once they put up that wall of defense it's hard to take it back down. This technique also ensures that you take ownership of your feelings as being your own. If the conversation involves conflict, *when/what/how* statements can also provide clarity. Referring to specific occurrences helps prevent people from feeling judged for their character as a whole.

It can also be helpful when addressing negative situations to use the feel good sandwich technique. It may sound silly, but when you add the jelly that is sincerity to your peanut butter that is your point, you'll end up with a great sandwich. Start with something positive, address the problem, then end on a positive note. It softens the situation and eases tensions. I use this technique often in political discussions, but most often I use it with kids. *Honey, you know I love you very much, no matter what. That does not make it acceptable to keep leaving these big messes. It is your responsibility to clean up behind yourself, and my responsibility to make sure you learn how to do that so you'll be a successful adult. Now please clean your room so we can spend some quality time together. I look forward to hearing about the book you've been reading when you're done!*

While generalizations can sometimes be effective for making a point, they can also be offensive. Avoid the use of the words *always* and *never* if you do dip your toe in those murky waters. As previously stated, these two words usually automatically make your statement false, because there are exceptions to just about everything. We've all been in that argument with a significant other where one claims something like, "*You **always** forget to take the trash out*". The other immediately responds with "*No I don't, remember that **one** time?*", and the argument escalates further because neither person feels heard. Nobody likes being lied to or accused of something, even if it was unintentional. Using these words will make people defensive, especially when your generalization is a stereotype and impacts them personally.

Stereotypes and profiling are a destructive by-product of a society oversaturated with labels. What begins as a simple word that identifies or classifies something/someone starts to form patterns which get noticed, and it leads to the formation of generalizations. When given a negative tone and allowed to be distorted by spiraling through rumor mills, generalizations turn into over simplified and inaccurate stereotypes that cause judgment and hatred to gain ground. To counter that, we must spend some time focusing on individual accountability and ditch the labels. This will eventually allow us to reclaim the true meaning of those words. In essence, we can detach the emotions from these labeling words through the use of rationality.

As an example, if you were born and raised in a small Midwestern town that was all Caucasian and you visit the south for the first time, *don't* tell an African American about how you heard they always like grape soda and fried chicken or fear that they will be violent. There is of course a chance you will say that to someone who happens to love grape soda and fried chicken. Fried food and soda of any variety are common menu choices in the south. There is a chance you could encounter someone violent when poverty amongst discriminated racial groups mixed with lower quality education systems can be a breeding ground for crime. The possibility exists.

However, that doesn't make it a universal truth, nor does it mean those traits are caused by their skin color. They are all choices any person of any race can make. You will likely offend a nice person, even if this was an innocent belief someone else shared with you and you honestly thought was true. Not having met an African American before, how would you have known anything other than what you were told?

On that note, the more people travel and experience other cultures, the less they make fear based judgments. As Mark Twain said, *Travel is fatal to prejudice, bigotry, and narrow-mindedness, and many of our people need it sorely on these accounts. Broad, wholesome, charitable views of men and things cannot be acquired by vegetating in one little corner of the earth all one's lifetime.*

Remember the golden rule in every interaction! Do unto others as you would have them do unto you. Treat people the way you want to be treated! It would be incredible to see more people adopt this mentality. It should be at the core of all interactions to not judge if you don't want to be judged, to not hate if you don't want to be hated, and to be loving towards others because you want to be loved.

Further, when this rule is neglected, the hypocrisy usually comes back around, often to smack you in the face in a pointed way. You can call it the spiral of life or karma or whatever else you want, but your actions will find a way to come back around to you. Make sure you can take what you dish out.

For many years I kept the spiritual things that were happening to me completely private. The difference there was a safety issue and a desire to know more regarding what I was talking about before I tried to explain it to someone else. I couldn't verbalize what I couldn't understand, especially when it was regarding a subject people can be persecuted for. I knew someone who was institutionalized for a brief time due to expressing what he felt was a spiritual experience to friends and family. It terrified me, because it terrified him. That brings me to the next communication tip - *tact*. Sometimes blunt honesty is called for, but more often than not tact is necessary. Tact is defined as a keen sense of what to say or do to avoid giving offense, a skill in dealing with difficult or delicate situations.

Applying the tips I've provided here will improve your tactfulness. However, tact also requires you to listen to your conscience and the guidance of the Holy Spirit. Tap into your soul and listen to the Spirit to know what's right. Sometimes omission is a lie. For example, telling your wife you went to the bar but omitting that you cheated on her while there is a lie. Other times omission is not sharing the truth until you find the right time, way, and words to express yourself clearly and rationally. That is what I chose to do regarding my experiences, being aware that they touched on sensitive subject matter. Knowing the difference between the two is tactful.

Last but not least, do not forget basic manners! This is something that seems to be getting lost through the generations, but a simple *please, thank you, you're welcome,* and *sir/ma'am* is just plain polite and respectful. This is not just something we teach children! Etiquette can be fickle to grasp when the rules are all social and not necessarily written down and taught in school, but anyone can participate in these courteous basics. While you're at it, please say *bless you* when someone sneezes and hold doors open for people. Small kindnesses go a long way!

At the end of the day, a liar is a hypocrite, and that is my biggest pet peeve. God is clear about his distaste for hypocrisy in the Bible (*Matthew 23:27-28, 1 John 4:20, Luke 6:46 & 20:46-47, Mark 7:6, Titus 1:16, James 1:22-23 etc.*). *Romans 14:23* even declares that doing anything that you *believe* is not right is a sin.
To know or feel the truth in your heart and mind and then lie about it when you speak is the definition of hypocrisy. Saying one thing and doing another is also hypocrisy. That means your actions are also a huge part of being honest. Do you do research and seek out validation that your thoughts and feelings are true *before* you speak or act on them (*Ecclesiastes 5:2-6*)? Do you pray about it? If we all did that with the pure intention in our hearts to gain the knowledge of the truth for the benefit of ourselves and those we interact with, this would certainly help us avoid false prophets.

Nobody is perfect. I've never met a person who has never told a lie. We can all accept that we have made mistakes. Perfect love accepts that we are imperfect people who need to learn and grow. Now it's time to be more aware of the words that pass our lips and choose them wisely. Make sure they all line up with our actions and God's will. Realize the product of the ripple effect is rarely seen by the one who started it, but it is always felt. Know that one lie can spiral out into the lives of many in negative ways. The truth is just plain better in every way, even if it can be difficult sometimes.

In the space provided, tell God you are sorry for all of the times you have lied in the past, and ask for forgiveness. Do you need to come clean with anyone you have lied to before and make amends? ***Where do you feel you fall on the spectrum of lies and manipulation***

versus truth and sincerity? What do you plan to do going forward to hold yourself more accountable to speaking truth? Why do you think honesty is so crucial? Do you feel that in looking back you have ever been a hypocrite? How do you feel about white lies? Reflect, then go pray the most sincere and honest prayer you have ever prayed. Pour out your heart to God in pure truth.

10. Thou shalt not covet thy neighbour's house, thou shalt not covet they neighbour's wife, nor his manservant nor his maidservant, nor his ox, nor his ass, nor any thing that is thy neighbor's.

To *covet* is all about what you desire. This command is about self control over our passions, not being overtaken by carnal lust, and not giving in to greed or jealousy. It is not addressing the necessities of food or clothing. Living things are specifically listed, as well as your house which is a word that can also double for family and the environment of a family. Then it is rounded out by generalizing not to covet any property as well (*1 Timothy 6:8*).

I appreciate that God made a specific point to separate people from things. Why did He do that? This command ties together many previous points that have already been covered. One of those points is that to desire something in your heart more than God and what He provides you is a form of idolatry (*Colossians 3:5, Psalm 10:3*). Recall that idols can be in your heart. Also, this reiterates the point that we love a God of life, and he despises when we place our focus and desires into inanimate objects.

Yet another point to look back on is how Christ qualified the desire for someone else in your heart if you are married as adultery even if it is never voiced. Clearly desiring your neighbor's wife would follow suit. You are just addressing the other perspectives in the situation and telling them not to interfere in a marriage or home. This command also tackles a main motivator for stealing. If you don't desire what belongs to someone else, you won't steal it. Pretty simple, right?

What else can we garner from the New Testament? *Ephesians 5:3-5* tells us that greed is improper and no immoral, impure, or covetous person will receive inheritance in the kingdom. *1 Corinthians 10:6-7* makes clear that the life of Christ was an example for us so we would learn not to crave evil things. Even *Hebrews 13:5* insists we abandon love of money and be content with what we have, because God has promised to take care of us. Christ also says in *Matthew 19:24* that it will be easier for a camel to pass through the eye of a needle than for a rich man to enter heaven, because we are not meant to focus on materialism and hoard wealth for ourselves. We are all meant to get a share in what is necessary to survive, so often the source of craving wealth is a desire to have more than others rather than giving. While coveting isn't as clearly called out in the New Testament, it is certainly clear from every angle that we are to control our desires.

When we develop characteristics like willpower, fortitude, and patience, we can beat back evil desires without indulging them and overcome them. Yet nobody wants to live a life where they are constantly battling themselves. Remember that a house divided will not stand, and you are a temple for the Holy Spirit. So how do we flip ourselves from rampant desire to being content?

This is where an attitude of gratitude will save the day (*1 Thessalonians 5:18*)! How did I get there myself? I admit, I certainly used to aspire to be famous and wealthy. In grade school I was in piano lessons, band, choir, speech, and every play and musical I could participate in. My major in college was a double in music and acting. I loved performing!

However, even though I had talent in this field, there were other people much better and more effortless at it than me. There were also people more attractive than I was, so I was frequently typecast as mother roles. Programs like these are very competitive when ten people want one role or solo. I won't deny that I experienced jealousy. It would then always come as a shock to me when someone would express jealousy to me over my talent. I would be so focused on how I wasn't good enough that I would forget that didn't mean I had no skill at all.

I learned that I try too hard sometimes, and it can be heard and seen. Competition was making me want to be like the people I idolized. I wanted my voice to sound like theirs and my technique to be the same as theirs. One day it occurred to me that was killing my spirit. When I finally let go of trying to be like everyone else and just embraced how God made me, my talent started to shine in its own way. I stopped idolizing them and just accepted myself.

I have always found it humorous that the songs my voice has sounded best at since childhood were always spiritual. God seems to have put a caveat on my gifts that they will only shine in service to Him. My voice never quite fit being a rockstar or pop artist or Broadway performer, even though I enjoyed those genres. I'm no Lizzy Hale or Eva Cassidy or Lauryn Hill or Adele or Idina Menzel (*though I've won some contests with a not too shabby Amy Lee and Jennifer Hudson*). I'm me! It's better to work towards maybe adding a new name to the list among different but equally talented musicians rather than trying to be just like them.

Then I became pregnant and dropped out of college to support my new family. My dreams collapsed under the stress of what I like to refer to as *adulting* and *momming*. I struggled financially for my whole life. It just became so much more important to stay on top of it once I had a child. There were many instances where I daydreamed of what could have been and hoped maybe I could get back to it someday like I saw my friends successfully doing. I knew people recording albums and making movies and admit I again felt jealousy from a distance.

I also became jealous of those who could afford to give their child more in life. I was stuck living in apartments when my credit took a hit. It took years to repair, and I'm just now barely at a point where I could get a loan for a home under very specific criteria. I began idolizing the American dream.

When I started to dig deep into healing my pain in life and found my faith again, a slow process began where those desires became less and less. They were replaced with just appreciating what I had. I stopped wanting everything shiny and new and focused on functional and affordable.

I also had the chance to see what the rich life looks like as a housekeeper. I have certainly seen some exquisitely beautiful homes full of high-end design elements. However, the upkeep just isn't appealing to me. Things still break. There are just way more things that can, and it is exponentially more expensive. Light bulbs still burn out, but there are a thousand to replace instead of ten. Dogs still pee on the carpet, but when the stain doesn't come out, cleaning or replacing it is way more expensive. It takes an estate manager to keep up with all of it and consumes a large majority of your time and resources. That just isn't my style, though some people do thrive that way.

In time I realized I had slowly become a bit of a minimalist. I am someone who could live in a tent in the woods and be happy if I didn't have a child to raise. It evolved even further when I shifted that joy to gratitude and openly gave thanks for my blessings. When I became grateful for a few clean outfits, food on the table, a car that runs, and a job that met my obligations, everything else was abundance I could give back. My gratitude evolved again into charity. In my faith journey I went from being someone who wanted everything to being someone who wanted to give everything to others.

Eventually I found a balance where I do what I can with what I have where I'm at, and I leave the rest to God. I do what I must to provide for my family and give when I'm able. I stopped trying to be like everyone else and started trying to be my best self. By accepting myself where I was at, I freed myself for true and meaningful change going forward.

I don't stress nearly as much as I used to or desire a bunch of things I can't afford. I rarely feel jealousy rear her ugly head. I just live in appreciation for the chance to take another breath, to hug my daughter, to sing a song in the shower, or to go for a walk in one more springtime. Even oxygen is a gift from God. Pure and sincere gratitude in your daily walk and prayers will breed abundance both by its very nature and supernaturally.

There are three lies you have been taught in this life. I think the truth will help set you free in this regard. We all grew up hearing the grass is greener on the other side, you don't know what you've got until it's gone, and the squeaky wheel gets the grease. The truth is the grass is greenest where you water it, we can appreciate what we have, and a regularly greased wheel doesn't squeak. A daily attitude of gratitude greases the wheel and waters our own grass. Saying thank you for ordinary efforts waters the grass of your relationships. Telling people you love them more often or sharing a hug once in a while greases the wheel of your bonds. It's important to remember that what we want for ourselves, others want from us. To be giving is to help yourself *and* others.

There are plenty of challenges in the modern world when it comes to desire. Everything is an ad! I participate in a social media group for Christian women to find fellowship and support, and people will even go *there* seeking customers for direct sales. They'll ask you to add them as a friend in Christ then hit you up to sell you stuff all the time. Sales has become so predatory! Your dollars are being hunted down by those who want them, like their eyes are laser focused on your wallet.

It creates a skepticism that is oddly both healthy and unhealthy at the same time. We must be skeptical these days to avoid being scammed. Seriously, when you study marketing, they have gone *deep* into the understanding of psychology and are being very precise about how their ad dollars are invested to create maximum success. It's almost scary how these tactics are precisely devised to reach into our minds and hit buttons. They aim to make us feel like we made the decision ourselves that we just *must* have what they've got to offer. It can be a form of mental and emotional warfare! At the same time, feeling leery of people all the time due to these manipulations is not a healthy state of being.

    This is just another reason I enjoy being more of a purist and minimalist. For example, if I'm not wearing makeup so I can be my most authentic self, it is super easy to say no to anyone trying to sell it to me. My reasoning is easily justified and accepted, and it shuts down further attempts to sell to me later. Being strong in who I am creates an environment where I can return to seeking out things I need when I need them rather than being bombarded by things I don't want. It is super clear when someone is trying to claim my money rather than serve my best interests. The way they respond to your *no* calls them out.

    One of the most effective sales tactics today is to put your product in someone's hands and ask them to share about it publicly. It's the foundational concept behind direct sales. There are people who will receive mountains of free stuff so that they'll wear it or share it on social media. They are encouraged to make other people envy what they have enough to spend money on it. They *know* we trust the opinions of our peers more than we trust the business name. When someone wears their dress in a social media post and we all rave about how beautiful it is, there will be people who buy it. The more we rave, the more people will buy.

    This is the premise behind celebrity endorsement as well. We look up to celebrities. Once we hit a point where we admire them enough to value their opinion, we will be more likely to buy things they are associated with. Ask yourself why taking a child to the store can be a nightmare. If they see something in their favorite color, they want it, even if it is completely useless to them. If they see a notebook or cereal box with their favorite cartoon character on it, they want it, even if they don't like the cereal or need a notebook. The relationship between the entertainment industry and advertising industry is pretty close knit on purpose.

    Even when I did direct sales, I was never a fan of cold messaging. I would share my personal experience with products and the work publicly on my social media and let people come to me if they had interest. I would offer product samples and do giveaways and always accepted no while still being informed enough to answer any questions people had. At the end of the day, people would come to me simply because they respected that approach above other salespeople. I was knowledgeable, authentic, and transparent.

I worked in car sales for two and a half years as well. I wasn't the one who helped the people that walked in the door most days. Statistics say these are the people who will likely buy within forty-eight hours. My client base was more focused around online conversion. These are the people who are likely to buy within the next ninety days. Someone would make an inquiry online, and I would follow-up with them. Following policy meant I had to continue calling them until they told me not to, so I tried hard not to leave the same voicemail twice and provide them with new options or suggestions to meet their criteria. This required some solid note taking and digging, but if I had to keep calling, I wanted to make it count for my customer.

That's why people bought from me. They would tell me they appreciated my patience, concern for their needs, and quality assistance. I didn't sell in high numbers like the guy who sat by the door and was a rockstar at playing hard ball on pricing. However, the clients I brought in were willing to take their time searching for the right vehicle from my dealership even if we didn't have a fit at first, because they wanted to buy from me specifically. I could sleep soundly knowing that.

I understand that spending money into the economy is what employs people and pays bills. I understand that if you don't advertise, it is less likely people will know your product or service exists if they do want it. Yet these points don't obligate me to support things I don't wish to support, buy things I don't want or need, or dignify a pushy salesperson's behavior. The consumer needs to take back control of dictating the market instead of being guided and corralled by advertising. If we stand up for reclaiming the integrity in business, I think it will heal a great deal of the downfalls of modern capitalism and still leave everyone employed. Stop trying to manipulate me into coveting what you're offering. Don't encourage greed and jealousy. Start asking what we need and just make it accessible.

In the space below, tell God you are sorry for any time you have coveted things that belong to someone else and ask Him to forgive you. Looking back, do you feel that you've fallen into the trap of being sold to, or do you feel you are in control of your spending habits? Do you have a lot of clutter in your life, or do you keep things simple? Are you happy with your answer to that question, or is it something you need to change? ***Where do you feel you fall on the spectrum of feeling greed, jealousy, and envy versus living with gratitude, comfort, and contentment?*** Do you feel confident and fulfilled through your faith, or do you feel like you are lacking things that opens you up to be susceptible to manipulation? Do you accept who you are the way God made you? Reflect and pray.

___
___
___
___
___
___
___
___
___
___
___
___
___
___
___
___
___
___
___
___
___
___
___
___
___
___
___
___
___
___

11. Thou shalt love thy neighbor as thyself.

The ten commandments were hinged primarily around what we are not supposed to do. Don't steal, don't lie, don't cheat, don't worship idols, etc. They draw the lines that form the picture, while the two highest commands are the colors that fill them in. The two highest commandments are about what we *are* supposed to do, and that is to **love**!

Both of the highest commands are phrased to reflect balance. Love yourself and love your neighbor equally, and love God with heart, mind, and soul equally. We covered the ten because they are like looking at the opposite side of the coin when defining love. If you are sincerely following the ten, you are already well on your way to following the two highest. These two additions serve to deepen the experience and sum them up in wisdom.

Pretend you are searching for the perfect wedding dress. Sometimes it is hard to identify what you want in a world full of choices. A helpful way to start figuring it out is to identify what you don't want. Maybe you are sure that you don't want a mermaid cut or a puffy skirt. Knowing what you don't like cuts off the choices that are outliers and narrows down your field of selection. Once you've drawn your boundaries of *no*, then you can look closer at the remaining choices to figure out what says *yes* to you. Did you realize after trying it out that a long train is more work than it's worth? Does the beadwork catch your eye or are you attracted to something more simple once it's on your body?

Apply this to our search to understand love and divine nature. God told us what not to do, and that list of commands implied love. In the New Testament, Christ came and flipped our perspective so we would see God's motives for face value. He spoke about love and got to the heart of the matter. He didn't just show us the picture on the front of the coin. He told us what material the coin was made of and that it was molded and carved out to look like a quarter. The quarter *is* love, even if we only saw one side of it at first.

We are now at the point where we are examining it more completely, why that specific material was chosen to make the quarter, and identifying the process that was followed to make it. We are diving deeper into the why and how of the matter of love. The only way to truly follow these two highest commands is to understand them 100%, which includes the why and how.

When invited, the Holy Spirit works in us to learn all of this. Truthfully, *I shouldn't even need to write this book.* None of this is secret knowledge, and the Spirit works to convict in each of us individually. I was *led* to write this by the Spirit so I could help people expedite the process and be more thorough while also providing a modern context. We have been taught not to hear or trust the Spirit anymore. Most people don't follow the conviction when it happens or understand what they're reading in scripture. This is the path to putting on white garments and salve for your eyes to see clearly (*Revelation 3:18*), because God loves you.

Hopefully as you have been reading, it has been providing you an awareness to the fact that God is truly working and present in your life. The very specific design of this journey is intended to help you label the way the Spirit moves, so that you will easily know that the feeling of uncertainty you had about a decision was the Spirit urging you to be cautious. You'll realize that tug on your heart to change a behavior was the Spirit working to convict you about what God wants. Open the eyes of your heart! It's time to see love through the lens of God. Are you awake now?

1 Corinthians 13:1-3 is very clear. *Though I speak with the tongues of men and of angels, and have not charity, I am become as sounding brass, or a tinkling cymbal. And though I have the gift of prophecy, and understanding of all mysteries, and all knowledge; and though I have all faith, so that I could remove mountains, and have not charity, I am nothing. And though I bestow all my goods to feed the poor, and though I give my body to be burned, and have not charity, it profiteth me nothing.*

Again, I almost quoted a different translation, because they used the word *charity* in place of *love*. In this instance, the translator even causes the text to contradict itself when choosing that word because giving all you have to the poor *is* charity. However, I kept it this time around to briefly acknowledge the idea that at a bare minimum it is positive to identify charity as a wonderful act of love. It is simply not all of love itself. This verse is stating that no amount of knowledge or good works matters without love. To understand that *completely* in your heart and live by it is **grace**.

Grace is the gift Christ gave us, the lesson he taught us, and the authority we are under. It is the elegance and ease by which you act. When you think of someone who is graceful, you think of someone who moves calmly and smoothly, like a prima ballerina. It is almost as if they float, right? Pure grace is light and free. The grace Christ offers us is liberating.

The real question to resolve then is whether this was new and a change to the law, or if it is a clarification of God's true intentions this whole time. The easiest way to determine this is to ask if the two highest commandments as identified by Christ in *Matthew 22:36-40* and reiterated in *John 13:34* were ever stated in the Old Testament. Most people don't realize it, but the simple answer has been there all along. *Leviticus 19:18* states *Thou shalt not avenge, nor bear any grudge against the children of thy people, but* **thou shalt love thy neighbor as thyself**: *I am the Lord.* Then *Deuteronomy 6:4-5* says *Hear, O Israel: The Lord our God is one Lord, and thou shalt* **love the Lord thy God with all thine heart, and with all thy soul, and with all thy might**. Boom. There it is.

I'm not even going to say feel free to go check if you don't believe me. Even if you clearly do believe me, I want you to pick up your Bible right now, turn to the page, and read. Read it in the Old Testament and read it in the New Testament. This action holds two purposes. One, it is intended to help people *finally* accept that the Bible is all one book with the same message *for a reason*, and it is ridiculous to keep fighting over whether our focus should be on the first thirty-nine books or the last twenty-seven. It's the same story about the same one God and His son - the Messiah - Christ. The New Testament is a continuation of history that corrected the errors Christ saw happening in the time, and it expounded upon greater principles, just exactly as God designed. Stop fighting and hear the message, folks. See its development rather than its conflict.

The second reason to read it on the page is because Christ is the Word! The Spirit resides in those pages just as much as it resides in you, and when you read them there specifically, it's like the words jump off the page at you with deeper meaning. It's a way that the Spirit speaks without an audible voice. Anyone with ears to hear, let them hear, right? Well sometimes the words are whispered. We should say anyone with a *heart* to hear, let them hear. If you're wondering where God is in your life, ask yourself how often you open the book that contains His message. Everything we needed to know is in there. You could spend a lifetime deeply studying it and still have more to learn. It's a *vast* well. Tap into it! Please, don't just take my word for it. Take God's Word for it!

In my personal opinion, the first five commandments are

details about how to love God with all our heart, mind, and soul. The second set of five commandments are details about how to love our neighbor as ourselves. The one about honoring your parents applies to both, but that is why it is the last of the five about loving God. It is there as a transition piece. Parents are a hinge of crucial importance, because what they teach to their children carries through the entire next generation. All the commands built upon each other in a fluid way. Studying them reflected a growth pattern that worked from the major principle at the bottom and worked through a progression. That's why a tower with twelve floors felt like the perfect way to battle through it. That's just how God designed it!

Population size must have something to do with the flow of the Bible as well. The whole world population during the life of Christ is estimated to have been around 300 million people. As a basis of comparison, the United States population alone was 325.7 million people in 2017. For a population to have survived in that time without modern advances like cars, plumbing, airplanes, and buildings designed to withstand major natural disasters, it would have been difficult. Add on top of that how each person would have to do much more of the labor which today can be divided between many, many people and machines.

It really makes you think. It only makes sense that there had to be strict protocols during that time. Never forget how blessed you are to have been born into this era. As our population grew and our intelligence advanced, love became more crucial to our existence so we wouldn't destroy each other. It prevents us from being our own worst enemy when we already have enough problems to deal with. It is now our greatest survival tool (*Psalm 118:22*)!

Now let's get focused on the point about loving our neighbor as ourselves. This breaks down into two subjects - the way we love ourselves and the way we love others. They are intended to reflect each other. This is pretty much exactly the golden rule in different words, which Christ stated in *Matthew 7:12*. Treat others how you would like to be treated! I find it interesting that seven is a number in the Bible representative of spiritual perfection, and twelve is one that represents governmental perfection. Finding the golden rule in *7:12* is pretty on point when you consider how this one verse is the pinnacle of divine law regarding how we treat others.

We have already covered in the previous sections how Christ taught this. In my attempt to help you transition from fear of God's commands to understanding their value, I shared why they matter to you/others and identified the behaviors that lead us to follow/break them. Embracing that process fully is love! When you can do your best to resolve all issues in a way that honors yourself, the other people involved, and God *all at the same time*, then you can enact love as a verb in your life.

To love is an action! It is not just a word. It's true that we are saved by grace and not works, but when Christ commands us to love, he isn't telling us to only do it in words. If making this level of effort matters to you, that is part of what love feels like. When you want others to be just as happy as you want yourself to be happy then do your best to make it happen, you honor this command. Breaking this command would then make being inconsiderate and selfish unholy.

On the flip side, it would appear that it would be just as unholy to always do for others and never take care of your own needs. That is a surprisingly big problem in the modern world. We have so many empathic people emerging who feel things so deeply. The sensitive people are often the first to be taken advantage of since feeling your pain inside themselves urges them to give freely without much thought for their own needs. Therefore, the divine nature of love can only exist when your internal world and external world constantly work to balance each other in healthy ways. That's why it takes time to learn and develop it.

Learning balance starts in conflict, but as God pours into you, peace and grace will abound. Love ascends to its most purely divine form and becomes *effortless* when you apply God to the formula. He *is* both your internal and external environment. The Holy Spirit is designed to tie that together, so that you can see His presence everywhere, including inside yourself. I feel this is yet another reason He said *I am that I am*. The three letters that form the words *I am* encompass everything! There is not a more concise way in existence to explain God than that. Don't strain your brain too much, but I believe He both has a form and is everywhere at the same time.

Where there is life, there is God. A point I have heard made before is that science tells us we need water, air, food, and light to survive on the most basic level. Christ gives us seven *I am* statements in the book of John. *I am the bread of life (6:48). I am the light of the world (8:12). I am the door (10:9). I am the good shepherd (10:11). I am the resurrection and the life (11:25). I am the way, the truth, and the life (14:6). I am the true vine and my Father is the husbandman (15:1)*. Also recall where we have talked about God giving us the breath of life and being the living waters and how Christ is the rock (*Colossians 3:11, 1 Corinthians 15:28*). God is life and all things that sustain it.

As you might expect, the sermon on the mount summed things up nicely in what is commonly referred to as the *beatitudes* (*Matthew 5:1-12*). In fact, these statements were his opening remarks.

And seeing the multitudes, he went up into a mountain, and when he was set, his disciples came unto him, and he opened his mouth and taught them saying:
Blessed are the poor in spirit, for theirs is the kingdom of heaven.
Blessed are they that mourn, for they shall be comforted.
Blessed are the meek, for they shall inherit the earth.
Blessed are they which do hunger and thirst after righteousness, for they shall be filled.
Blessed are the merciful, for they shall obtain mercy.
Blessed are the pure in heart, for they shall see God.
Blessed are the peacemakers, for they shall be called the children of God.
Blessed are they which are persecuted for righteousness' sake, for theirs is the kingdom of heaven.
Blessed are ye when men shall revile you and persecute you and shall say all manner of evil against you falsely, for my sake.
Rejoice, and be exceedingly glad, for great is your reward in heaven, for so persecuted they the prophets which were before you.

On the next page, tell God you are sorry for the times where you have not acted out of love, and ask for forgiveness. Take a moment to review what you wrote in the previous sections, and identify in this section if you feel these truths have sunk in. Have you felt the shift in your life, even if it has not fully matured yet? Is there something that has been harder to work through than the others? Write down what characteristics are central to the expression of divine love in your life and define them. Are you able to explain the concepts we dove into in a clear and concise way? **Where do you feel you fall on the spectrum of love as a whole? Is that where you want to be?** If it is, congratulations! Well done! If it's not, write a brief plan on how you plan to reach your goal. Reflect on everything we have covered so far, and pray for God to fill you with his love and peace as you continue your journey with Him.

12. Thou shalt love the Lord thy God with all thy heart, and with all thy soul, and with all thy mind.

Here we are, at the top of the tower! You are so brave! If you have been taking this journey seriously and working through the emotions that surface from it, then God has surely been filling you like a glass of the waters of life. We no longer have to debate whether the glass is half empty or half full. It has been filled to the brim and is about ready to overflow! It will too, because He will keep pouring so that you will share the gospel! Remember when you first entered the ground floor and I said to fulfill that command God needed 51% controlling shares of your heart? Well to fulfill this command, He needs 100% controlling shares in your heart, soul, and mind.

This in no way means that you can never make decisions for yourself or have fun or anything absurd like that. You are still you, living the life that God gave you. It means that you are fully committed to walking as God instructs come hell or high water. You will allow Him to lead and teach you. You will pray and love and be gracious and wise. What offends Him offends you. What He loves, you love. You have done the work to unify your desires with His and are prepared to execute His will. Go back and read *Colossians 3:11-17* again. Everything up to now is summed up so perfectly right there. Hopefully it will take on a new meaning for you.

Ask yourself this - if God weren't real, would that change the value in the behavioral message here? Of course not! That is a true sign of discerning if something is of a divine nature. It is true no matter what. I have heard some Christians say to atheists that if I am wrong about God, then I wasted my life, but if you are wrong about God you wasted your eternity. The thing is, even if I'm wrong about God, I certainly didn't waste my life by being a good person with morals and believing in something greater than myself. My faith in God means I win no matter what with my life. That sounds pretty divine.

It makes complete sense that God would hang His message on such a timeless understanding of the human condition! *Matthew 22:40* says of loving God and loving our neighbor as ourselves, *On these two commandments hang **all** the law and the prophets.* Only a being who has observed and overseen an eternity of life could execute the teaching us this kind of wisdom. How amazing is it to consider that God created everything, knows everything, has endured everything, and loves so perfectly?

If we are getting closer to an understanding of perfect love, it's time to evaluate the word *perfect*. According to the dictionary it means *absolute, complete, having all the required or desirable characteristics/elements/qualities, as good as it is possible to be.* In short, perfection in the divine sense is graceful precision. Doesn't that remind you of somebody - perhaps Christ?

As you can see in my testimony, I have broken many of the commands at some point in my past, some more than others. Most often I didn't even realize it. By the Old Testament standard, I would die and burn in hell for it. Before Christ, nobody could meet the standard. There is at a bare minimum a certain age and intellectual level we must reach before everything we have discussed here sinks in. Mistakes and bad choices happen.

Christ truly changed everything with his sacrifice! He gave us a chance at change, and who he has set free from the bondage of sin should always cherish that freedom (*John 8:36*)! He lived one perfect life, which he had to do in order to make this a possibility. It was a procedural necessity. In doing so he also demonstrated what perfect looked like. He set the bar high and gave us goals we will spend our whole lives striving to come as close to as possible, knowing and accepting that we can never be as perfect as he is and can only aim to grow.

Providing a clearer explanation of that transitional space between being a sinner and fully following Christ is my purpose. That gap is what I have written this book to address. I am not here to model perfection. I am here to model *redemption*. I bit the bullet and aired my flaws for the sake of explaining the change process in detail. In turn, while Christ is lifting and pulling you up from above, I'm trying to get underneath the core of the problems and push you up so our bottom line standards as a society can be raised. As the Amish say, very few burdens are heavy when everyone lifts.

Together, I hope that my efforts to explain Christ's message of the gospel in a modern context while providing process you can follow aids him in his mission. Hopefully I have helped give voice to the Holy Spirit so that you can hear it for yourself. I pray this all leads you to the Father. I want to help as many souls come to a pure experience of salvation as possible.

I made many mistakes in my life. Through a science focused mind I justified those actions, but they were wrong. I now see how things I thought were ok were causing me pain. So often now I realize how things that hurt me hurt God and vice versa. Christ is a best friend. He held my hand while we walked through the grueling process of erasing my sins. Then he pulled me into that beautiful peace, love, and joy.

Don't get me wrong. You will still be tested in your faith. You will face attacks both in the physical and spiritual sense. That armor of God should be carried with you every day forever. God will keep you safe if you cling to your faith, but that doesn't mean He will prevent you from experiencing troubles for the rest of your life. That will be in heaven. Keeping you safe and keeping you absent are two different things, and you would have to be absent from earth to avoid any confrontation. Total trust is essential to following this command.

You may lose friends when you profess your love for God. Within one month of starting to talk about the Bible on social media, forty friends dropped me without a goodbye. The good news is that God removed people from my life that didn't want to be there and gradually started replacing them with people who did. He started helping me connect with others who shared in faith, and that made the journey exponentially easier. It is so powerful to have solid support in fellowship, especially when people start to criticize your beliefs. Birds of a feather flock together, and God gives us wings as eagles. We are all a family being one in Christ.

We are meant to joyfully love God. In turn, what we send up to Him trickles back down to us. The exchange is similar to how a battery works. The battery and the device both don't do anything or use energy until the batteries are installed and the circuit is completed. Think of the Holy Spirit indwelling inside you like the batteries that power your connection with God. Once you have been filled with it to the brim, blessing can flow freely in that circular motion. The power on your stereo has been turned on. Send up love, and He sends it right back. The caveat is that it won't work until you go through the motions as we just did. Nobody gets to skip steps. I believe God will still be working in your life before this process is enacted, it's just not a functional relationship at that point.

This exchange happens on a thought, word, and deed level. That means many passages in the Bible will come to fruition in your heart first, then your mind will analyze the feelings. Then you will speak about it for clarity. Then you will act on it. This impacts the environment which is part of a planet in a galaxy in the universe. Everything interacts, and the single mustard seed of faith that is planted in you through salvation gifted by Christ can ripple out to effect everything. This also means that every parable in the Bible can have layers of meaning in the internal, physical, and spiritual levels. It all actually happened in real life events, but it happened how it did for a reason to teach spiritual lessons (*Mark 8:31-33*).

A relationship with God holds a responsibility, but it is something He makes worth your while. The joy alone is priceless. He is not a genie, but once you get to this place with Him, you'll certainly feel wealthy. *That Christ may dwell in your hearts by faith; that ye, being rooted and grounded in love, may be able to comprehend with all saints what is the breadth, and length, and depth, and height; and to know the love of Christ, which passeth knowledge, that ye might be filled with all the fullness of God* (*Ephesians 3:17-19*).

Gravity is what pulls us to the earth. It holds us down. To me, it is symbolic of our desire to be here made manifest. When we love God wholly and focus our lives on love taught by Christ and refined through the Holy Spirit, it pulls us slowly away from concern about materialism and our physical plane of reality. In essence, when Christ returns for us, we will be so elated that we will abandon the physical entirely, and in metaphorically overcoming gravity, we will fly. The Bible says he will call us into the air with him. I feel that the strength of our faith and love for God will be what lifts our feet off the ground. To become a butterfly, we have to give up being a caterpillar, right? All we need is to hold onto our patience until he returns to collect.

Whether you are righteous or not is defined by your behaviors. Behaviors are actions, and actions are works. Faith without works is *dead*, so you don't have *true* faith in Christ unless your actions that build your behaviors begin to reflect his righteousness one step at a time. To accept him in your heart - to love him - is to follow his commands (*John 14:21*), because his laws reflect what is loving and righteous behavior (*Romans 13:10*). Whoever loves him and follows his commands *will be loved by his Father*. So again, doing these things is part of loving God completely. Strive to be righteous a little more each day. Allow yourself to be absorbed into divine nature. It will save your life on so very many levels. Your faith is what saves, but your sincerity in living by it is what heals.

In summation, I would like to return to the idea of prayer, something at the foundation of our relationship with God. When Christ was asked how we should pray, we were given what has become known as the *Lord's Prayer* (*Matthew 6:9-14*). It is so perfectly composed and is a wonderful prayer to recite. I am going to share it here worded as I learned it growing up, though you'll find slight variations in different translations. As you read this, I want you to reflect on each line. After all the territory we have covered in our mission to reclaim your tower of self for God, do you now understand the deeper meaning behind why these exact words were chosen? Give it due meaning.

> *Our Father, who art in heaven,*
> *Hallowed be thy name.*
> *Thy kingdom come.*
> *Thy will be done*
> *on earth as it is in heaven.*
> *Give us this day our daily bread,*
> *and forgive us our trespasses*
> *as we forgive those who trespass against us.*
> *Lead us not into temptation,*
> *but deliver us from evil.*
> *For thine is the kingdom, and the power, and the glory*
> *forever and ever. Amen!*

In the space below, tell God you are sorry for the times where your love did not include Him and ask for His forgiveness. Thank Him for everything He has done, is doing, and will do for all of us. Affirm that you understand what divine love looks like, and share ways in which you have seen Him express it. ***Do you feel like you love God with your whole self? Do you feel you will continue to in the future?*** Identify ways that we nurture relationships over time to keep them healthy, vibrant, and full of love. How can those things be applied to your relationship with God? Have you fully accepted the authority of Christ? Reflect and pray for God to send the Holy Spirit and fill your cup to overflowing. Ask the Spirit to help keep you in check so you don't lose your way from this place going forward.

Therefore, leaving the principles of the doctrine of Christ,
Let us go on unto perfection;
Not laying again the foundation of repentance from dead works,
And of faith toward God,
Of the doctrine of baptisms, and of laying on of hands,
And of resurrection of the dead, and of eternal judgment.
And this we well do, if God permit.
For it is impossible for those who were once enlightened,
And have tasted the heavenly gift,
And were made partakers of the Holy Ghost,
And have tasted the good word of God,
And the powers of the world to come,
If they shall fall away, to renew them again unto repentance;
Seeing they crucify to themselves the Son of God afresh,
and put him to an open shame.
For the earth which drinketh in the rain that cometh oft upon it,
And bringeth forth herbs meet for them by whom it is dressed,
Receiveth blessing from God:
But that which beareth thorns and briers is rejected,
And is nigh unto cursing; whose end is to be burned.
But, beloved, we are persuaded better things of you,
And things that accompany salvation, though we thus speak.
For God is not unrighteous to forget your work and labour of love,
Which ye have shewed toward his name,
In that ye have ministered to the saints, and do minister.

And we desire that every one of you do shew the same diligence
To the full assurance of hope unto the end.
That ye not be slothful, but followers of them who
Through faith and patience inherit the promises.
For when God made promises to Abraham,
Because he could swear by no greater, he swore by himself,
Saying, Surely blessing I will bless thee,
And multiplying I will multiply thee.
And so, after he had patiently endured, he obtained the promise.
For men verily swear by the greater: and an oath for confirmation
Is to them an end to all strife.
Wherein God, willing more abundantly to shew
unto the heirs of promise
The immutability of his counsel, confirmed it by an oath:
That by two immutable things, in which it was
impossible for God to lie,
We might have a strong consolation, who have fled for refuge
To lay hold upon the hope set before us.
Which hope we have as an anchor of the soul,
Both sure and steadfast, and which entereth into that within the veil.
Whither the forerunner is for us entered,
Even Jesus, made a high priest forever
after the order of Melchisadec.

Hebrews 6

7. *Meeting with the Goddess* & 8. *Woman as Temptress*

And be not conformed to this world,
but be ye transformed by the renewing of your mind,
That ye may prove what is that good, and acceptable,
and perfect will of God.
Romans 12:2

Congratulations! You have conquered and reclaimed your tower of self! You have been removing what is dark and replaced it with the light and love of God, being filled with a better understanding of divine nature that will guide you forward in every step. Thanks to your dedication and works of faith, you understand intimately that love is the fulfillment of the law (*Romans 13:8-10*). With time, following God's instructions will simply be your instinctual behavior, not rules you're following. The rules will still be there, but they won't need to reign you in.

This process is *how* He writes them on your heart and turns it to one of flesh. I had a revelation one day that I would like to share. While I am confident that all of the events of Moses actually physically happened, I also believe it was meant to parallel a spiritual experience we undergo with God. He wrote the commandments with His own hand on the two stone tablets. They are now said to be stored somewhere in the ark of the covenant with Aaron's rod and a pot of manna. They were placed in a box covered in gold and guarded by two cherubim (*Exodus 25:10-22*). Some claim to know their true location, others believe they are lost. Ron Wyatt claimed to have found them. We are told in *Revelation 11:19* we will see them in God's temple in heaven in the end times.

No matter where they are physically, the truth is once God writes His commands on our hearts of stone, we learn to stand strong in our faith. When we are filled with the Holy Spirit, we become a type and shadow of the ark of the covenant. The rod is like our backbone, and the Holy Spirit is the manna. All of the contents of the ark are placed inside you on a spiritual level. Furthermore, you have two lungs constantly breathing that breath of life and a dual sided rib cage. Just like the cherubim guard the ark, God built your anatomy protecting your heart. It is the organ that pumps blood through your body, and the Bible says blood is life (*Leviticus 17:10-14, Deuteronomy 12:23, etc.*). **You** are now metaphorically the ark too, carrying such precious cargo inside you.

If you have gotten this far, you have chosen of your own free will to hang in there and show God through your words and actions that you truly appreciate the gift of salvation Christ gave on the cross. You have not just asked God to clean the slate of your sins, but instead stepped up to personal accountability. You know you made these mistakes, and you are working to fix them with God's help. You have chosen to improve your mental, emotional, and spiritual health and develop it in a way God finds pleasing. You embrace the grace the Holy Spirit has infused in you as you went from level to level. Your armor is of respectable quality.

In the time under the law of sin and death, it was only your works that could save you. We were all born into sin, so it set a near impossible standard. Grace was a change to faith first. If your heart isn't in your faith, it isn't real. That is how God created us. If you don't value the motives behind the laws and thusly God as their author, then they are nothing more than words. This process gives the words meaning.

What could possibly be left to cover? Well, here's a key point to learn. Demons run when a good man of God goes to spiritual warfare. Every choice going forward from here is like a game of chess against the devil, because once you are strong in faith *and* morals and are walking in God's love, that makes you a threat to him! You simply living your life by God's standards will make you stand out. You are in the world, but not of it (*John 17:14-16*).

The world is still broken and following sin, but you are not. People around you will definitely be impacted by your presence. They will see your love and your strength of character. They will see you be calm in a crisis, giving of yourself more for others, and even if you never preach about your faith, your life will minister. It will catch peoples' attention so they stop being hypnotized by the wiles of the devil and look at you to see the Holy Spirit at work. They will want what you have, that glow of peace and joy, causing the sin of coveting taught by the devil to be turned back against him! If the devil is the poison, then your presence is a dose of the remedy. If Satan wants to take as many people to hell as he can, then he certainly won't want you around.

Luckily you built up your armor in your trials, so you should be fine, safe in Christ from the enemy. However, as I said before, that doesn't mean they won't attack. These two sections about the goddess and the temptress are being tackled together for one important purpose - the lesson of discernment. We are going to work on honing your skill in quickly and accurately identifying good versus evil. Christ returns wielding a double edged sword, just as we have a sword in the armor of God. Walking with him in Spirit helps him wield it. We are going to sharpen the blade so fine you could split a hair with it blindfolded because your discernment is that excellent. This is the beginning of the rockstar level hero training that establishes our ability to be quality leaders who share the gospel openly.

In the book of *Revelation* there are two major females at odds with each other. The woman with the crown of twelve stars on her head in chapter twelve has been most often paralleled to symbolizing the true church or the 144,000 first fruits based on verses like *Jeremiah 6:2* and *Ephesians 5:25-27*. Here is another way twelve represents governmental perfection. She is viewed in a positive light, a mother who births what is to come. It's hard to say whether she is one person or a group of people or both, but you can now consider the concept for yourself. Some believe her to be wisdom who Solomon was so enamored with. Others say that when Christ returns, she is the bride. Whoever she is, the dragon that archangel Michael casts out of heaven becomes angry with her and her children that follow the commandments of God and have the testimony of Christ. He tries to destroy her, but she is protected.

Later, *Revelation 17* describes the whore of Babylon, a harlot, a Jezebel, who is overcome. I love how yet again seventeen represents victory here when she is cast down. She is described in a vile and haughty way, a representation of the false church. This is the feminine parallel of the dispute between Christ and Satan. While we are not going to explore any kind of encounters with a female spiritual being, we will look at the way we discern between good and evil, whether it be expressed through a male or female.

In the parable about unleavened bread (*Matthew 13:33, Luke 13:20-21, 1 Corinthians 5:6-8*), we read about a woman who adds yeast into the dough. The living organisms in it will grow overnight, affecting all of the dough by morning. This parable is about how the false church likes to take the Word and weave and blend in things that aren't true. Christ is the bread of life (*John 6:25-59*), so his message is the unleavened truth. The leaven spoils it. That is the message at the foundation of the feast of unleavened bread during Passover.

As a woman writing this book, I want you to remember that not every single woman that exists reflects the woman who adds leaven. In fact, by using Strong's Concordance to clarify concepts and asking you to identify where you stand against scripture, I have been hoping to help remove the leaven from the modern church as much as I can being one person. Obviously if I were making real bread in a physical sense, that would be impossible. You would just have to make a new batch of dough. However, it's interesting to consider that Christ says we must be born again (*John 3*). We metaphorically junk the old dough and make it right without the leaven.

You can study all you want about red flags that indicate falsehood or behaviors of those who are truthful, but the best way to truly learn discernment is to be put in a position where you are forced to discern and test the spirit (*1John 4:1-2*). That is exactly what happened to me. I was unaware I was being deceived until I had the experience where I saw the light being in the white room during my first fast. I believe when Christ searched my heart, he saw my pure intention and deep desire to help people. In a world this thick with confusion and deception, it is understandable that people will be deceived about things that rely on faith.

When this being appeared, it forced me to discern by seeking Christ in study of the scripture and history. Since he can see into our hearts, he knew my desire was to be good. If I had to discern between him and the devil who tries to imitate, I would seek him and learn his character. He knew what I would do! Plus, I truly did believe in God at the time and shared it openly. I was just confused and uncertain about Christ. That is no longer the case.

Inevitably, once you start seeking God, these experiences will seek you. I would like to help you be prepared with some key basics for such an occasion. This is going to give you another upgrade to your armor! Before tackling a list of things to watch for, I feel obligated to separate the definition of faith versus trust. They are words we have a tendency to confuse in the modern day due to their overlap.

Faith exists based on *hope*. It is a belief formed *without* indisputable evidence. **Trust**, however, is built through *experience*. It is earned by actions that reinforce the *belief*. I have faith in the potential of humanity, that each individual is capable of love, compassion, and growth. That doesn't mean I trust everyone I meet. I do trust God, because He fulfills all of His promises.

Often through demonstrating my faith in a person's potential, they will rise to meet it like an expectation, and they will earn my trust. Truthfully, though, it is more often my faith in their potential that causes me to earn *their* trust. It is powerful to believe in the good in people, and even more powerful to show them that belief exists. At the end of the day the saying is true that what you think, you become (*Proverbs 23:7*). When we teach people they can be good and help them believe they are, they will typically become it. Just be careful not to confuse that faith with trust. That is intended to be earned. A healthy small dose of skepticism when initially confronted with a situation can save a lot of trouble down the road.

It is also worth pointing out that discernment is a key element of **wisdom**. There are said to be seven pillars of wisdom (*Proverbs 9:1*). A pillar is essentially a concept you must develop, and they proceed in sequential steps towards developing wisdom. The first is *knowledge* - the facts/information you acquire. In this context the scripture we have consulted is the main source of knowledge. The second pillar is *understanding* - when someone helps you piece together that information so it makes sense. Hopefully I have done a decent job of that so far. The third is *discretion* - the ability to discern. That is where we are at now.

The fourth is *equity* - the ability to utilize the previous three steps with anyone you meet. It is defined as being fair and impartial. On the surface it is about fair treatment to everyone built on what you have learned. It also implies an ability to be adaptable in delivering your message so it can reach many and put large concepts into simplest terms. That is why we will proceed from here to the discussion of sharing the gospel and leadership. The fifth is *justice* - this basically boils down to living righteously. A wise person knows it is better to execute justice by being a good person rather than acting unrighteously causing a need to be corrected or reprimanded. Yet they will also accept that if they do wrong, there are consequences.

The sixth pillar is *judgment* - to be able to encounter a

situation and judge it correctly and soundly, then do what is necessary. While true and final judgment belongs to God, that does not mean we never have to exercise sound judgment ourselves. We are just not meant to place our judgments onto others. Instead we are supposed to address situations as they arise and proceed as necessary based on the internal conclusions formed. There was a time in the Old Testament where there were no kings or rulers, only appointed judges and counselors who would resolve disputes (*Book of Judges, Isaiah 1:26*). They were regarded as a high authority in all situations. If you ever intend to enact the use of judgment in any way, you better be totally sure you have fully developed the previous five pillars through Christ first. Without them you are nowhere near qualified.

There's a reason it is the last pillar before the seventh, which is *wisdom* itself. I feel wisdom boils down to being authentic on every level and knowing how to apply emotions to your logic. *James 3:17* then becomes a perfect summation in one sentence. *But the wisdom that is from above is first **pure**, then **peaceable**, **gentle**, and **easy to be intreated**, full of **mercy and good fruits**, without **partiality**, and **without hypocrisy**.* Do you see where each of those pillars is laid out in each part of that statement?

In this verse, the word translated to *from above* is *G509 - anothen*. This word is the same one that is translated to *again* in *John 3:3* and *3:7* where we are told that we must be born again. It's root meaning is *from above*. This implies to me that being born again is a spiritual rebirth from above, and it is intended to give us this kind of wisdom that comes from there.

Wisdom is often depicted as a woman, just like the church. This is especially true in *Proverbs*. These two things tie together in the parable of the wise and foolish virgins. In *Matthew 25:1-13* the kingdom of heaven is compared to ten virgins who took their lamps and went to meet the bridegroom. Christ is called the bridegroom returning for his bride in *Revelation 19:7*. The foolish did not bring oil with them for their lamps, but the wise virgins did (*Exodus 27:20*). While they slept, the bridegroom worked.

At midnight, he cried out for them to come meet him. The foolish virgins ran out of oil and asked the wise to share theirs so they could come along. The wise virgins said no and told them to go buy some. While they were gone, the wise virgins went to meet the bridegroom and the doors were shut. When the foolish virgins returned, they tried to get in to the wedding, but the bridegroom denied them saying he knew them not. The parable ends with a warning that we do not know the day or hour Christ will return. Wisdom knows to be prepared.

Let's tackle the third pillar - how to discern words and actions. How can you prepare for the return of Christ if you cannot discern what is true or false about his message? *And this I pray, that your love may abound yet more and more in knowledge and all judgment; that ye may approve things that are excellent; that ye may be sincere and without offence till the day of Christ. (Philippians 1:9-10)*. The very first rule is that it is only by the Holy Spirit that one can declare that Christ is Lord (*1 Corinthians 12:1-3, 1 John 4:1-3*). Any spirit that speaks against Christ is scripturally deemed false. It is important to clarify that this is only true in the supernatural sense. In the physical world, any person can say they are a Christian and still be false in their other words and deeds.

This makes rule number two that all divine messages can be verified in scripture. The Bible is your strongest tool! God will never instruct you to go against His own Word. It's true that some of the mysteries are just described as mysteries in the Bible, and you might get the privilege of deeper understanding as you build your relationship with Him. However, understanding them still won't directly contradict scripture.

Rule number three from scripture is in *Matthew 7:15-20*, straight out of the sermon on the mount. People are often metaphorically referred to as trees in scripture, and this passage talks about the fruit we bear. A good tree produces good fruit, an evil tree produces evil fruit. What your words and actions produce is a clear indicator of who you follow. What is in your heart is what comes out of it. If God is in your heart, His nature flows from you. That is why Christ said our love for one another will prove to the world we are his disciples (*John 13:35*). If we truly follow him we will begin to shine his love. If we don't, it won't.

Another common sign I have noticed isn't specifically called out in scripture, though I don't find it to contradict scripture. It's more of an observation about modern behaviors. Watch out for those who repeatedly develop doctrines based on one verse or partial verses. This is a red flag that should caution you to turn on your discernment meter, not necessarily a guarantee of falsehood. I have seen some people who have a true deep understanding of what they are sharing and can preach an entire sermon on one verse with accuracy. They are often people with a strong understanding and presence of the Holy Spirit. However, in the thousands of sermons I have listened to online and in person, I would say about 80% of people I have seen do this one thing get caught up more in their own interpretation rather than the true context of the Word.

We touched on this somewhat in the very beginning, but here's another example. It is incredibly easy to lose the meaning of a bit of scripture when it is pulled out of its own context and applied to someone else's. For example, *Romans 10:9-10* is commonly abused. *That if thou shalt confess with thy mouth the Lord Jesus, and shalt believe in thine heart that God hath raised him from the dead, thou shalt be saved. For with the heart man believeth unto righteousness, and with the mouth confession is made unto salvation.*

People like to use the first sentence to say that as long as you step up in church one day and say you love Christ, you are saved and there is nothing left for you to do. It neglects the second sentence that supports how our belief allows the Spirit to convict us and pull us towards better behavior. It points to the power of the heart and the reason why we must accept him beyond simple words. Public confession is what you do at your baptism, so this also supports the need for that event to take place. Further still, they neglect how this sentence reflects perpetual confession of Christ, not just in one moment, but not denying him ever.

There is a lot of context lost when you only use one sentence. I don't think these people intend to be false, but their lack of effort to dig into fuller context makes them unprepared to be leading. It's important if you want people to see the Bible for its truth that you don't teach it as contradicting itself. If confession was all that was necessary, then Christ would not have said anything he did in the sermon on the mount. That again doesn't mean you must be 100% perfect to enter heaven, but you do need to try your best, and repent and learn from your mistakes.

Another key to discernment is that if it sounds too good to be true, then it *may* very well be untrue. As I have said, God is not a genie. He is not going to grant whatever wish you pray for just because you prayed for it. There are tons of people out there teaching a law of attraction application to God, claiming if you just declare something by the four winds or pray and focus on something a certain way, it will come to you. The law of attraction in and of itself is essentially a fancy form of idolatry. You are told to focus on this certain thing until it basically manifests. For example, if you want a new car, you are supposed to visualize like you already have it, even pretend that you are driving it. You're just focusing on a thing that you want instead of praying to God for what you need and trusting Him to provide. He is not just going to hand you a winning lottery ticket.

I have prayed for a new car. The difference is, we only had one and our family depended on it. Without it, nobody would be able to work. I wasn't asking for a fancy sports car or an extra one. After my car accident, even though it had been repaired, it started breaking down every three weeks for one reason or another. I tapped all my resources fixing it including taking out a lease for $2500 in repairs, and I was out of options. It broke down again after that, so I prayed for God to help me get the financing to trade for a more reliable vehicle. I didn't end up getting the exact kind of vehicle I hoped for, but I did get a brand new car that met our needs and improved my fuel economy. It had three years of warranty and less than fifty miles on the odometer. *Hallelujah! Amen!*

When I went to sign paperwork, I was told they hadn't rolled my tax, title, and license into the loan. I panicked at having to come up with $800 out of pocket when I was putting every penny into the down payment and living paycheck to paycheck. Instead of backing out, I trusted that God had blessed me with this opportunity to fulfill a need and signed on the lines. On the drive home I was starting to panic again, worrying over what I had just gotten myself into. Then I saw a rainbow shoot up out of the ground and a calm washed over me. I felt God saying trust me, I am taking care of you right now. Surely enough, my boyfriend was given a new and better job opportunity, and we came up with exactly the amount of money needed the day before it was due, which was 7-7-17.

When people start pushing God's abundance like a trip to the toy store, it sets off a discernment meter for me that they are focused more on the desires of man than on the will of God. Again, I don't think these people are trying to be false. I don't see bad intention behind a lot of the misconceptions being spread in the modern world. We just get so caught up in the fantasy, that we forget that God is smarter than us and doesn't simply cater to our every whim. He knows what we really need better than we do. In some cases we will see people who experience supernatural healing, and that is certainly a wonderful blessing! It's all up to God, though. We can't make Him do what we want.

There is a passage I see floating around on social media often by *Claudia Minden Weisz* that seems appropriate. While I think there are always going to be exceptions based on His will, this gives a better idea of what prayers are intended to be for. *I asked God to take away my pride, and God said No. He said it was not for Him to take away, but for me to give it up. I asked God to make my handicapped child whole, and God said No. He said her spirit was whole, her body was only temporary. I asked God to grant me patience, and God said No. He said patience is a by-product of tribulations. It isn't granted, it's earned. I asked God to give me happiness, and God said No. He said He gives me blessings, happiness is up to me. I asked God to spare me pain, and God said No. He said suffering draws me apart from worldly cares and brings me closer to Him. I asked God to make my spirit grow, and God said No. He said I must grow on my own, but He will prune me to make me fruitful. I asked for all things that I might enjoy life, and God said No. He said He will give me life, that I may enjoy all things. I ask God to help me love others as much as He loves me, and God said "Ah, finally you have the idea!".*

Always remember *Matthew 22:40*. **ALL** the law and prophets hang on the two highest commandments. Love God, and love your neighbor as yourself. Love is the highest law. Applying reason and logic to feelings is wisdom. Solomon provided an excellent example of using this knowledge about emotions to discern the wisest course of action. In *1 Kings 3:16-28* two women approach him claiming that the same infant was their child. All he had to go on was their word, and both shared a contrasting story. He tells them he will cut the baby in two and give each woman a half.

One woman said to go ahead and cut him in half so that neither of them would get what they wanted. The other woman pleaded with Solomon not to cut the child in half, because she loved him too much. She would rather save his life and let him go than let him die. Solomon tested their emotional response in order to determine who was speaking the truth, and he gave the whole child to the woman who pleaded for its life. This was the moment that showed God had blessed Solomon to be a wise and fair judge.

There are plenty of other specific examples I could give of discernment, but these are the most crucial foundations. It is important for your own journey to be certain you can test things against scripture for yourself without the perpetual need for outside guidance. You never know when it might be up to you and only you to determine if something is of God or not. Take some time to dig into this subject for yourself and even further sharpen your blade. You won't always get the chance to step back and contemplate. You need to be so good at it that you can identify when even a thought that pops into your head does not feel like your own. That way you can get ahead of it if it's bad and follow it if it's good.

  I recall a day where I was sitting in my living room relaxing, not realizing I had my guard down. All of a sudden I looked up and thought I saw something flying at me. It felt like I had been smacked in the head by some invisible gust of wind compacted into a dart or something. It took me a few minutes to realize that the thoughts I then started having were far outside my nature. I was suddenly angry, judging people on social media, and feeling depressed. If I hadn't been aware, who knows where that could have led.

  The good news is I realized something was off, and I prayed, rebuking the evil thoughts and whatever was causing them in the name of Christ. It cleared up like a fog lifted, and I was fine. When scripture says that our armor helps us withstand the fiery darts of the enemy, it felt like I had managed to get hit by one when I wasn't paying attention. Honing my discernment and self awareness was what allowed me to overcome. It only further assured me my armor was crucial at all times, and that knowledge is power.

Write your list of rules for discernment then recite them until they are memorized. Work on making these part of your instinctual nature through repetition. Would it be helpful to carry them around in your pocket? Share about an experience you may have had where you needed to be able to discern whether someone or something was truthful. Do you feel you got it right then, or do you see it differently now? How did the Spirit speak to you at the time to help you understand the situation?

_____
_____
_____
_____
_____
_____

9. Atonement with the Father

Create in me a clean heart, O God;
And renew a right spirit within me.
Psalm 51:10

God's timing is *perfect*. Over and over He demonstrates this point to me. Today was no exception. I'm going to hop out of the flow here for a moment to share a blessing with you, but no worries, there's a reason! On the day I am typing these words to the page in my unedited first draft, my daughter and I were baptized together (*April 8th, 2018*)! It was seriously such a beautiful experience. We attend New Life Church, a non-denominational Bible believing church whose mission is to bring people closer to Christ wherever they're at in their walk. I have always enjoyed the way the Spirit can be felt moving through their music and sermon. I initially chose them because they honor the concept of full submersion baptisms.

Photos taken by Destiny Wipf, used with permission, www.newlifechurchsf.org

My daughter turned ten years old this week and had been requesting baptism for almost two years. She wasn't baptized at birth, because her dad and I came from different faith backgrounds and neither of us was really practicing at the time. We decided we wanted faith to be her choice. I spent those last couple years answering her questions, letting her participate in a children's Bible study, and helping her build an understanding. She needed to have that relationship with Christ first. I was baptized at birth, but I wanted to do it again as an adult when it was my fully informed choice. Doing this together was a priceless experience I will cherish for a lifetime.

I had planned to write about baptism in this section. It just so happened that I reached this section and began to write it on the *very same day* we were scheduled to get baptized. This church does baptisms in groups once every couple months. On Easter Sunday, my family wanted to attend the huge cathedral downtown so we could see how beautifully it was decorated, but we were late leaving the house for the 11am service. I then followed my instinct to go to the 11:15am service at New Life where we were exactly on time. During that visit they announced the plan to do water baptisms on April 8th, so I followed the nudge of the Spirit to sign us both up. I wouldn't have known if we hadn't been late that morning.

When my daughter smiled her huge smile getting in the water, I could no longer fight back the tears that had been welling up in my eyes. When she came out and walked over to me, I hugged her, and I just let the tears roll. They were very happy tears! Luckily, this amazing church knew how special these moments are, and they had a photographer on hand to perfectly capture one of the most powerful moments in my relationship with my daughter. Even just writing those words has my eyes welling up with tears again. What a joyful day! Perfect timing, perfect execution, perfect *forever moment.*

There are churches out there that want you to dive into baptism as quickly as possible. Their doctrines typically revolve around the idea that baptism is a requirement to save your soul from hell, and by doing it immediately upon accepting Christ you are covered in the case of accidental death. That is why babies get baptized. It is believed we are born into sin right away and having sin on you upon death without having received salvation will send you to hell. They believe that even though God created us and intimately knows how we function, He would not make exception for an innocent and unaware baby if there were a tragic and unexpected loss of life. Some other churches will proclaim baptizing a baby is a sign of your parent's intentions, like their declaration that they want you to be a believer when you grow up. Some will call this a dedication rather than a baptism, which I find more fitting.

My take on it is a little different. I see baptism as your moment of identifying yourself as a follower of Christ. I believe whole heartedly that you shouldn't do it until the Spirit moves you. You need to be ready for that commitment in your heart! Some people need more time than others to get past their doubts and fears. Part of the baptism is affirming your belief that Christ is Lord and that your sins are forgiven. It is intended to be a public declaration of the internal, personal, and private commitment you have made. If you cannot declare that to be true where others can see and hear, then you are not ready. You'll know when it's your time. If you want to dedicate your child to God, I see no problem with that, but baptism is a different thing.

To reiterate this point, let's examine the perfect example of Christ. There is no record of him being baptized at birth. According to scripture, he began his ministry around age thirty (*Luke 3:23*), and John the Baptist conducted this rite for him at this time in order to fulfill all righteousness (*Matthew 3:13-17*).

In *John 3:5-6* Christ says that nobody can enter the kingdom without being born of both water and the Spirit. *Luke 3:16 & Matthew 3:11* tell us John baptized with water for repentance, but that one would come after him that baptized in the Holy Spirit and fire (*Luke 12:49*). I see that as indicating three separate baptisms, not just one.

I think the baptism of fire serves two functions. One is to burn away what does not belong in us, and the other is to refine us. This is present both in the womb phase where we learn and struggle through conviction as well as any trials we face that refine us down the road. It's not so much a baptism by fire in my eyes as it is a trial by fire. Don't worry though, because God is faithful and will not allow you to face anything you cannot handle (*1 Corinthians 10:13*).

Have you ever made pottery? (*Isaiah 64:8, Jeremiah 18*) You start with soggy clay, mold it, then put it in a kiln. Often this has to happen more than once. The first time hardens the clay. Then it comes out to apply lacquer or paint, and you put it back in for the polished finish. I see it in much the same way as part of solidifying our faith. Not everyone shares this perspective, so I encourage you to do a study for yourself.

Baptism by water is like being born! Scripture says that is when the spirit descended on Christ, and that is what I believe is the baptism of the Holy Spirit which continues to pour over time. It starts pouring when you accept Christ, and reaches a filled point at baptism. Everything from there is overflowing to share with others. John helps us identify in *14:26* that the baptism of the Spirit is about garnering wisdom and understanding. The Spirit brings it all together like the breath of life being added to you in your new life. We are transformed.

Basically, I feel this process burns away the chaff in us to be more righteous. The water baptism then quenches the fire, washing away what we have released. The Spirit fills us with new life as we emerge from the water fresh and clean. Any future trials are refiner's fire, polishing. There are many other scriptures that discuss baptism such as *Matthew 28:19, Acts 2:38-41 & 8:12 & 10:47-48,* and *Romans 6:1-11.* It's a great study to undertake and all ties into *Luke 17:20-21.*

If you're concerned you have not completed a piece of this process, pray for it. Ask God to show you what you're missing, even if it is difficult. Ask Him to guide you into understanding, burn away what is holding you back, cleanse you, purify you, sanctify you, and prepare you for what is to come (*Matthew 5:6*). Read *1st John*. It's short and rich in content. If you can read that and your heart understands and accepts it, then I would say that is a strong indicator of your success.

It is my obligation to warn you that Satan is not a fan of people getting to this point. Not everyone, but many have expressed that after their baptism they felt they were under spiritual attack. If we are truly following Christ in the Spirit, then it only makes sense, because after Christ's water baptism by John was when he spent forty days fasting in the wilderness being tempted by Satan.

Expect similar treatment. Be prepared for it, and it will be less difficult. He will try to tear down your faith and push you to sin, very reflective of *Revelation 12:4 & 13-17*. If he can't make you sin, he will try to steal your peace. He will rattle you, shake you up, and try to pull you away from God right out the gate of your new life. Remember the authority you have in Christ to cast out evil (*Luke 10:17-20*). You will overcome! Just like Shadrach, Meshach, and Abednego, when all is said and done, you will have the strength of God to stand in the spiritual fire and not be burned (*Daniel 3*). When the storm passes, you will stand firm in Christ (*Proverbs 10:25*).

It's important to identify how God communicates with us once we start building that relationship with Him. It's not much of a relationship without communication, right? How do we atone with the Father if we can't speak with Him? To someone who has not come to this point in their faith, the idea of God answering prayers or communicating with us sounds like lunacy. Recently a high-ranking politician identified that he feels Christ speaks to him, and a national talk show host stated that she felt he needed his mental health examined for this. It is a perfect example of some of the condemnation you may face.

Until approximately the last twenty years or so, saying that you heard voices or had visions would likely land you in a mental institution. While there are some people who really do need help with their mental health, there's a difference between communication with God and things like schizophrenia. In fact, it has been identified by mental health organizations that many people who are in all other respects healthy will still report that they hear voices. How do we discern the difference? In *John 10:27*, Christ says his sheep will hear his voice. He will know them, and they will follow him. There is a video on the playlist about scientists doing brain scans of people speaking in tongues as well, and showing that something is happening which supports it as truth.

Personally, I have had some dreams as well as waking visions. There have been a handful of times where I heard an audible message, though they have always been very short and to the point. All of these things were verifiable in scripture in some way and validated when I saw many other people having these same experiences, though I didn't know any of that before they happened. I only realized it when searching for explanations.

Truly, my strength lies in feelings. I am what new age people would refer to as an empath. I feel things deeply. Sometimes I can just read people by an internal feeling. It's hard to explain, but I think of it like the notes on a piano. There may be eighty-eight keys on a full piano, but each one has its own name and pitch. Different combinations make different chords. With time, I have just learned how to label each feeling like a note on the piano. I just know that one feeling is about a certain friend, or another is pointing me to something. Other times the Spirit will move me to look a certain direction, then place an emphasized focus on something like a number or word. It will just jump out at me.

I believe God works to develop a communication system with each person to fit their strong suits, so what works for me might not be for you. Instead of numbers you might see animals. I saw a video once where a woman had asked God to confirm that she understood something by showing her sea turtles, and everywhere she went for the next few days they were there. Her kid had seen them on a tv show, and a store she went to had a huge painting of them on the wall. Once you are certain you can trust the source, He will develop a process with you and you will know.

Some skeptics will say that receiving signs and communication like this is the sign of a false prophet. That is the most ludicrous thing I've ever heard! The entire Bible is written based on communications from God to people such as the prophets and apostles. Disbelief in the source of the message is the reason the Jews crucified Christ! He was claiming to speak for God as His son, and they didn't believe him. We don't have tons of scripture about the Holy Spirit, but that is explained in *John 16:7* when Christ said he had to leave in order to send us what has been translated to the Advocate, Comforter, or Holy Spirit. *John 14:26* tells us this Spirit will teach us and help us remember what he taught. So if you believe in scripture, then you believe this is truth. The *content* of the communication can determine a false prophet, but not the act of receiving a message itself. Some verses to start your study about ways God communicated with others are: *1 Kings 19:11-13, Job 38:1, Exodus 19:18, 1 Samuel 2:10, John 12:29, Psalm 77:18, Hebrews 1:1-2.*

My friend sent me a message on this exact topic of communication from God eight hours after I started writing about it. She had no clue we were focusing on the exact same subject, so that is a perfect example of one of the ways the Spirit will communicate. Sometimes a friend or family member will be moved to reach out to you about something so specific. God loves to utilize His people! Her questions, concerns, and perspective helped me with the writing process. In turn, the fact that I was already presently thinking about the topic allowed me to be prepared in sharing my perspective. It created a wonderful exchange that I felt benefited both of us. If you've ever had that feeling in the pit of your stomach that something was wrong with a loved one only to call them and find out you were right, I think that is the Spirit communicating with you.

There is definitely a cause and effect correlation present. If you pray on something and feel you get a response, that is different than just hearing things at random. I prayed my way through writing this book, so the timing of my friend felt like God answering in His own way. That doesn't mean it's impossible for God to send random messages, but it is less common. It also doesn't mean that everything you think is an answer from God actually came from Him. It is easy when we are hoping for a response to see what we want to see.

These communications are not something I have control over. I can pray and hope for a response, but there is no guarantee. In fact, I have found that if I'm hoping for a dream or vision for the wrong reasons, they don't happen. It's when I relax into the feeling of peacefully trusting God that they occur. He makes sure I remember that He is in control.

Another point is that God is not the one who wants you to be confused. That is about division and inner conflict, not peace and balance. You might feel convicted to correct your perception about something and it may initially feel confusing, but it will be about bringing you to a point of clarity and understanding. So, if you are receiving some kind of communication over and over that is sending you into a tailspin of confusion, it is most likely not from God. It could be demonic, or it could be a mental health issue.

That being said, I read an article once where a man who claimed to be able to see beyond the veil talked about mental health issues. He claimed when he walked into a mental health facility for the first time, all he saw was people being plagued by dark spirits. I don't know how much weight that holds, but scripture does suggest that they can cause disease. For example, when Christ healed the blind child, he cast out a demon and returned his sight. It certainly makes you think about all the modern afflictions we face. While it is clear some things that make us sick are of our own creation, how much of it is spiritual?

If you are ever uncertain, call on the name of Christ. Ask him to help and protect you. All evil spirits respond to the authority of his name. As stated previously, fasting and prayer in fellowship are effective for stronger cases. You will hear the word **rebuke** often said, which is defined as expressing sharp disapproval. In the Biblical sense it is about casting out evil, declaring that you are against it by name and description in the name of Christ. You tell it to leave with authority.

At the end of the day, the Spirit will lead us in God's ways. *Matthew 13:3-9* explains the parable of sowing seeds. It shows us how God will work with us if we simply choose to follow Him, and by doing so we produce good fruit. All of it hinges on ***trust***.

In previous sections I've already covered two of the three tests of Satan while Christ was in the wilderness for forty days. What was the third? Satan approached Christ and said *Your Father swore to protect your life. Go to that highest temple in the city and jump! He will make the angels come save you!* Christ replied *It is written again, thou shalt not tempt the Lord thy God* (*Matthew 4:5-7*). We are not supposed to test God's protection. We are supposed to trust it. If you want to atone with Him and show your love, trust is paramount.

This will require heavy endurance. *Here is the patience of the saints, here are they that keep the commandments of God and the faith of Jesus* (*Revelation 14:12*). That doesn't say faith *in* Jesus, it says faith *of* Jesus. That one little word can totally change the meaning. We are meant to reflect the same level of faith in the Father as Christ did, and show it by following instructions we were given through the gospel.

It's easy in the modern world to lose your gusto, your commitment. The world dwindles it with time and feeds your desires, so patience is crucial to success. The changes you make for God need to be lasting. I assure you, I have suffered much in my life. I definitely paid for my mistakes, even if I have made it sound easy. It wasn't. God helped me pass the endurance trial. His love made it all bearable. Then it healed. Then it brought me joy. Then I had so much joy that I shared it. You will come out of the darkness. Have faith! Now I am equipped with relatable experiences regarding overcoming many different obstacles.

Pain is transformed into wisdom. There is a reason that scripture so often refers to long suffering as a good thing (*Ephesians 4:2, Galatians 5:22, Hebrews 2:10, etc.*). It is what helps perfect us. If you fell and scraped your knee wide open, chances are it would hurt, right? Your body has utilized your nervous system to create a feeling of pain that alerts you to the fact that you are wounded, maybe even bleeding, and it requires your attention to heal. You then become consciously aware of the problem so you can clean it up, as well as internally aware so your immune system can step in and do its job.

Have you ever considered that your emotional pain holds the same purpose? Feelings are invisible and internal at their foundation. There's no cut you can see to wash and bandage. Pain is not a punishment. It's a necessary part of a healthy mind, body, and spirit in this reality. Ask yourself what the world would look like without it. Would we care whether anyone lived or died if we never felt grief or mourned? Would the ego never have a check in place to balance it with humility? In heaven these won't be issues since we are told there will be no more pain, but here they are things we face daily. A psychopath is defined by their inability to feel pain or any range of emotions while still being able to emulate the behavior when necessary to meet certain ends. *That* is a mental health problem.

While pain certainly sucks, perhaps we can find a silver lining in the fact that it has purpose, just like anything else. The more aware of that we are, the faster we can work to alleviate the pain when we feel it. Eventually that can evolve into being better able to avoid painful situations in healthy ways. If we avoid facing pain, it festers and grows. When we face it head on, we take away its power, just like shining light on your shadow eliminates it. I used to ask myself why God would allow us to endure pain. Then I survived my own struggles and realized how it molded me into a better person and taught me endless things, nuances so precious to life.

There is a fine balance to be discovered between holding on and letting go, because what I do for you, you do not learn to do for yourself. I think God knows this intimately. He used to walk with Abraham. Then His son and the angels came as messengers. Now we have the Holy Spirit. As He backed away in the physical aspect, He increased His spiritual presence. There's always a guiding hand helping you to stand up on your own two feet. You just have to trust that it's there. That doesn't mean you don't still have to use your own muscles to stand up. That hand will just help make it much easier.

Submit to God, and the devil will flee as your path is made straight (*James 4:7, Proverbs 3:5-6, Romans 8:38-39*). Seek His kingdom and righteousness first, and all things needed shall be added to you (*Matthew 6:33*). God makes it clear that if we offer him faith and love, He will take care of us in many ways. All we have to do is trust him instead of worry (*Philippians 4:6-7, Matthew 6:25-34, Luke 12:24-34, Psalm 55:22, etc.*). There is a short and easy prayer commonly referred to as the *Serenity Prayer* that I feel is perfect for times of inner conflict. *God, please grant me the serenity to accept the things I cannot change, courage to change the things I can, and the wisdom to know the difference.* It is simple yet elegant, and exactly the message we need to hold close to our hearts in times of distress.

The Seven Letters to the Churches

True atonement with the Father is finding peace in Him and allowing it to become peace within yourself. That is why we went through the process of studying the divine nature in the commands. I want to wrap up this section with a recap provided to us in Revelation. Christ wrote seven letters to the seven churches, detailing his thoughts towards each of them. He ends each letter by saying to let anyone hear what he is saying to the churches if they have ears to hear. That means their reprimands were not just for them. They were for everyone. There is a real city each church is named for, but remember that we are a temple of the Holy Spirit. In that sense, we are all a type of church. Check yourself against each, and ask if you feel you are compliant with the message.

For each church, I have provided what the name translates to mean. All names have meaning in the Biblical context. Your name was meant to reflect you. When God gives new names, He sometimes likes to add an *h*, like a breath of life from the divine. For example, *Abram* became *Abraham* (*Genesis 17:5*). *Israel* is the name God gave Jacob (*Genesis 32:22-30 & 35:10*). God told him this name was given because he had wrestled with God and man and overcome. Ask yourself what it means to be a part of spiritual Israel based on the meaning of the name. Christ's appointed name (*Matthew 1:21, Luke 1:31*) means *salvation*.

Most of us still have Biblical names in modern times. My birth name, *Ann*, means *graceful* or *merciful* in Hebrew depending who you ask. They are words that are often used interchangeably given their related uses, though they do mean different things. What does your name mean? Look it up!

Ephesus (Revelation 2:1-7) - The word means *desirable* according to *Hitchcock's New and Complete Analysis of the Holy Bible.* Christ commends this church for their works, labor, and patience. He likes that they can't tolerate evil and have tested the apostles with discernment. He praises their endurance for his name's sake. It is indicated that at some point they fell away from their first love. The word translated to *love* here is *G26 - agape -* which applies to a more universal love, goodwill, and benevolence. They are strongly commanded to repent of abandoning this and return to their first works. Christ also says he appreciates that they hate the work of the Nicolaitans. While we don't know much about them, one of the other letters suggested they were guilty of eating things sacrificed to idols and fornication. Those who overcome will be granted to eat of the tree of life.

Smyrna (Revelation 2:8-11) - The word comes from the Greek word *smurna*, meaning *myrrh.* Christ states that he knows their works, tribulation, and poverty. He also knows the blasphemy of those calling themselves Jews but are really a synagogue of Satan. He says some of them will be thrown into prison for ten days to face tribulation. Sometimes in the prophetic, a day is not a day as we know it on earth, but instead on a more heavenly time clock. It's possible this is a longer time period like ten years on earth. I couldn't say for sure, though. If they are faithful unto death, they will receive a crown of life and not experience the second death.

Pergamos (Revelation 2:12-17) - The word either means *citadel* or *united by marriage.* In this letter, Christ identifies that he knows their works, and that they have held to their faith in him even though they lived in the place where Satan resides. He chastises them for holding to the doctrine of Balaam wherein they would cast stumbling blocks in front of the children of Israel. They are also accused of eating things sacrificed to idols and fornication as the Nicolaitans did. If they do not repent, he will come fight them with his double edged sword. He says it is the sword of his mouth! The overcomers will be given some of the hidden manna and a white stone with a new name on it that no man knows but the one who receives it.

Thyatira (Revelation 2:18-29) - This can translate to *castle of Thya*. According to Dr. Arnold Fruchtenbaum in his book *Footsteps of the Messiah* he says it means *sacrifice offering*. Christ commends them for their works, charity (*G26 - love again*), service, faith and patience. He applauds that their last works are greater than their first. However, he says they tolerate Jezebel who taught people to fornicate and eat things sacrificed to idols. He says he gave her space to repent, but she didn't do it. He insists they repent of their deeds or be cast into tribulation with her. He will kill her children, and everyone will know that he can see into our hearts and gives to everyone according to their works. However, those who do not hold that doctrine like Jezebel will not be burdened and are instructed to simply hold out for him. The overcomers will be given the morning star and power over the nations. There are a handful of references to the morning star in the Bible, and almost every one of them is translated from a different word. If you would like to undertake that study for yourself, check Strong's Concordance for *Job 38:7, Isaiah 14:12, 2 Peter 1:19,* and *Revelation 22:16* alongside this verse.

Sardis (Revelation 3:1-6) - There are three potential meanings of this word. Some say *prince of joy,* some think it's *that which remains*, and some believe it to be *those escaping*. Christ says he knows their deeds, and while they think they are alive, they are dead. He warns them to wake up and strengthen what remains, because he does not find them perfect or complete before God. They are to remember what they know and repent, otherwise he will come for them like a thief. They will not be ready for him because they didn't prepare and watch. The few in this church who are not defiled will walk with him in white, because they are worthy. Those who overcome will be clothed in white and not be blotted out of the book of life. He will confess their name before the Father and the angels.

Philadelphia (Revelation 3:7-13) - Most people are familiar with this word. It comes from the Greek word *philadelphos* which means *brotherly love.* This is another of their six words for love. Christ says he knows their works and has set before them an open door. They had little strength but kept his word and did not deny his name. He will make those who claim to be Jews but are found lying to worship before their feet, and they will know that Christ loved them. The word translated to love here is *G25 - agapao* - meaning to take pleasure in, esteem, wish well, and denotes a love of reason. It is the same word translated to love every time it is used in *Matthew 5:43-46*. Since they kept his word and patience, they will be kept from the hour of temptation or trial that the rest of the world will endure. They are told to hold fast so that nobody takes their crown. The overcomer will be made a pillar in the temple of God and stay there, going out no more. The name of God, the name of the city of God which is New Jerusalem, and his new name will be written on them.

Laodicea (Revelation 3:14-22) - This word refers to either *people ruling* or *people judged* and comes from the Greek word *laodikeia*. It combines *laos* referring to a group of people and *dike* which means *justice* or *judgment*. This is the church that is condemned for being lukewarm. They are neither hot nor cold, and if they stay that way he will spit them out of his mouth. They say they are rich and need nothing, but are really poor, blind, naked, wretched, and miserable. I think naked is in reference to *Hebrews 4:12-13*. It means your heart is exposed to Him. He instructs them to buy gold tried in the fire and white raiment, and to anoint their eyes so they can see. He says he rebukes and chastens those he loves and instructs them to be zealous in repentance. He will stand at the door and knock, and he will come and eat with anyone who hears his voice and opens the door. Those who overcome will sit on his throne with him, just as he sat with his Father.

The Lord is my shepherd, I shall not want.
He maketh me to lie down in green pastures: he leadeth me beside still waters, He restoreth my soul: he leadeth me in the paths of righteousness for his name's sake. Yea, though I walk through the valley of the shadow of death, I will fear no evil: for thou art with me; thy rod and thy staff, they comfort me. Thou preparest a table before me in the presence of mine enemies: thou anointest my head with oil; my cup runneth over. Surely goodness and mercy shall follow me all the days of my life: and I will dwell in the house of the Lord forever. Psalm 23

In the space given, write what progress you feel you have made in making amends with God. Did you truly feel remorse for your sins and try to turn from them? Do you understand His will for you as it has been laid out in scripture? What are you still struggling to work through? Reflect and pray over everything you write down. Do you believe you have been tried by the fire? Have you been baptized in water and declared your faith yet? Do you feel full of the Holy Spirit and baptized by it? If not, are you ready? Do you understand how God communicates to you? Reflect and pray asking God to help you develop a way to hear Him that is clear to you. Be sure to tell God in your own words how much you love Him and why. Thank Him for all He has done, is doing, and will do for you. Thank Him for sending Christ to give us second chances, and let him know that you plan to do your best to honor that gift.

10. Apotheosis

And I will bring the blind by a way that they knew not.
I will lead them in paths that they have not known.
I will make darkness light before them,
and crooked things straight.
These things will I do unto them,
and not forsake them.
Isaiah 42:16

    This may not be a word you are too familiar with, so let's define it. *Apotheosis* is a noun meaning the highest point in the development of something. It represents the climax. In other uses, particularly in mythology, it can also mean the elevation of someone to divine status or deification. For our purposes, we are going to bring our understanding of divine nature and what Christ taught us to a climax.

    What does the word *apocalypse* really mean? While most think it means the end of the world, I think a more accurate definition would be the end of the world as we currently know it. The true meaning of this word in Greek is *an uncovering*, or a *disclosure of knowledge*. Thusly, it means just about the same exact thing as Revelation - a revealing. What has been revealed to you in this journey?

    A *disciple* is one who is taught. *By this shall all men know that ye are my disciples, if ye have love one to another (John 13:35)*. This is *G26* love. Learning divine love is a journey over time built on the experience of trial and error and the guidance of God. My personal interpretation is that the journey is mapped out by the four beasts/living creatures mentioned in *Daniel, Ezekiel,* and *Revelation*.

    The lion represents where we start with our more primal nature as carnivores and kings of the jungle. We have a heart of stone. This is related to our physical health. We then evolve towards the ox, an herbivore found in agricultural settings. The commands of God are written on our hearts and waters of life are pulled from it. This is related to our mental health. When we finally wake up to Christ, we become the man. This also reflects our early industrial age where we become more cerebral and intellectual and veer away from the farming atmosphere. We receive the heart of flesh and develop our emotional health. When we truly accept divine nature and purify ourselves in the sight of God with His light in our hearts, we become like eagles, able to fly like angels. That is about our spiritual health, and Christ returns to drive that home. Again, they are real, but I hypothesize that they each represent a certain aspect of our development.

Science is knowledge. It is the mind's ability to reason. It doesn't care, it just observes and analyzes. It must be objective by its very nature because feelings create variables. They can't be part of the equation or results will be skewed. Wisdom sees knowledge through the eyes of the heart. It applies love to logic, taking your facts and putting them to their most beneficial and efficient use.

I think the early church did a decent job summing up divine behavior in the *seven deadly sins and blessed virtues*. Contemplate what you have learned from scripture about each of these concepts. They are:

Wrath versus Patience
Gluttony versus Temperance
Greed versus Charity
Envy versus Kindness
Sloth versus Diligence
Lust versus Chastity
Pride versus Humility

Do you want to know what one of the most profound experiences was that I have ever had? I started reading the Bible as though I was every person in it. I'm sure that sounds incredibly conceited at first, but hear me out. It started out as simply meditating on the words (*Psalm 1:1-3 & 19:14 & 104:1-34, etc.*), trying to imagine what the scene looked like. For example, let's look at when I was reading about Moses helping free the slaves that were captive in Egypt.

I can't fathom living an entire lifetime as a slave, fearing beatings and constantly working just to survive for another day of the same. It made me value my personal freedoms and opportunities more. Then again, it felt like that was also my metaphorical relationship with money. I depended on it, measured my worth by it, and let it define my goals. We all need money to live in this modern world. I wanted to be free of it, so I sought to be self-sufficient, but even doing that costs money to make it happen legally. It made me feel stuck.

I then considered the life of the pharaoh. I suppose it would be nice to have more money and responsibility, allowing me the ability to make a more positive impact. Did he really think he was doing the right thing for the people or for himself? I wondered about his logic. I have considered running for political office before, but I honestly felt my talents would have been wasted. I prefer not to spend all my time fundraising for a campaign to plaster my face everywhere when I could fundraise for suicide prevention or diseases that need cures or to help the homeless. I want to get my hands on doing good things rather than hit the campaign trail.

What about the people who worked for pharaoh? If your leader asked you to do something against your morals like kill or beat slaves, would you do it out of loyalty to them? I am non-violent, because God says not to kill and it's the right thing to do. I would not betray that because someone told me to. I would rather die with a clean soul than live with the guilt of murder.

Then I imagined myself as Moses, the one so devoted to following God and the basic principles of love which he would later share outlined in the ten commandments, that he risked his life on faith. He made sacrifices to help the slaves become free. It was quite noble, and I aimed to be a better person by beginning to find ways to volunteer my time. I wanted to help people see that anyone is capable of making the choice to help others.

Then I evaluated all of these positions in conjunction. I asked myself why all that conflict needed to happen. Why couldn't we all just make better choices and choose love? Why can't we work together? What are we waiting for? Then I realized that must be how God feels looking down at all of this. We are a bunch of people unwilling to set our ego and self-importance aside in order for everyone to win. Somebody still wants power and control, and it always gets distorted. When do we finally hear and live the message instead of fighting about who gets to say it? Just treat others the way you want to be treated. If you want to be forgiven for your failings, you must believe forgiveness is possible. If you want to see the world change, you are part of it and must be willing to change with it.

By reading the whole Bible this way, I evolved as a human being. That is the point of being told history and stories - to learn from them. I saw that the devil, while still real, was also representative of everything dark in ourselves, even the dark side of positive things like love. He was pride and deceit and gluttony and greed. He was ego. I looked in the mirror and saw the potential in myself to become dark, just like everyone can. I saw what pride could turn me into, even if it was about doing good things. I used the stories to define what was dark versus light and asked myself if I was doing that. I prayed about it continuously, fasted in penance and positivity which helped me reclaim my personal strength and control, and spent time reflecting on where I have made mistakes in life.

I identified my pure intention to do the right thing and how I struggled in identifying what was right in the moment, because life is complicated sometimes. Logic and love don't always get along, so I made it simple for myself. Starting the moment I realized any error, I would commit to understanding and correcting it in line with God. I would live love as best I could and forgive myself and others, because I know I'm not perfect. I ask God almost daily to forgive me even if I don't think I screwed up, because it keeps me humble to the fact that I could make a mistake and not realize it. I also ask God all the time to forgive everyone else that isn't me, because we are all at least a little lost and imperfect, and I am compassionate to the struggle that right answers can be hard to find in the moment. Unfortunately, positive intention does not always breed positive results when deception exists.

Once you are in the Spirit, this is an important part of your growth. *Matthew 18:18* says *Varily I say unto you, whatsoever ye shall bind on earth shall be bound in heaven, and whatsoever ye shall loose on earth shall be loosed in heaven.* Then in *John 20:23* it says *Whose soever sins ye remit, they are remitted unto them, and whose soever sins ye retain, they are retained.* Both times Christ was talking to the apostles about the weight of their responsibility once they carried the Spirit with them. It gave them authority to forgive or not forgive, bind and loose. The purification of self is practically a safety precaution for everyone around you when you look at it that way. It emphasized the power carried behind their words and actions.

So here I am, musing out what's been on my mind. I can't claim to know everything, but I can share some of what I have learned from my efforts and failures. Maybe someone else will be struggling with the same things I experienced and will find some light while in a dark place. Maybe someone will think twice before responding to another person in anger. Maybe someone will go volunteer their time somewhere after reading this, because it sounded like a good idea in their heart. Maybe someone will finally accept Christ. If even one person reads this truth laid bare and any of the above happens, then it was worth the time and effort it took to write it all down.

This is how we spread love, by just being it because we choose to. It's much easier to show people your perspective through your example than to force people to do or agree about anything. Sum it all up and we are basically being told not to be jerks and think we are better than anyone, and we will be just fine. God says judgment is not my place, so I trust Him on that one.

Faith has kept making me feel lighter and lighter. One day it may even lift me right off the ground light as a feather, healthy and pure. I refined myself step by step over time. It all just felt like something was missing until Christ was in my heart and that peace finally felt real. I used to feel tiny, depressed, and cursed. Through faith I began to feel tall, happy, and blessed. Even when feeling tall, I brought myself down to worship and be humble. I found joy in my ability to persevere having followed Christ to put God in my foundations. I chose to try and be the best version of myself possible every single day out of love. Looking back from this point in my journey and seeing how God was always there walking me through it was the number one strongest solidifier of my faith.

I understand now that while I will never forget the lessons learned from the real struggles, I barely remember feeling so sad and numb, because I worked with Christ in cleaning my slate. When it says that Christ will remember your sins no longer, I think it's because he forgave us and saw us change. In this process he sees the purity emerge in our hearts, and he trusts that. If the Holy Spirit indwells in us, then we have to be able to forgive ourselves as part of the process. If we don't, we will continue to hold a grudge against our past actions and they will control us, pulling us back into sin.

One of the biggest fights I see in the church today is the fight over whether the Old Testament is still relevant anymore or not. It has been clear in my study that those who live in only one half or the other are the ones typically missing some major bits of understanding that are contained in the books they neglected. Even in all of this writing, I haven't fully examined every verse against

Strong's Concordance or developed an understanding of all the mysteries. I hold some strong educated guesses on deeper matters, but it would take a lifetime for anyone to fully grasp the knowledge and wisdom in every word of the true scripture. I am trying my best to share the overarching principles that appear to be most important and somehow lost, but I will be continuing to study and learn for the rest of my life.

Christ was following the Old Testament. He preached out of its scriptures at synagogue on the Sabbath. He was supposed to have lived the perfect life, so he sets an example. To say the Old Testament is irrelevant is like denying that he was the prophesied Messiah, which is a huge part of validating his claim to being the son of God. That is like saying all the laws he fulfilled perfectly and preached about came out of thin air instead of those scriptures. Hopefully this book has turned on a light for people and helped connect these two sections.

My personal climactic revelation of truth was that we crucified Christ on the division (*Ephesians 2:14*). He was placed on the cross with one hand nailed to the right side and one nailed to the left. He was crucified right down the middle. To me, this is symbolic of how we constantly crucify our compassion on the cross of conflict. Wasn't that a major theme of his message, that we should stop being so angry all the time? We divide everything down the middle and fight about it instead of loving each other enough to try working together. Democrats versus Republicans, the battle of the sexes, we fight about everything. Every time we rise to true anger and violence, it is metaphorically like crucifying him again (*Hebrews 6:4-6, James 1:19, Ephesians 4:31*).

I'm sure he would have preferred to bring both of those arms down and hug us, but we basically said *no, you're not the right one to give us a hug.* I once saw a quote while doing some online study from GK Chesterton. He said *Christianity is not a faith that has been tried and found wanting, but a faith that has been wanted and never tried.* I now think of it anytime I see someone rise to anger instead of rising to the occasion and showing love and logic. Stop crucifying your salvation and compassion! Once was more than enough. Hear the words of the gospel and let it speak love into our lives. I respect and appreciate his sacrifice on the cross, but look at how rich his *life* was too!

Thought exercise: Christians wanted to separate themselves from the Jews who crucified Christ. Here's the thing, though. What would happen today? If someone stepped up and claimed to be Christ in the modern day, they would likely be committed, scoffed at, and ridiculed. They would be made fun of on the world news to anyone with ears to hear, picked apart by vultures. We have lost our childlike ability to believe, and most people look at the pages of scripture like they are dead trees and nothing more. We may need to be discerning and cautious about what we believe, but that doesn't mean we should abandon belief all together or turn to such hateful solutions.

Ask yourself - are our modern selves any better than those who crucified Christ, or are we ready with torches and pitchforks in hand? The Jews of Christ's time believed deeply in the importance of the ten commandments. The heritage passed down to them were the stories of Moses. He was a hero to them. Then this guy showed up claiming to be the son of God working miracles? Their ancestors were punished severely for idolatry and worshipping false gods. They were incredibly skeptical of this new guy telling them they were doing things wrong. Imagine the fear and confusion they must have felt trying to decide for themselves whether he was telling the truth or not.

Was this Christ truly the son of God? *We grew up with him, no way! He was like us!* I mean, can you imagine how panic stricken some of them must have been? Think of how it would be handled today with 7.5billion people. Would he get lost in a crowd? Would he publish a new scripture that never even made the best seller list like *Harry Potter* did, because people thought he was crazy? If he did gain traction, would he ignite a world war?

We are told Christ will return descending from the sky (*Mark 13:26*), so as I said, this has just been a thought exercise. However, if he had just been born a baby somewhere in the world today and been raised in a human life as was the case 2000 years ago, would anyone today believe him? Maybe now that I have asked these questions you would consider it, but if I hadn't I'm guessing not. If he didn't make a show of his return it would be hard for most people. He wouldn't be heard above the roar of bickering. The only way we will know it's him is seeing it fulfilled exactly as scripture states. We are warned that the anti-Christ will be widely popular and reign forty-two months before the true Christ comes. People will be deceived all across the world. If you are not reading your Bible to prepare yourself, it is literally part of prophecy that you will likely be deceived! Do your best to be certain you aren't misled.

In the space below, write what has been the most profound revelation you've had on this journey to build your relationship with God. What do you understand now that you didn't imagine you would before? What doubts and concerns do you still have that are holding you back from truly submitting to God's will? Collect various interpretations about the topic and identify what you feel aligns with scripture and your heart. Can you identify what is a healthy way to submit to God versus what is not a healthy way? Do you feel like God loves you and you love Him in a mutual exchange? Reflect and pray. Thank God for the understanding He has provided you thus far, and ask Him to continue guiding you in your study.

11. The Ultimate Boon

*The night is far spent, the day is at hand.
Let us therefore cast off the works of darkness,
and let us put on the armour of light.*
Romans 13:12

A *boon* is the ultimate item you were seeking on your quest. An example from mythology would be the quest for the holy grail. The grail itself was the boon. In this case, we sought to develop the perfect armor of God (*Hebrews 13:20-21*). Let's review all the upgrades we've given to it so that you can claim your top of the line gear!

What are the qualities we have covered that represent each piece of your gear? Do you remember? They are *salvation, righteousness, the Spirit, truth, faith,* and *peace*. **Salvation** was the first step, when you accepted Christ in your heart. That shined up the helmet that protects your head. Then we discussed the commands of God and divine nature, which helped you on the journey to pursue **righteousness** in word and deed. That upgraded the breastplate that protects your heart (*Isaiah 59:17*). When you got baptized, that was what filled you with the **Spirit** which is your sword (*Acts 2:38*). It is like Christ fighting battles with you and through you using his own double edged sword. We discussed how to discern **truth** which not only sharpened that blade but bestowed you with your belt (*Hebrews 4:12*). All of these steps helped build our **faith** and trust in God, strengthening our shield as we atoned with the Father (*Proverbs 30:5*). At the climax, we had the revelation that the message of the scripture is **peace**, and we will embrace it in each step we take going forward. That gave us the perfect shoes (*Isaiah 52:7*).

It's *very* important when you visualize putting on your armor each day to remember that spiritual warfare is *not* physical warfare (*John 16:1-4*). This book is not your license to pick up a gun for God. This is about our souls. *For though we walk in the flesh, we do not war after the flesh. For the weapons of our warfare are not carnal, but mighty through God to the pulling down of strongholds. Casting down imaginations, and every high thing that exalteth itself against the knowledge of God, and bringing into captivity every thought to the obedience of Christ (2 Corinthians 10:3-5).*

If we each individually conquer the beasts within, we will be able to conquer the beasts of men and of Satan. Christ has taken up his sword to lead you in spiritual battle! Notice how he was composed, strong, unafraid of his emotions, and full of wisdom from God to guide him. In turn, when you follow him, you are blessed with these same gifts. He is shouting a triumphant cry to charge forward by loving fearlessly! Going to physical war is fighting to bring death upon yourself. *Then said Jesus unto him, Put up again thy sword into his place, for all they that take the sword shall perish with the sword (Matthew 26:52).* It is those who answer the call to spiritual war that are truly following the message of the Bible. We aren't fighting flesh and blood. We are fighting powers, rulers of darkness, and spiritual wickedness (*Ephesians 6:12*).

This is also not your license to be on the attack towards people all the time. It is one thing to speak truth, which we are instructed to do in love (*Epehsians 4:15*). It is another thing to force or coerce people. This armor is built up for your protection, your *defense*. The next section will talk about leadership in faith, so if you feel called to speak openly in any form of ministry, please finish the book first and consider how best to approach such a delicate subject. We don't attack when we minister, we lead. There is a difference, and it is one that is incredibly important if you want the message to be truly heard.

Your knowledge of scripture is your strongest weapon. Being able to cite the Word of God in a dispute is like calling in the cavalry to your defense. When you specifically reference the words of Christ, he is fighting your battles for you. His word is God's Word, and it holds the highest authority in how to resolve conflict. In the Old Testament, two or three witnesses was all it took for a conviction to be punished, so having two or three verses that support your perspective is like bringing witnesses to the table.

The sword is of the Spirit, and Christ wields it. After everything we have covered, why do you think it is specifically referred to as a *double edged* sword? Remember in the beginning when I talked about thirds? The far left and far right extremes of the spectrum are where evil lies. The center is solid. A double edged sword is sharp on both the left side and the right. If you try to find your balance on either one of them alone, you will get cut. That sword will cut off the extremes creating a narrower field instead of a wide spectrum, one that is more peaceful. If you simply choose to embrace that battle is about controlling yourself instead of others so that they cannot push you to anger, then you will win the war.

In the space below, explain in your own words what spiritual warfare really requires of you. First share in the general sense of the lesson. Then share about what personal hurdles you will be focusing to overcome so that you can bring the peace of God to any conflict. Identify any triggers you may have that you know will be difficult to encounter, and outline how you plan to gradually heal them so the opposition can no longer push your buttons. Reflect on your journey as a whole, and the comfort God gives you to walk in peace. Pray whatever is in your heart.

12. Refusal of The Return

For God hath not given us the spirit of fear,
But of power, and of love, and of a sound mind.
      2 Timothy 1:7

      Let's face it. Once we are comfortable in how we live our own lives, it's hard to step away from the bubble of learning and personal growth. We have worked so hard to develop that strong relationship with God and walk in His will, it would be easier to just stay in the comfort of His arms, waiting for the return of Christ and living out our normal lives. It would be easier not to go any further, because it just sounds like too much work sometimes. I mean, I wouldn't complain if I could just spend my life learning.

      At the same time, developing a moral conscience in the sight of God develops a deeper sense of compassion in us that is simply impossible to turn away from. This is the point at which we toil over how vocal we want to be about our faith. You have a calling to share what you've learned. Knowledge is a responsibility, not a secret. This section is devoted to finding the courage to burst your bubble and throw away the crutches. This is a *hero's* journey! *(James 5:19-20)*

      Being asked to live in the world but not be of it can feel like a bit of a stretch. I want you to understand that even those who have rock solid faith will still feel doubts creep in sometimes. Christ knew he was going to die. He knew exactly what was coming. In *Matthew 26:36-46* he went to Gethsemane to pray. He was sorrowful and pleaded to the Father saying *If it be possible, let this cup pass from me, nevertheless not as I will, but as thou wilt.* It's not like he wanted to die. However, he refused to fight the guards who came for him. He knew His Father's will and placed his trust in Him completely despite his fears. That is what the perfect example demonstrated for us. He trusted God with his life, even unto death.

      Not only did this show how to trust, but it showed us how we should approach our fears. *James 1:5-7* says *If any of you lack wisdom, let him ask of God, that giveth to all men liberally, and upbraided not, and it shall be given to him. But let him ask in faith, nothing wavering. For he that wavereth is like a wave of the sea driven with the wind and tossed. For let not that man think that he shall receive anything of the Lord.* When you experience doubt, pray for wisdom and guidance. Speak your heart to God in faith, and let Him know that you will respect and trust His decision on how to handle things. Christ was trusting God in perfect faith, so even when he didn't get the answer he hoped for, he accepted it. If God had granted this request, would any of the world have been granted the chance at salvation? Christ also told the apostles he would be resurrected, and he trusted that action would be fulfilled.

Have I not commanded thee? Be strong and of a good courage. Be not afraid, neither be thou dismayed, for the Lord thy God is with thee whithersoever thou goest (Joshua 1:9). Believe me, I know how incredibly difficult it is to face our fears. I know how hard it is to lose a friend in an irreconcilable conflict. I know the shame you can feel at first when you are new to your faith and attacked by someone who is strong in their disbelief (*Romans 1:16*). I know how easy it is when faced with *fight or flight* to choose flight and just scoot right out of dodge.

Unfortunately, running from our problems not only doesn't solve them, but it can often just make them worse or dump them on someone else's lap. Christ didn't run. He stood his ground and accepted God's plan. He was beaten and still carried his own cross on his back to the hill where they crucified him on it (*Luke 9:23*). Wow...

You can do all things through Christ who strengthens you (*Philippians 4:13*). Look at his example, and imagine the fortitude his actions must have taken to face all odds and not break away from God's instructions. Feel in your heart his commitment and perseverance for what he knew was right (*Hebrews 10:36*). Then pull from that image in your heart and mind. Feel his same amount and quality of strength and willpower through the Holy Spirit indwelling in you, and use it. Tap into his peaceful, composed stature and **walk in that faith towards freedom**. You got this!

> *If you hear a voice within you say "you cannot paint", then by all means paint, and that voice will be silenced.* - Vincent Van Gogh

In the section below, write your battle cry. If Christ were standing in front of a field of troops, preparing them to go forward into spiritual battle, what do you think he would say? As the man who *is* the Word, what are the precise words he would declare to speak directly to your heart and ignite a fire? What would compel you so deeply to advance through this world in strength and virtue unafraid? Pray, and ask God to guide your words and make them personal. When you are finished, go stand in front of a mirror on your own, and speak those words to yourself as though Christ was speaking through you. Speak them with conviction. Make every word matter. Let God motivate you! If you feel these words will be inspiring down the road, rewrite them on sticky notes and put them up around your house. Don't ever let yourself forget the power of conviction.

Part Three:
The Return
(aka Mature Trees Bear Fruit)

13. The Magic Flight

*Grace and peace be multiplied unto you
through the knowledge of God and of Jesus our Lord.
According as his divine power hath given unto us
all things that pertain unto life and godliness,
through the knowledge of him that hath
called us to glory and virtue:
whereby are given unto us exceeding great and precious promises:
that by these ye might be partakers of the divine nature,
having escaped the corruption that is in the world through lust.*
2 Peter 1:2-4

There is still plenty left to cover on our journey and how the things we have learned apply to our lives. Now we must identify the internal flight from finding courage to speak openly in faith towards the joy and confidence of doing it. That joy is what will allow your message to be so infectious. We want love to go viral! Living as a joyful, balanced self in Christ will feel like flying everywhere you go (*Isaiah 40:31, Revelation 12:14*). Forward momentum and action in our lives is also a wonderful way to move us out of a season of stasis and reflection into a season of activity. It's time to run to win (*1 Corinthians 9:24-27*), with purpose and discipline!

First thing first, we come back to trust. This is a concept that will remain forever tested and forever necessary. Trust is at the core of perfect love. God says He knows the plans He has for us (*Jeremiah 29:11-14, 1 Peter 2:15, 2 Peter 3:9, Micah 6:8, Proverbs 3:5-6 & 16:4, etc.*). Believe in His plan for you and that it will prosper your life in the most authentic and valuable ways. *Ayn Rand* is quoted as saying *All you have to do is look straight and see the road, and when you see it, don't sit looking at it - walk.* I like that sentiment.

No matter how diligently we work to avoid it or how blessed we are, we will inevitably face struggles, hardships, and failures. It is honest and humble to acknowledge, accept, and prepare for our imperfection. *Steve Maraboli* said *Happiness is not the absence of problems. It's the ability to deal with them.* It will be incredibly useful to have some coping skills in your back pocket. Our ability to stay positive and push through is the advantage that helps us overcome the long-suffering parts of life. While God is infused in every part of that ability to overcome (*2 Corinthians 12:8-10*), there are still personal efforts we can make to improve the quality of our days (*1 Timothy 4:16*) and maintain the quality of our temple (*1 Corinthians 6:19*).

God doesn't pick what you eat every day, buy your groceries, cook your meals, pick your outfits, choose your job, or any of these menial tasks. You can choose to pray about all these things and follow God's guidance on them, but ultimately you still make these choices. The little things add up fast, and neglecting your overall health seems to be a door for Satan to attack in subtle ways. What you decide daily impacts your mood which in turn can bring you down overall. Plus, we serve a God of order. That doesn't just apply to a hierarchy. It also applies to the way we live our day to day lives and how stability is vital to success.

What are some things that will help uplift and keep us positive? I'm a believer in preventative and routine maintenance. Everything in this section is about healthy actions that will improve our ability to think clearly and face challenges with strength and ease. This is like keeping your armor well maintained in like-new condition and being prepared as an individual before you step out to work with others. A regularly greased wheel doesn't squeak, right?

These same actions often double as being therapeutic in times of stress. I see it as an efficient and beneficial way to cope. Choosing where you place your focus and making sure it is on positive and constructive things can help us get through challenging times with more ease. God does that too, and you should never neglect prayer in crisis. Absolutely have faith that God will carry you through, but if you have a broken arm, God is not going to teleport you to the hospital. You still have to get in the car and go. He might make sure there's no traffic on the way there to help you out, but please, go to the hospital if you break your arm!

We must maintain a balanced focus on self care. Perfect love is balanced, which means we care for ourselves too. This was touched on briefly in the command about loving our neighbor as ourselves, but now it's time to dig deeper in order to fly freely. If you don't have any self love, then the fruit of loving your neighbor as you love yourself will be bitter, won't it?

Through the experiences of myself and others as well as piles of research, I find it necessary to be clear that true wellness reflects balanced physical, mental, emotional, and spiritual health and a lifetime commitment. Each category is interconnected. They play off of each other. When one area lacks, the other areas suffer. This also means when one area flourishes the other areas benefit. It parallels well to the four elements. Earth is physical, fire is mental, water is emotional, and air is spirit/soul. Together the elements form an ecosystem, just like each balanced area of health forms your high functioning, happy life. Someone who is balanced in all four areas is remarkably harder to rattle in a crisis.

    I have taken courses and done private study from many sources which provide illuminating references to research studies. Also, having struggled with weight issues and faced many emotional hardships, I have consulted with numerous professionals in their fields regarding health including doctors, dietitians, personal trainers, psychologists, college professors, and more. While I am not any of these professionals, I feel I have collected enough data to provide the conclusions that have molded my perspective.

    On top of that, I am a certified life coach. While therapy is about digging into your past for understanding, these practices I utilize focus more on building the future. They are all beneficial life tools related to how God created the mind to function. I simply made the personal choice to help people focus forward outside the professional office setting in my life's work. I do not wish to diagnose or prescribe. That doesn't mean there isn't a time or place for these other fields.

    If you feel that your coping requires guidance and peer support, medication, or that through prayer God is leading you to connect with people, do not hold yourself back or feel ashamed. Emotions exist to be felt and expressed. Suppression is unhealthy. The sooner you face things, the less awful they will be to deal with.

    Please, if you decide anything I share speaks to you, consult with your doctor or other health professionals before making any changes to your lifestyle. One time I recommended a nutritional supplement to a friend, because it really helped me, and the nutrition label was about as harmless as it gets. It turned out she had an uncommon medical condition that gave her migraines when she ingested too much vitamin A, so this product that would have been great for most people wasn't a fit for her. Taking control of your life should not mean avoiding assistance to be sure you're on the right path for you. We should honor that we are all a little different. That was meant to be a blessing (*1 Corinthians 12:4-31*).

Let's tip things off with an analogy! Imagine one of those old televisions from the 1980s with the bunny ear antennas. I am going to use this as a metaphor for your body. The purpose of the tv is to display the images and sounds you choose so you can be immersed in the rest of the world by seeing the news and other media. It receives signals then projects them on the screen. In other words, your body is receiving the signal of your soul energy and allowing it to be in charge so you can interact with the world. You choose the channel, *aka* you make decisions.

If the internal wires were snipped or the tv was dropped and the casing cracked open breaking the glass, then it might stop working. The parallel here is your physical health, and it is of course crucial to your ability to survive in a physical world. Your body is your vessel as well as a temple for the Spirit, and it must be taken care of so it will operate at peak efficiency thusly giving you the full life experience God intended for you. This only becomes more important when you add any form of ministry to your life. You also become an example for others.

What happens if the antenna gets bent and signal is weak? You may get static or lose your channel. What if something happens to the cathode-ray tube? You may lose colors or parts of the picture that are important to the show. This is how I'm correlating mental and emotional health. These two are typically referenced together. While your mind is not your feelings, it impacts them a great deal. People are often diagnosed with mental health problems when they exhibit deep emotional distress or erratic behaviors.

If the antenna gets broken, you no longer receive signal. If the power knob breaks off or cord isn't plugged in, you won't be able to turn it on. Both of these are examples of the need for spiritual health. If you're not plugged in with your faith or at least able to connect with your soul, an imperative part is missing. Most people with this issue tend to keep reaching for things they feel will make them happy or even suffer from depression, but true happiness that fills that void is never found in material possessions.

For the whole tv to work exactly the way it is intended, all these areas need to be functional. Even one piece of the tv having a problem in one category can mess up the whole viewing experience. When you apply this to yourself, remember that you need a balanced focus in mind, body, and Spirit to really get the full picture.

It is one of my biggest pet peeves that all of these areas of health are so divided. When you go to a general doctor for a problem, they aren't usually analyzing your mental state. If there's an issue with that, they refer you to a therapist who in turn is only focusing on your mental state. Your therapist does not give a physical. Neither of them give much credit to spirituality in their practice either. They focus so hard in scientific fact that the spirit is taken out of the equation entirely. However, if you are feeling lethargic, there could be any number of reasons. You may feel spiritually unsatisfied, have a malnutrition problem, be developing cancer, be struggling with bipolar disorder, have a chemical imbalance, just be bored with a monotonous lifestyle, etc. The list of options that cause basic symptoms is too broad.

My other huge pet peeve is that most of these professionals like doctors and therapists spend the majority of their time helping fix what has *already* been broken, whether it's your arm or your heart. There is very little focus on preventative maintenance. Even from a spiritual perspective, many people attend church out of a desire to repent of sins more than to motivate them towards good. It is understandable that this problem happens based on need, and even when focused just on fixing, these professionals take on overwhelming workloads. That means it is important for people to take the personal initiative towards preventative efforts. Church should be something you look forward to as a way to fellowship and worship!

This is an appropriate time to revisit the point that most generalizations are inherently false, because they reflect a majority and ignores outliers, even if those outliers come together to form 49% of your data. Rest assured I know there are professionals out there that go beyond being repair men and women and people who attend church because it invigorates their soul. My goal here is to identify what is happening common place that can be changed for the better so that positive outlier behaviors become the norm.

Physical Health

Let's address our body first (*Romans 12:1*). When talking specifically about physical health, cars provide a great analogy. Fuel is like the food and water we ingest, and quality counts. Oil is like our blood, and we need to keep the system from getting clogged.

Wheels are like our arms and legs that take us where we need to go. The engine is like our heart, constantly firing off pistons to keep the flow going. It wouldn't surprise me if Henry Ford hadn't designed the first automobile with the human body in mind.

If you don't want your car to break down on the side of the road, you have to invest in it. Low quality or the wrong kind of gas can ruin your fuel system. Also, leaving a car to sit too long without being used can cause the oil to become gunky and blow your engine, metal can rust, tires can rot, and so much more. They are designed to move! You will feel it if you are not being active, whether it be physically or spiritually (*Proverbs 10:4 & 12:24 & 19:15, 2 Thessalonians 3:6-10, 1 Timothy 5:8, Genesis 2:15, etc.*). There are endless parallels. The human body is designed to be used and needs proper maintenance and fuel to continue working at peak efficiency.

What you put into your body impacts your output performance. First and foremost, water is vital to existence. The human body is 50-75% water! While doctors recommend drinking a bare minimum of sixty-four ounces per day, many say the actual goal is half your body weight in ounces. My cutoff is around 100 oz a day personally.

As a child I didn't like the taste of water, so I didn't drink it *at all*. To be fair, the water that came out of our tap had to settle for a couple minutes before you could see through it, and water filters weren't commonplace yet. Instead I consumed substantial amounts of orange juice and soda. A significant bit of my weight gain is likely attributed to that practice and the subsequent damage it did to my body.

As an adult, I committed to changing my habits. It took a little over a year for me to fully transition to drinking only water and getting an adequate amount daily. I started by scaling back on soda and juice. As I started incorporating water, I used flavoring additives. Eventually I just drank the flavored water, and with time I stopped using them all together. As a child, I could drink six cans of soda in a row without flinching. Today I only drink water and cannot have a single can of soda without getting an upset stomach. I will occasionally partake in a glass of wine, some ginseng tea with honey, some orange juice, or almond milk, but it's a treat, not a daily thing.

In the modern world, the quality of your water is also a factor. Studies have literally found medications like epilepsy meds, mental health prescriptions, ibuprofen, sex hormones, and others in tap water all the way across the country! In places such as Philadelphia, traces of as many as over fifty different medications were found, and water treatment facilities have no way of scrubbing these out. (*MSNBC reported this study conducted by Associated Press*). Oil and coal companies often have runoff that goes into our streams as well, and water processing plants don't get all of that out either.

On top of it all, some things are intentionally added to our water supply such as *fluoride*. This was done on a national scale to improve the quality of our teeth. Recent studies have suggested fluoride is actually a neurotoxin (*The Lancet Neurology, Volume 13, Issue 3, March 2014*). The best thing you can do is get water processed through reverse osmosis. This removes all the junk while still leaving water drinkable. There are fancy machines that can ph balance your water and purify it even further if you're willing to throw down some serious cash, but I can get three gallons of reverse osmosis water at the grocery store for $1, and it has been sufficient for me. I have certainly felt the difference. Distilled water is not intended for daily consumption, but it can be good on occasion to help pull junk out of you. Switching to clean drinking water was like removing heavy chains from myself that I didn't even know were there.

Being hydrated sufficiently is the easiest part of the equation. When it comes to food there is such a massive haze of confusion built around what is considered healthy. It almost feels intentional, because it allows every new diet to appear as the cutting edge science that will turn the tide for you. Let me simplify it all for you in two categories - quantity and quality.

As far as quantity is concerned, any dietitian I have ever talked to will tell you eating smaller portions more frequently is best. I aim to eat 200-400 calories every three hours (*9am, noon, 3pm, 6pm, and on a late night a snack at 9pm*). This reflects my work and family schedule appropriately. It is also fitting for my height, weight and personal goals. For someone with a different height or build that might be too little or too much in one sitting, but to me it is just right.

Eating less at one time but doing it more frequently gives the body the energy it needs to get by without overdoing it. Extra unused food in one sitting will be converted to fat and stored. Also, if you are one of those people who is so busy they only eat once or twice a day, it leaves your body unsure of when it's next meal will come and also promotes storage of fat for emergencies. Balance and moderation are key.

When it comes to quality, I am a bit of a purist and stick to as many *non-gmo organic whole foods* as possible. Studies are now beginning to show evidence in the long term that gmo foods can have a negative effect on the human body, though it is heavily debated. Even without that information, I just don't like the idea of people messing with the way God made things. As far as buying organic, as a general rule, if someone is required to wear a hazmat suit to spray a pesticide, then I don't want to eat it in my food. You can't wash pesticides off of foods that have absorbed them through either saturated soil or sprays. Whole foods will maintain the highest nutritional benefit and not have added sodium, sugar, preservatives, and chemicals.

In short, what God gave us to eat should be enough. He made it that way for a reason. Thankfully this is becoming more affordable and accessible. That doesn't mean you can never treat yourself to something like chocolate or ice cream, but your body is far more capable of handling processed foods as occasional treats rather than every day. The Bible also speaks against gluttony pretty strongly (*Proverbs 23:20-21 & 28:7, Philippians 3:19, etc.*).

Food breaks down into three major categories - carbohydrates, fat, and protein. Carbohydrates come from things like starches, grains, and sugar. They are your body's first resort for energy. As I stated previously, when you don't use all the energy you ingested, your body stores it in your fat cells for later use.

The majority of eating plans on the market today are based in some way on a low carbohydrate structure (*typically something like 20-50g per day or less*) where you eat higher healthy fats and protein. When looking at a nutrition label, dietary fiber is subtracted from the total carbohydrates. You eat more meat and veggies, low amounts of fruit and dairy, and cut out things like bread and sweets. Call it whatever fad name you want, with minimal variations the science will point back to eating low carb. When your body runs out of carbs for energy, it will then use the stored fat as a secondary source, hence the weight loss effect. Again, if you happen to be hypoglycemic, an approach like this could be dangerous, so always consult a physician before making major changes.

When you consider that one burger from a fast food chain can have on average 400-600 calories with forty or more grams of carbohydrates *before* fries and a soda, and stack on top of that how the world has become more sedentary with technological advances, it is clear to see how weight gain has become a serious problem. Gluttony is commonplace. According to the Center for Disease Control, 1 in 3 American adults are considered medically obese as well as 1 in 6 children age 6-19. Our high intake of sugars and overeating are largely to blame. All processed and fast food has added sugar anymore, even bread.

Obesity has become an epidemic, and unfortunately it is the source of many of the top leading preventable causes of death including but not limited to heart disease and diabetes. Furthermore, the mentality that thin wins which dominates popular culture is creating a subculture of eating disorders which are considered a mental health problem. According to the *National Association of Anorexia Nervosa and Associated Disorders*, anorexia is the third most common long term illness in teens. 95% of eating disorders belong to youth age 12-26, and anorexia is the leading cause of death up to twelve times higher than any other condition in ages 12-24.

The best thing we can do is promote health being a balance between both ends of the spectrum. You should not starve yourself, nor should you over indulge. There is a centered sweet spot and it takes awareness and effort. Make *health* more important than appearance!

After carbohydrates, we come to fats. Eating fat is not the same as storing or having fat, so don't get them confused. Some fats are good, and some are not. Typically lower carb foods are higher in fat (*and/or protein*) like for example avocados. This is good, and doctors have begun to suggest eating healthy fats may even contribute to reversing the effect of diabetes. Essentially if you count your *carbs*, *calories*, and *chemicals* you are doing pretty good.

Understand that this is all highly simplified, and there is plenty of research you can and should still dive into. For example, products with labels that say *fat free* will replace the flavor lost from the removal of fat with sugar. They use complex carbs that are harder to break down, so avoid them. Fresh fruit has simple sugars and are not the same as processed sugars. Also, when you reduce your carb intake, you become less effective at retaining water. Sodium if not overdone is helpful with that problem. As you can see, tips, tricks, and details exist in abundance.

Yes, you absolutely can get all the nutrition you need from food alone. I will even go so far as to say that I think it will be the medicine of the future; however, most people don't eat a diverse enough selection of foods to meet their needs. If you are not getting balanced and satisfying nutrition, your body may communicate that to you through cravings or health problems.

The color of your fruits and vegetables is one indicator of what nutrition they consist of, so enjoy the whole rainbow! Green foods typically purify and detox, yellow support joint health, purple support longevity of life, and red are great for your heart. If you struggle to diversify your selection or are on a reduced calorie plan, consider finding a quality multi-vitamin or mineral to fill in the blanks.

Foods that are good for maintaining balanced health are really the same foods recommended for weight loss. Don't be fooled, your health is not a fad. It's a lifetime commitment! Don't shift your eating habits thinking that when you hit a certain goal you can go back to the old way. There's no turning back. Focus forward on better health, and the scale and your clothing will eventually reflect your effort.

Next we have protein, which is a great segue into exercise and body output. Your muscles fulfill many vital roles, and protein is their fuel. Making sure they get that fuel is important. The most prevalent source of protein is meat, though it can be found in plenty of other foods as well such as broccoli, spinach, and mushrooms. We have already discussed my view on eating meat, so I won't rehash it, and I won't judge your perspective. I just know that I have been somewhere between vegetarian and vegan for a year now, and my health has improved, so meat is not essential. Ideally if you do choose to eat meat, lean meats like chicken, turkey, and fish are the healthiest and most affordable options. Keep red meats to a minimum. You might also find it interesting to do a *scientific* study on the meats that are considered unclean in the Old Testament (*Leviticus 11*).

Mobility is the major job of your muscles. The cool thing is that they are also the furnace that burns your fat. This is one of the reasons exercise is necessary not only in weight loss but a general healthy routine. When you exercise, muscle fibers become damaged and even tear. They rebuild stronger and larger with repetition, and protein aids in that healing process. The larger the muscle furnace is, the more fat they can burn. Exercises that lift and support your body weight are great if you need an at home regimen. Your glute muscles are some of the largest in your body, so engaging them in your workouts with things like walks or jogging can be very effective for weight loss. God's design for the human body is seriously fascinating!

Everyone will have different preferences and limitations when committing to an exercise routine. I used to enjoy yoga for how it improved my energy flow and built core strength. I stopped doing it when I accepted Christ. There are Christian alternatives to yoga. If that is something you would enjoy, check out *Streth 'N' Praise* by *LMM* at *www.LeaMichelleMinistries.com* for more info. My family likes to engage in fun activities that breed exercise benefits like hiking or swimming. Plus, doing these things together not only teaches appreciation of healthy habits to our children but provides more family bonding time. Yes, I'm a fan of lifting at the gym and appreciate the way it allows you to target muscle groups. I just don't like staying in one place all the time.

It's good to push hard, don't get me wrong. Just don't hurt yourself. When I first started planking, I could barely hold it for five seconds without wanting to cry. Each day I held out for a couple seconds longer, and now I can consistently hold them for over one minute every time. Your muscles have their own sense of memory, and progress only comes when you push yourself further. If you don't, eventually the same routine won't breed results anymore and you will plateau. Changing up your routine once in awhile is good for overcoming that.

At the end of the day, just realize that all body movement requires calorie expenditure, even shivering and laughter. Get off the couch and live a hearty life! It is good for your health (*Psalm 16:11*).

What about the things we put in our body that aren't food or water? Since I am a purist, I apply that principle to medicine and choose to be something closer to homeopathic, though I don't use the diluted drops. I recall even as a child I was nervous about the idea of taking any medication, even antibiotics, and would do my best to wait out my sickness to let my immune system build strength on its own. If I had to take medicine, I would, but I always tried to wait it out first.

I'm not necessarily recommending that, but healthy caution

is never ill advised. As common diseases like for example gonorrhea or malaria have developed drug resistance over time, they are edging towards incurable. Super bugs can develop as bacteria become exposed to antibiotics and adapt ways to protect themselves. Prevention in many cases can be as simple as cleanliness and sound judgment. Wash your hands!

Aside from the occasional Advil or expectorant, I have treated every cold and ailment for the last several years with things like echinacea for sore throats, elderberry for colds, and so on. Since making this decision, the couple of times I felt sick enough to go to the doctor they told me there was nothing they could do to help. I was not given a prescription, and they told to me continue doing what I was already doing.

As I mentioned previously, I also experienced a car accident awhile back. While nobody was hurt, it gave me anxiety to drive again feeling as though history could repeat itself. I went to the doctor for a therapy referral and was immediately offered two prescriptions without so much as even a stethoscope to the chest. I refused to even bother filling one of them seeing as it was a class IV substance, but I opted to try the other given the doctor's confidence. It had an adverse effect on me, and I was overrun by depression. The first week I was on it my employer even noticed the difference. I quit taking it after that. The experience unsettled me. Not every medicine is for every person.

Overall, I have been very pleased and successful with this approach, even enjoying the use of essential oils and probiotics. While I never personally invested in drops, I have friends who do use them with incredible results. There is a lot of contention around this subject, so look to credible sources backed by experience if you choose to look into it.

Mental/Emotional Health

I have a riddle for you! *I am your constant companion. I am your greatest helper or heaviest burden. I will push you onward or drag you down to failure. I am completely at your command. Half of the things you do might as well turn over to me and I will do them - quickly and correctly. I am easily managed - you must be firm with me. Show me exactly how you want something done and after a few lessons, I will do it automatically. I am the servant of great people, and alas, of all failures as well. Those who are great, I have made great. Those who are failures, I have made failures. I am not a machine though I work with the precision of a machine plus the intelligence of a person. You may run me for profit or run me for ruin - it makes no difference to me. Take me, train me, be firm with me, and I will place the world at your feet. Be easy with me and I will destroy you.* **Who am I?**

The answer is your habits! Studies show that it takes twenty-one days of consistency to establish a new healthy habit, but once you get through the hard part, life gets much easier. It takes commitment, a reason you want it enough to do the work, accountability, and a plan to move forward. Prayer is also way more helpful than you think. If you reread that riddle, several of those statements apply to Christ too. He helps us develop good habits! My prayers for energy boosts, willpower, and support always get answered.

Taking care of your physical health through daily habits allows your emotional and spiritual health to not only operate better but also to have more of your focus. Emotional health can be trickier to address since it is often heavily impacted by our interactions with others. However, that doesn't mean your self talk isn't incredibly important.

What do you see when you look in the mirror? While the technical function of a mirror is to reflect a physical image so we can see what we look like, the truth is most of the time they reflect our emotional state as well, consciously and subconsciously. Not only do we see the body language we are presenting to the world of our current mood such as frowns or smiles, but most people use a mirror to determine what they want to change. That could be as simple as brushing or styling your hair, wanting to whiten your teeth, or seeing that pesky acne breakout. It can also show sadness, tiredness, sense of style, and other things we feel and then judge ourselves about. If the Bible says we aren't supposed to judge because that is only for God, that should include no longer judging ourselves so harshly. The command said to *love* your neighbor as yourself, not *hate*.

Humans are very visual as a species. Self reflection, both literal and metaphorical, is a crucial part of forming personal identity. Therefore, when you look in the mirror or even at photographs of yourself, it is important to remain positive. I like to encourage people to say positive affirmations out loud in front of a mirror like we did with the battle cry. It reinforces the formation of positive beliefs to our brains through sight, thought, and voice.

The language you use with yourself is taken very literally by your subconscious mind. In Neuro Linguistic Programming you learn that simple shifts have powerful impacts. For example, it's not good to tell yourself or even a friend off handedly that you just don't have time for exercise or how much you hate your job. Your subconscious mind (*which I feel has some connections to the Holy Spirit*) wants to form a true reality. Therefore, if you say you don't have time, your mind will be working in the background to make that true, helping you search for excuses.

If your brain is a computer, what search criteria are you giving it with your words? People will so often use this excuse with faith saying they just don't have time to read the Bible or pray, but I call baloney on that! You make time for what is important to you. Dramatized readings of the first four books of the New Testament are on the video playlist to help you get started if that will be easier for you. Listen while you do housework.

Another example is words like *but* or *should*. I want these words to set off alarms in your head to pay attention! *But* is a word that typically comes in front of excuses. *Should* is a word that typically comes in front of limiting beliefs. Being aware of how often you use these words can help enlighten you to where you are creating problems for yourself and provide opportunities for you to change things up.

Eliminating limiting beliefs often starts with diving into conditioning, which put simply is what we were subconsciously taught to believe is true. The majority of who you are is developed by age seven, because the young mind is in one of its highest states of learning at that time. Infants will observe the facial expression of their mothers to learn what emotional response is correct to a stimulus. They learn responses, whether they are loving or hateful.

If you grew up with both parents working a 9-5 traditional job, then you might become an adult who feels that is the only way to provide for your family. This limiting belief could stop you from trusting yourself enough to start your own business, work from home, or even work a different shift. It might even stop you from ministry. It's not exactly a high paying gig, but if you trust in God to provide, you will always have everything you need, and your career will be satisfying. Limiting beliefs can be overcome through a process of identifying them, debunking their validity, and replacing them.

If I dig any further into that, this book will become a really long coaching session. So just know that these little shifts make a significant impact on your success. Little things make up the big things (*2 Corinthians 10:5*)! Instead, it is better to tell yourself that you *will* make time for what is important and that you *can* find the resources if you look, ultimately developing confidence in your ability to succeed (*Matthew 6:33*). In turn your subconscious mind will work towards those goals with you, helping you identify ways to fit things into your schedule and locate those resources. Again, I find that when I pray about these things, opportunities will fall into my lap if I'm taking a good course of action. Obstacles will repeatedly surface when I'm not.

In essence, you teach your subconscious mind how to perceive yourself and your life. The more frequently you engage more of your senses, the better what you are learning will stick. Bible verses and positive quotes can be written on sticky notes and put on your mirrors or other places you visit often such as the refrigerator or your desk at work. This way you have constant reminders of your positive intentions. Support the image of yourself that reflects traits like love, strength, respect, dignity, tact, perseverance, compassion, intelligence, and humility. These are all traits the Bible praises! A couple examples of verses that would be great for some sticky notes are *Philippians 4:8* and *Proverbs 3:5-6*.

Morning is the best time to start a healthy routine. The first twenty minutes of your day will set the tone for the rest of it! Morning exercise, a balanced breakfast, and a glass of water help your body systems and metabolism get fired up after a night of rest. This is the optimal time for carbs as fuel for your day. Furthermore, a morning prayer and attitude of gratitude can help you set a tone of positivity that carries forward. Start by stating things you appreciate about what you will be doing and reinforcing that you are a person worthy of love, respect, and happiness. Don't forget to throw on your armor!

For example, if you have a job, express gratitude to God that you are employed and have money coming in rather than being bummed that you'll see that annoying coworker. If you have a dentist appointment that day, tell yourself how glad you are to be able to have your dental health taken care of instead of thinking about how much you hate the process of getting a cleaning. Then proceed with your prayers and affirmations, and please be sure to say them with a smile and as much sincerity as you have in you. Here is something I wrote back when I was focusing on my weight loss. I wasn't focused in my faith at the time, so I *challenge* you in the space below to modify it to reflect God's role in your efforts. If it doesn't fit your personal goals, then write a brand new one.

I love myself, and that means
my physical, mental, emotional, and spiritual health are a priority.
I am loved.
When I am happy and healthy, it benefits my friends, family, and society.
I set personal goals, and I will not allow myself to make excuses.
Nobody else can do this for me.
I can and will surround myself with supportive people.
I am completely capable.
My struggles do not define me.
My weight does not define me.
I define me, and I choose to take the necessary steps to succeed.
Balance is healthy.
I will not starve myself.
I will not over indulge.
I will increase my physical activity and make time for exercise.
I will remember the importance of quality rest.
I will tell myself I can, because I am honest with myself.

Make a choice to see the positive, and eventually with time and consistency that habit will become your natural response to situations. It allows you to take personal control by not letting the outside world change your inner state. That is ***willpower*** and ***fortitude***! Choosing to reinforce the fact that not every situation is negative will reduce stress and disease and breed more inner calm and peace. That control is at the basis of emotional health.

Studies suggest that those who spend time in reflection tend to demonstrate more qualities of success. Harvard conducted a study where one group of employees used the last fifteen minutes of their day journaling, while other employees continued work during that time. Performance and productivity increased 22.8% for those who used that time writing a review of the day in a journal. I recommend closing out your day reviewing the events and how they were handled. Journaling can also have a secondary benefit of allowing you to look back on change and progress over time. Personally I have a prayer journal, again bringing God into my personal efforts. I couldn't do any of this without Him, so I do my best to honor that even in my personal efforts.

Another under rated stress reliever is nature. This is part of why I love to go hiking. I call it fresh air therapy. Get outdoors and take it all in! Dr. Joe Dispenza says, *"In clinical studies, we have proven that two hours of nature sounds a day significantly reduce stress hormones up to 800% and activates 500-600 DNA segments known to be responsible for healing and repairing the body."* Clearly God designed it this way!

The last facet of physical health I want to touch on is rest. Obviously if God designated that we should take a whole day for rest on the Sabbath each week, He knows it is important for our health. It is recommended to get an average of 6-8 hours of uninterrupted sleep per night. That can be difficult for some people whether they have a new baby waking up for feedings, work third shift, or even just have trouble getting comfortable.

Melatonin is a popular recommendation for those who have trouble initially falling asleep, though it should be cleared by a doctor and not abused. For those who sleep during the day, curtains designed to completely block out sunlight and hgh supplements have been successful for me in the past. Whatever you need to do to make it happen, get it done. Sleep is a crucial time for your body to recover. It does *so much* healing work during that time, which is why bed rest is often recommended when you're sick. In turn, lack of it can also cause problems, such as for example throwing off your cortisol production causing sweets cravings.

Rest is not just about sleep, though. When it comes to your muscles, there is such a thing as overdoing your exercise. Personal trainers will often suggest a 2:1 split, where one day is spent focusing on the upper body, the next day is spent on the lower body, and the next day is a rest day to allow proper time for recovery.

Spiritual Health

When all is said and done, I honestly feel that simple self awareness and positive self care *is* a large part of spiritual health. It involves honoring your personal needs and the gifts you've been given by God in a way that creates a deep sense of fulfillment. When you nurture the relationship with Him, He nurtures you. The Bible supports all these things, so be sure to include some time meditating on the Word. As I stated, your subconscious mind wants to shape a reality that is true, so if you are a doubter about spirituality you may be reinforcing a disconnect from yourself and the experience of life.

Take the time to practice mindfulness and generally honor that your spiritual self has a voice. We may live in the physical world, but as we have discussed, the point of being here is based more in the spiritual realm. Allow the body to amplify the soul, not the soul to be controlled by the material world.

Charity work is also a wonderful way to nurture your spiritual health. It is the cornerstone of brotherly love, and the reward is the way you are uplifted by seeing someone else smile. They say there are three T's of giving, but I believe there are four - *talk, time, talent,* and *treasure.* Even when you don't have money to give, there are other ways to be of service. This is also a very healthy way to practice humility and remove yourself from constantly focusing inward. We are all here together! We are told not to do our good deeds in front of others in order to be seen (*Matthew 6:1*), which reflects a need for pure intent. Do acts of kindness because it is the right thing to do and you *want* to help. Don't just do it for attention or praise.

I am also a believer that spiritual health grows through seeking your soul's purpose. This can be a challenging task if your physical and emotional health are not in decent shape, which is why

I saved it for last. People tend to talk about destiny and fate as though it's either all or nothing, but as I have said, I see a blend of both perspectives.

I believe everyone is here with a God given purpose, whether it is to make an impact on humanity or to learn personal lessons. God has a plan in mind for us. That doesn't mean everyone lives up to their calling, and we must still make personal efforts to get there. Many people find career paths tied to these missions. A person who experienced loss or abuse in this life and learned how to cope with their grief may find a calling in being a social worker or therapist. A person who discovers a joy for creating with cloth and color might find themselves designing clothing. Someone who realizes their natural leadership skills might get into politics or ministry.

Everything you experience can be translated into a service. We thrive as a community where everyone contributes. Don't commit to the limiting belief that there is only one way to earn a living in this world. The most successful people have passion and determination behind their career choice and will pioneer a way for their passions to support them financially. Trusting God to lead that path all but assures success. Just keep your head on straight. ***Gain is not godliness, but godliness with contentment is great gain*** (*1 Timothy 6:5-8*).

I bounced around so much in earlier life. I found passions in artistic self-expression like music, photography, writing, and dance. I experienced a heavy amount of loss, struggles with weight and health, and relationship difficulties on many levels. I discovered talents in public speaking, writing, teaching, and compassion. As a whole, I learned a multitude of things that culminated in my ability to self publish this book. I combined every experience into what I hope will be an extensive career of reaching into peoples' lives and helping guide them to God through Christ, lift them when they fall, and bring their joy and truth to the surface.

I had to live countless experiences to collect the pieces of this puzzle. That doesn't mean when I saw for example the blue puzzle piece that I knew whether it was sky or water or someone's clothing in the finished picture. I may have seen it wasn't an edge piece, but most pieces aren't. It just didn't all make sense when it was happening, and it wasn't intended to. I spent close to thirty years thinking *why me*, and eventually I said *oh, that's why*.

The journey to discovering your soul's purpose is for you, to challenge and change you. If it doesn't make sense, that's ok. With awareness and focus it will come together in time. If you need help, ask for it. Guides are everywhere, both in prayer to God and in the physical world. Interaction is a gift. There are plenty of people like me who want to help you piece together your own puzzle.

Every topic covered here could practically have a whole separate book written that expands on each individual paragraph. The overview provided is intended as a guidepost and an arrow as you go, not to replace your ability to experience the journey. However, health in particular has been so clouded with confusion and poor guidance for so long that I hope this has helped make it more simplified and manageable. Take care of the vessel which allows the steps your soul takes to happen gracefully. If you trip on one of these steps, realize it's a rocky path for a reason. The greatest growth and love will occur when you allow yourself to learn from experiences with appreciation and gratitude. Don't worry if it takes time. If it were easy, it wouldn't be worthwhile.

In the space below, write down any bits of routine that you feel have been helpful or might uplift you in your walk. Address all four categories of physical, mental, emotional, and spiritual health. Do you feel that you know what God's plan is for you, or are you uncertain? Given everything we have covered to this point, do you feel that you are on track with God's plan, or have you been hitting detours? If so, what are they? Sometimes writing things out can help you find clarity and form connections when things are unclear. Reflect and pray about God's will for you, and ask him to help you fly through all things with grace.

_____
_____
_____
_____
_____
_____
_____
_____
_____
_____
_____
_____
_____
_____

14. Rescue from Without

*Brethren, if any of you do err from the truth, and one convert him;
let him know, that he which converteth the sinner
from the error of his way
shall save a soul from death,
and shall hide a multitude of sins.*
James 5:19-20

Rescue is about saving someone from a dangerous or difficult situation. In our context, there are two meanings. The first we will address is how we rescue each other through fellowship. Our interactions as a unified body in Christ need to be exactly that - *unified*. When we fight amongst ourselves, we are missing the whole message of scripture and not even remotely demonstrating it for others to see its benefit (*James 4:1-3*). Leadership will be a separate topic. In the current climate of the church, it feels important to differentiate fellowship from leadership and clarify this part comes first.

The second application you could potentially fit under this heading would be a discussion about the rapture. Honestly, though, I have less than zero desire to crack open that can of worms. While it is certainly a fascinating and relevant study with *at least* three major interpretations floating around to evaluate, it is simply not the point of this book. The point here is to focus on preparing for the return of Christ. No man knows the day or hour (*Matthew 24:36-44*). It is only logical to focus on how to behave here and now, not play into the devil's distraction tactics by trying to set a date. Feel free to pursue a study on your own. However, if you want to hear the perspective I have found to be most scripturally sound in my own study, I will refer you to the YouTube playlist for videos from *Leeland Jones* and some others.

In reading an article about this step of the hero's journey, this rescue is often designed as almost an act of reaping what you have sown. It is implied that this rescue always comes from someone who previously appeared in the journey, and that it was earned. They also identified how it most often appears as a surprise. This is where our friends come to the rescue. If we had not made friends previously, we wouldn't have this grand rescue. It also alludes to our friend

Christ, who has promised the resurrection and rescue at his return.

Right now, this is a call to ***fellowship***. We all know that where two or three gather in the name of Christ, he will be there (*Matthew 18:20*). Hold close to your brothers and sisters in Christ! I would never suggest to anyone that they should segregate from people who do not believe if the friendship can be peaceful and respectful. Even if you never speak of faith, the way you live a balanced life in Christ is a ministry in itself (*1 Timothy 4:12*). In *1 Corinthians 7:12-14* the apostle Paul suggests a similar principle in reference to being married to a nonbeliever.

People won't always confront you regarding what they observe about you. There are people I haven't spoken with in ages who will message me out of the blue saying they've been following my journey on social media for a long time and they feel like they know me personally enough to open up to me. I earned their trust by just being an open, honest person, so they respected the advice I could give when they were troubled. If they appreciate that advice, ministry can be as simple as planting the seed that it was all Biblical, then respecting their space to process that thought. If you are feeling brave enough to strike up a conversation about faith with a friend who is not a believer, feel free to blame me. You are welcome to tell them you've been reading this awesome book that has you in thought, and if they don't mind you just wanted someone to talk to about what was in it. There you go, *excuse provided*.

Not everyone will be at that place like you are, and that's ok too. Trust that God's timing for each person is different and plant seeds when you can. If it causes tension, remember what was covered about a scriptural approach to conflict resolution. Do your best to follow Christ's instruction and pray diligently rather than making hasty decisions. The way you handle your problems is just as much a reflection of you as it is of your faith. Sometimes you will have to cut ties with someone for your own wellbeing. That can't be denied. I never reach for the scissors, though. I acknowledge that I only need them when someone hands them to me.

At the end of the day, having quality fellowship with others of the faith will more often than not be a lifeline for you. They will be people who understand and respect your love for God. They will turn to scripture just like you, and often help you see things from a fresh perspective. Again, *Romans 14* makes a strong point about not judging others for not being at the same stage in faith as you are.

Where you are weak, your neighbor may be strong. Down the road you may find the opposite to be true. We are all on a journey that doesn't happen overnight. Respect their process if you want them to respect yours.

Keep all interactions at a level of loving exchange (*1 Thessalonians 5:11, Romans 1:11-12*). Never talk down to people, especially if they come to you in confidence to discuss a matter. Break down the word fellowship - we are all *fellows* on the same *ship.* Be hospitable without complaint (*1 Peter 4:9, Romans 12:13*). Most importantly, never forget the most important message of Christ. Forgiveness is part of the essence of love.

It is good to be honest with each other if we discern someone may have false understanding or is straying from the path. Scripture refers to this as admonishing each other. *Behold, thou hast instructed many, and thou hast strengthened the weak hands. Thy words have upholden him that was falling, and thou hast strengthened the feeble knees* (*Job 4:3-4*). I feel like the times I have spoken up in this capacity have been led by the Holy Spirit, so if you feel that urge in your gut, follow it.

Sometimes you will be approached for advice. Other times, once you reach a more leadership capacity or even just form a deeper friendship with someone, you may reach out of your own volition (*1 Samuel 23:16*). Just be certain that your words are shared in love, not judgment. Placing people in a defensive position will shut them off from hearing you, and it has the potential to push them away from faith instead of drawing them closer to it.

And let us consider one another to provoke unto love and to good works, not forsaking the assembling of ourselves together, as the manner of some is, but exhorting one another, and so much the more as ye see the day approaching (*Hebrews 10:24-25*). We are meant to build each other up, not tear each other down! We are to interact with humility, patience, tolerance, love, and peace, and to do all of them diligently (*Ephesians 4:2-3*). It is therefore incredibly important to choose your words wisely as well as your method of communication.

While the internet allows us to connect across great distances in ways we would never have been able to before, remember again that only 7% of communication is words. Message services or commenting on posts is like asking for someone to misinterpret your words when it comes to sensitive topics. I have learned over the years that when I don't take the time to choose my words carefully in written mediums, my point is often misconstrued or missed entirely. However, when I overcompensate and get wordy, either nobody has the attention span for that or they will sometimes take it as being preachy. If I don't specify that I'm not judging and only conversing, people make assumptions. Yet when I do specify, it can sometimes plant a thought that wasn't there. It seems to me that it is just more effective to speak on the phone, via video chat, or in person. My friend and I like to use the mic voice recording feature in messenger apps so we can talk, but the exchange is still on our own time like a text message.

  Fellowship is more than just conversation, though. A family that prays together, stays together! That doesn't just apply to parents and children, but our church family as well. *Acts 1:14* provides an example that this was a widespread practice in Christ's time. Of course applying *Matthew 18:20* to prayer can create powerful results! There are also many verses about singing together, as a form of unified worship (*Ephesians 5:19, Colossians 3:16, etc.*). A church that comes together as a whole for charity can also move some mountains! I have seen some phenomenal church led programs like backpack giveaways, food drives, and even free medical services.

  To wrap this up, I would like to share what the apostle Paul said in *Philippians 1:3-8*. He holds such an affectionate feeling towards the fellowship he had with these people. I can only hope that we all get the chance to experience this same level of quality in our connections with one another. *I thank my God upon every remembrance of you, always in every prayer of mine for you all making request with joy for your fellowship in the gospel from the first day until now. Being confident of this very thing, that he which hath begun a good work in you will perform it until the day of Jesus Christ. Even as it is meet* (meaning equitable, in character, innocent, holy, just) *for me to think this of you all, because I have you in my heart; inasmuch as both in my bonds, and in the defense and confirmation of the gospel, ye all are partakers of my grace. For God is my record, how greatly I long after you all in the bowels of Jesus Christ.*

In the following space, write what you think makes a good friend in Christ. What characteristics do they have? How would they treat you? What would they do if you came to them with a problem or concern and needed counsel? How would they respond if you tried to offer them correction or advice? After you have outlined how you would like to be treated in fellowship, agree to treat others the same way in the spirit and name of Christ. Reflect on any past experiences that could have been better. What could you have done differently? Pray for God to help strengthen your communication skills and love for your neighbor so that you can honor Him going forward.

15. Crossing the Return Threshold

O give thanks unto the Lord; call upon His name:
make known His deeds among the people.
Sing unto Him, sing psalms unto him:
talk ye of all his wondrous works.
Give ye in His holy name:
let the heart of them rejoice that seek the Lord.
Psalm 105:1-3

You've returned home from your studies, a victorious champion over your trials! You've found the courage to step out of your bubble and are trusting God to lead you. You've taken the time to engage in Christian fellowship, and hopefully that has built on the depth of your love for God and added a width by sharing it with others in fellowship. Perhaps you now feel ready to add height to your faith and test the waters of leadership. Crossing that threshold should start simple and pure. Let's look at how to dip our toes in that water.

I think every true Christian at some point will have that moment where they fear for those who will be lost in the end times. It goes beyond just sharing truth with people, because *saved people save people* (*Proverbs 11:30*). The first time it occurred to me that we might see *Revelation* play out in our lifetime, it made me panic stricken to wonder how much time we had left. It propelled me forward in many ways. As my faith grew, I feared that less and less. The peace of the Spirit helped me realize that we cannot save time. We can only spend it, but it can be spent wisely or foolishly. If you think others are not ready and you know in your heart the scripture is true, it becomes time to step up (*Isaiah 6:8*).

You will encounter many people who will be downright offended at the thought that they need to be saved. Choose your words *carefully*. I used to be one of those people, because I thought I understood more than I really did. I didn't like answering the door for people holding a Bible in their hand. I felt uncomfortable if someone asked me if Christ was my Lord and Savior. The bolder these people were, the more uncomfortable it made me, which would push me away more than it would draw me in. Fishing from the right side of the boat means lighting the spark of curiosity and leading people towards asking questions rather than just approaching them bluntly. There is some dispute about who actually said this quote originally, but *Antoine de Saint-Exupery* is credited as saying *If you want to build a ship, don't drum up the men and women to gather wood, divide the work, and give orders. Instead, teach them to yearn for the vast and endless sea.*

The best place to start is at home. Begin the conversation with friends, family, and if you have them your spouse and children. If you cannot lead your home, you cannot lead others (*1 Timothy 3:4-5*). Truthfully, that may be harder in the respect that we are often not accepted by those closest to us when we first enter the faith (*Matthew 13:57, Mark 6:4, Luke 4:24*). Their opinion is more important to us than that of a stranger. If we offend them, we can't just avoid them later. If they criticize our beliefs, we take it way more personally. At the same time, they are more likely to take you seriously than a stranger. In that respect, it is easier.

We live in a time where people are finally starting to pay attention to how our words line up with our actions. Talk is cheap if it isn't supported by your deeds. When you are first crossing this threshold, the easiest way to start is through your example. If your behavior matters, then it is a service to both you and those around you to live in truth and be a light through your life. It's a two birds, one stone kind of deal. Be *doers* of the Word (*James 1:22*)! Share openly and invite others to participate with you. Invite people to attend church with you or participate in your Christian support group. Draw people in to the fun and community part of faith!

Revelation 13:10 says those who kill by the sword will die by the sword. You cannot *fight* for peace. Conflict is the polar opposite of peace. You can only choose it instead of conflict. Then you will have it. The final battle was meant to be an internal one. That doesn't mean there won't be people who fulfill prophecy through physical war. As I have said repeatedly, I can't choose for you, only offer up the lessons I've learned and hope you will take them to heart.

Just know that as *Ghandi* said, *There is no road to peace, peace is the road.* That is why the blanket name for all of my ministry projects is *Peace Is The Road*. The Bible teaches us to walk in peace, not just dream about it. This is at the foundation of any leader that steps up to spread the gospel. Christ was called the Prince of Peace (*Isaiah 9:6*). *Blessed are the peacemakers, for they shall be called the children of God (Matthew 5:9).*

Recall the parable of the fishermen I shared in the beginning. Fish were not being caught out of the left side of the boat, but then Christ summoned them to fish from the right side and they caught plenty! If you reach out to strike someone, they will cower back in fear. When you reach out to people in love, they will reach back. You may need to adapt a little to meet the person where they are at, but love is a universal language God built everyone to be able to speak.

Revelation 11:18 says those who destroy the earth will be destroyed. A leader will demonstrate a desire to work together instead of escalating conflict. They will show love and respect to the earth rather than being destructive. For example, our household recycles everything we can and follows a minimal waste policy. We buy most of our clothes second hand and pass them on to others if they are in decent shape. We will pick up trash when we go hiking. We walk when we're able, and carpool when we can. These are some simple efforts to help reduce our impact on the environment. *Reduce, reuse, recycle!*

As far as leading in your words, I think a safe place to start is simple yet thought provoking things like occasionally sharing a Bible verse on your social media page and letting scripture speak for itself. You could share Christian content like videos or blog articles, and just be transparent about the steps you take in your faith journey. Find other leaders you like and share what moves you for others to appreciate.

In turn, be more conscientious that you are *not* sharing things God would not like. That doesn't mean everything you post has to be about God. That means don't share things that are crude, vulgar, or directly in contradiction to scripture. Definitely don't air your dirty laundry online or go there to vent. There's a difference between criticizing/name calling/shaming/judging and *sharing* what you learned from an experience. Know how you influence people. Choose your words wisely.

When I learned that baptism was meant to be a public declaration, I decided to share photo and video on my wall and leave the privacy setting to public. Literally anyone can see, and all I did was model an action we are told we must do! I thought I might get some criticism for it, but it rallied so much support around me. In turn, other onlookers had a chance to see all that love. I feel pretty blessed about the whole experience.

Take time to be supportive of others as well. Don't just project your inner state. Respond to the inner state being projected by others. Sometimes the most profound moments of ministry are found in consoling someone who is sad, hurt, or lonely. A hug is like connecting your bodies so the Spirit can be felt by a friend or loved one. *Jimi Hendrix* is attributed for saying *Knowledge speaks, but wisdom listens.* These are profound words indeed. Provide an ear that allows others to be heard, and truly try to understand how they feel. Mountains of pain can be moved away in an interaction where love is present.

Once you have the light in your heart, just let it shine. *Matthew 5:13-16* explains it elegantly. *Ye are the salt of the earth, but if the salt have lost his savour, wherewith shall it be salted? It is thenceforth good for nothing, but to be cast out, and to be trodden under foot of men. Ye are the light of the world. A city that is set on a hill cannot be hid. Neither do men light a candle and put it under a bushel, but on a candlestick, and it giveth light unto all that are in the house. Let your light so shine before men, that they may see your good works, and glorify your Father which is in heaven.*

Just let your light shine in its natural beauty, friend. That is what it is designed to do! Keep focused on that pure intent Christ placed in your heart. In a health sense, salt also helps us retain water and adds flavor. This is a great metaphor for how disciples as the salt of the earth help us retain the waters of life.

Simple and subtle things go a long way. They plant seeds and allow people to be drawn in magnetically to your positivity rather than trying to yank or push them towards God. For many people, this will be as far as they go in ministry. As long as you are not denying your faith and live actively in your truth, you are doing your part (*Luke 12:8*). Focusing beyond your own salvation to that of others is a beautiful thing. You don't even need to have the right words ready, because Christ promises the Spirit will give them to us when needed (*Luke 12:11-12, Acts 1:8*). The goal of your ministry is to help people walk in truth and love, accept Christ in their hearts, and choose to be baptized. Even if you simply plant a tiny mustard seed, have faith that God will help it grow (*Matthew 13:31-32, Mark 4:30-32, Luke 13:18-19*).

In the space below, write three things you plan to do to share about your faith. Remember to keep them simple and to allow the scriptures to speak for themselves at this stage. Reflect on ways you have been successful sharing a message in the past, and write examples so you can compare them to find common elements. Pray, and ask God to guide you forward in how and what He wants you to share. Thank Him for giving us a message worth sharing.

16. Master of the Two Worlds

*Not many should become teachers, my fellow believers,
because you know that we who teach the law
will be judged more strictly.*
James 3:1 (NIV)

This section is devoted to leadership in its purest state. This is the maximum level of being in the world but not of it. Being open in your faith, having strong fellowship, and even helping people accept Christ and come to the Father are things we are all called to do as a duty of faith. There will inevitably be times where it makes sense to bring it up in conversation, like when you tell a friend no to their invitation to a social outing because you are already planning to attend a Bible study group. Your devotion will shine.

However, teaching is a horse of a different color. To desire leadership is a noble thing (*1 Timothy 3*), but it is meant to be undertaken by those who are capable of both setting a proper example in their personal lives while still speaking truth in all teaching. You are a master of your spiritual understanding as well as your understanding of the way the world currently works as you walk in both worlds. You are metaphorically like the angel in *Revelation 10*, with one foot on land and one in the sea, ready to make the truth known to others. Just like John, you swallowed that scroll and found the truth to be bittersweet. Your heart will always be in the kingdom, no matter where your feet are planted.

I have been observing and absorbing leadership knowledge from a Biblical perspective the entire length of my study. That is one of the benefits of beginning to speak openly in faith by sharing the work of other leaders. It also establishes a unified message when many people can agree.

I have always been a leader in some capacity, whether it be tutoring, management positions, owning my own businesses, or being appointed to lead group projects. I even had an algebra teacher *and* a music teacher who both asked me to fill in for them when they had to miss a class. As stated previously, I am also a certified life coach who has studied things like goal setting and success skills. God put leadership in my blood. Even still, explaining it in words as best I can will only go so far.

Leadership in faith is still somewhat new for me, and I aim to tread carefully. I value the guidance of quality leadership. Slowly becoming immersed in the church I attend and submitting to their authority I feel is part of my journey (*1 Peter 5:1-6, Galatians 4:1-2*). God led me to the *right* people, and I trust I have been planted there to learn and grow from their experience and wisdom. I pray more churches rise up in their likeness. If you truly wish to step up in this capacity, I highly recommend first taking the time to study under a leader you respect. Ask them to take you under their wing and nurture your gifts together.

This is the stage where you start to create your own content instead of sharing that of others. It is not a job for everyone (*Matthew 9:37-38*). I still recommend starting small. When I first began speaking my own thoughts openly, I only shared universal truths. Some people viewed this as sugar coating the harsh truth. I saw it as a foundation to build upon as I strengthened in my understanding. I wanted to share, but I didn't want to mislead. I wasn't wasting time not talking about God when I could, but I also wasn't getting ahead of myself or God. This is still valuable, because it helps build the credibility of the Bible to those who see it as just another book. Even an atheist can be a humanist, and we all value a message of love and peace whether we believe in God or not.

Another suitable place to start is speaking from personal experience. This plays off of *Matthew 7:1-5* where Christ instructs us to first remove the plank from our own eye before we try to remove the speck from someone else's eye so we can see clearly in order to do it. Knowing this, I want you to go back and read all the answers you wrote to the questions I presented throughout this book. Combine them all together and read them in sequence. You should see the rough outline of your story growing and changing in faith.

Congratulations! This is the foundation of your testimony! I challenge you to paraphrase it and share it somewhere. Compile the things you have overcome and how you did it through faith. Maybe you want to speak at church, or perhaps you'd like to share on social media in videos, blog articles, or posts. Give an honest account of your journey to faith and what Christ has taught you (*2 Timothy 2:15*). I want to see them, so use *#perfectloveherojourney*!

There is a difference between honesty and transparency. You can be honest and still be hiding or withholding a heck of a lot. Be as transparent as possible without compromising your safety as well as the intimacy of your relationship with God. Some things are private for a reason. This level of balanced transparency is so incredibly powerful. It teaches by your example instead of just preaching down at someone. It is relatable for others to hear instead of being high and mighty.

Don't forget that when it comes to honesty, we must be certain what we think is true is actually true before claiming it as fact, *or* identify that we are sharing an opinion when that is the case. When a teacher stands before a student, their words are taken to heart. Their words hold more weight, because they will guide other souls in their journey. To speak falsely, even out of ignorance, is to jeopardize the soul of every person with ears to hear it or eyes to read it. As I said in the beginning, *Christ is the only teacher*.

We are all students who have studied well enough to share what we have learned. We will never stop learning. A teacher is also perpetually a student. In Hebrew, *lamed* is a letter/number, but it also means both to teach and to learn. In this way, you can help people learn or you can learn with them, but you don't really teach as Christ does. If you ever think you have learned everything there is to know, then you need to step back and practice your humility (*Matthew 11:29, Romans 12:3*). Only God knows all things. We just have a slice of that cake (*1 Corinthians 13:9-12*).

True leadership will also require some trial and error. God didn't build us all to have the same gifts, but He did give us all the same material to teach from (*1 Corinthians 12*). There are *so many ways* to lead! Some people choose to embrace their artistic gifts like music or art. Others might run workshops. Some will settle down and make one town their home, while others will be jetsetters and travel with the message. We all have diverse backgrounds and dialects, strengths and weaknesses. Our God is one of order, and he has hierarchies and offices in place you may be called to as well (*Ephesians 2:20 & 4:11-12, 1 Peter 4:10-11*).

Prayer and trusting God to guide you should eliminate a good bit of the trial and error to find what suits your talents best. There are also some decent spiritual gifts assessments and personality profiles you can work through if you are struggling to piece it together. Just be aware that sometimes we will start a project we are passionate about and it won't take off like we hoped. Pride comes before the fall (*Proverbs 16:18*), so be able to accept failure and course correction rather than beating a dead horse. Often these moments that feel like failure are building blocks to something bigger and better. *And we know that all things work together for good to them that love God, to them who are called according to His purpose. (Romans 8:28)*

Another angle to consider is playing nice with other leaders. I have seen many leaders get so focused in on delivering their message that they isolate themselves in a negative way. They stop conversing with others of the faith, tell people they don't have time to answer their questions, and just talk *at* people all the time. This is the type of behavior that prevents the body of Christ from truly coming together. Sometimes leaders will need to collaborate to be more successful in sharing the message, and that should be celebrated as a special level of fellowship reserved for those who lead. My heart is blessed in a special way when I have heart to heart discussions with other leaders willing to go deep. It can be illuminating and inspiring!

The best way to determine if you are ready to teach is to identify if you can take a complex concept and explain it in simple, concise words. I may have dug deep into the details behind the concepts here to help create a feeling of depth in your heart, but I started by summing up the entire message of the Bible in six words - the balance of law versus love. If your shorthand statement is true, then theoretically just about any verse or passage regarding the topic should support your point.

Leadership is not just about standing at a pulpit and trying to sway hearts by any means necessary. It is a responsibility where lives are in your hands (*Ezekiel 3:17-19*). Leadership isn't always behind the pulpit. Many are being called to serve outside the four walls as well. You must be prepared to follow Christ where you are led to go in order to fulfill the work. Excuses don't cut it (*Luke 9:59-62, 14:16-24, etc.*).

Christ reminds us in *Matthew 10:34-39* and *Luke 12:51-59* that although he taught principles of peace, he comes creating division with the double edged sword. This is how he will separate the sheep to his right and the goats to his left. The key point to realize is how many times he told us to follow him, pick up our cross. I feel we are truly meant to be able to discern as he discerns, not necessarily fall to his right or left. As a faith leader, are you able to be divided, or are you built on the rock that is Christ and unable to fall? One who cannot be divided is a pillar, an embodiment of the straight path (*Revelation 3:12*).

This does not give license to attack people. We minister, and people choose how to respond to it. That helps Christ sort and sift, because he can see your true heart. We minister in peace and he will see all he needs to see. People will ultimately sort themselves based on the way they respond to the truth being shared.

The more vocal and confident you become, the more opposition you will face. In *2 Corinthians 11* apostle Paul speaks of the suffering and persecution he faced in choosing this path, often inflicted by his own people. I feel it ties to *Hosea 2:14-23* where God says he will lead the woman into the wilderness where struggle will produce a change of heart and lessons. Conflict will teach so that peace can be restored and *appreciated*. Yet as I said before, we don't get to skip that part. Can't go around it, can't go under it - you have to go through it.

Here's an example. I typed a comment on a video once sharing a translational clarification I had found through Strong's Concordance. This guy had made a forty minute video about how women are to blame for everything wrong in the world based on one verse, so I shared an alternate scriptural perspective. There are clearly good and virtuous women in the world and in scripture. I chose my words nicely, and not once attacked him or his belief keeping it strictly scriptural. Another man, not even the original poster, later replied to my comment threatening that it was *off with my head* if I didn't retract my words. This man never bothered to verify anything I shared. He simply jumped to threatening my life.

I have watched people wince at the mere mention of the name of Christ, even if I was just responding to a question they asked me without ministry in mind. I have seen plenty of people ask questions in online forums and be absolutely attacked for it. My friend, *the bubble has been burst*. It is my duty to warn you that you will face some hatred for choosing love and truth. *John 15* is a message from Christ regarding the subject, and how he was hated without a cause.

My sincere hope is that building up your armor here as we have done will help deflect the hatred so it bounces off of you without struggle. It has simply been my experience that some people feel so judged or hurt by past experiences that they take it out on you, and they may find ways to jab and twist in your weak spots. They would rather bring you down to their enjoyment of mediocrity than rise to the occasion, because that would require them to admit things about themselves they are not prepared to face. Misery loves company.

I say that knowing I have been that person a time or two in my past, and I regret it now. Turn to prayer, stay strong, and discern with trust when it is not appropriate to engage or escalate conflict. To say *turn the other cheek* is one thing. To be able to do it is another, especially when the subject is as personal to you as your life calling to share about God.

Be aware that you will be under a microscope. I understand that being reborn in Christ forgives my past sins. By that reasoning, it should take them off the table as a way to attack me. If Christ can forgive them, nobody should be able to judge. However, going forward, people will watch you and nitpick everything you do, and I have to say rightly so *to a degree* (*John 15:22*). It is downright hypocritical when you hear about the politician charged with adultery who campaigned on Christian family values. It often ends their career.

You *cannot* be a good leader if your words and actions are not in line with each other. Mistakes will happen, because nobody is perfect. There is a difference between impossible standards and realistic standards. That doesn't justify intentional major transgressions, though. Practice what you preach to the best of your ability, because people will be ready to pounce the second you don't. If you can't practice it, don't preach it and get to work on removing that plank from your own eye so you can share about that experience in a positive way.

The really angry ones will be like the Pharisees and Sadducees and try to trip you up (*Matthew 22*). Don't let them! This brings us back to stumbling blocks. When we entered the trials, I clarified that my approach to studying the commandments was specifically worded not to put stumbling blocks in your path. It was all intended to help you be more self aware so you can avoid tripping in the future. As a leader, it is simply unbiblical and unethical to test people or try to make them stumble. That is not now nor should it ever be your teaching strategy. Allow people to learn from past mistakes. Don't cause them to potentially make new ones. This is another reason why your example is crucial. When people look up to you, they will model your behavior.

A fitting example of living as an example others can follow

is about how we dress. I was listening to a video from *David Johnston* about the scriptural ideal woman, and he touched on the topic of dressing modestly. I would like to share his assessment, which you can hear in the video on the playlist I previously referenced. He said we dress the way we think, feel the way we dress, and act the way we feel. Therefore, the outside reflects the inside. He shared that the scripture stated four reasons for clothing. They protect us from the elements. They can be symbolic of our position, such as police uniforms or doctor's jackets. They differentiate gender. Last, they provide modesty because a person who knows their worth doesn't need to sell their worth with their looks. Dress appropriately for your calling.

Our gentleness should be evident to all (*Philippians 4:5*), but perfect love isn't just sappy and sweet, *especially* in a leadership capacity. It is strong, protects, and guides. Speaking truth in love is not about sugar coating it, but we are more than conquerors (*Romans 8:36-39*)! When the message is love, it must be delivered in a like manner.

Nothing can separate us from God's love. Don't let the way you deliver the message attempt to sever that. Coming back briefly to the significance of the number seventeen, *Romans 8:35-39* lists out exactly that many things that cannot separate us from the love of God. *Who shall separate us from the love of Christ? Shall **tribulation**, or **distress**, or **persecution**, or **famine**, or **nakedness**, or **peril**, or **sword**? As it is written, for thy sake we are killed all the day long. We are accounted as sheep for the slaughter. Nay, in all these things we are more than conquerors through him that loved us. For I am persuaded that neither **death**, nor **life**, nor **angels**, nor **principalities**, nor **powers**, nor **things present**, nor **things to come**, nor **height**, nor **depth**, nor **any other creature**, shall be able to separate us from the love of God, which is in Christ Jesus our Lord.*

People make mistakes, and your job is to help them learn from them. Speaking evil of your brother makes you a judge of the law (*James 4:11*), and that is disrespectful to God. Respect the sacrifice of Christ. Respect each person's journey to come out of the wilderness. Respect the point of the message. Respect that everyone is at a different place than you and change does not happen overnight. Christ called out what needed correction to prevent people from being misled, not to insult or ridicule them (*Psalm 15:1-3*). In turn, by doing this, you demonstrate self-respect by not sacrificing your integrity at the altar of truth.

So many of these aspects of leadership all come back to one thing - *keep your pride in check!* That is not as easy of a feat as it may sound. Praise feeds the ego whether we want it to or not. Remember the parable that tells us not to exalt ourselves (*Luke 14:7-11*). It is our duty as leaders to deflect praise towards God rather than accepting it all for ourselves. We are sharing His message, doing His work, and are a vessel for His Holy Spirit that brought us where we were. So little of true leadership comes from ourselves. Credit should go where credit is due.

A leader must always keep themselves in submission to God. If you aren't sure how to submit to God, try attempting to identify what equality would actually look like and realize that is just way more responsibility than anyone could want or handle. The scope of His existence alone is too infinitely grand to perceive, so to suggest any of us could do things better is pretty haughty.

In contrast, we do still need to be confident. We need to be meek and humble, but not so much that we cannot be heard. We are also exhibiting authority in Christ. If you cannot speak the message with confidence, nobody who hears you will bother to listen in any way that impacts their heart. Confidence is the key to any good salesman. While you are not selling anything, nor are you a con-artist, it is helpful to realize that a man who is confident in what he's saying and how he is saying it could sell snow gear to someone in the jungle or ice to an eskimo. You have the advantage, because you are sharing something people actually need in their lives! Shouldn't you be even more effective at conveying that message?

I struggled over stepping into a leadership capacity for a long time. I kept praying about it and kept feeling pointed towards it, but I just wasn't trusting myself to be someone who could make a difference on team Christ. I was scared I might say something wrong and hurt someone's relationship with God. I was scared that what I shared might be too much for people and my safety could be in jeopardy. Looking back, I realize now that those fears were being planted by the devil to hold me back. If God says all things are possible when He is in your court, I will most certainly choose to believe it. Once we are in the body of Christ, we are one with him acting in his authority.

I had a dream one night that changed how I felt entirely. In this dream I was in the back seat of a car, and two old friends from high school were in the front. One of them dropped something, and I warned them to just leave it until we were stopped. They didn't listen, and in an attempt to reclaim the item they started to swerve slightly to the left in the road. The front passenger realized what was happening and tried to correct the steering wheel to the right at the same time the driver did, and the car went so hard right that it flew in the air and started spiraling sideways like a football.

In that moment of the dream I knew I was going to die. Rather than being scared, I used my last moments to pray. I was calm, composed, and sincere as I was upside down then right side up then upside down then right side up, being held firmly in place by my seatbelt. Then all of a sudden we landed, right side up. The whole outer body of the car had come off somehow, but there was no fire or explosion, and all three of us came out of it without a single scratch. We just sat there, frozen in our seats in the open air, trying to figure out what had just happened.

I've had a few dreams before where my life was at risk, being chased or shot at, but this was the first time I ever knew in a dream that I would *die*. When I woke up, I felt a peace and confidence wash over me. It was in that moment I knew that God was looking out for me. Just like Christ in the wilderness, I trusted that God would have my back and had no need to test it. I accepted that if it is His will, He will protect me. If it is not His will then that will mean it was my time to go and nothing could have prevented it. I trusted that I will be part of the resurrection, so death would only be temporary rest.

My trust became complete, and it was the foundation of my confidence that led to writing this book. Whether that dream was simply a manifestation of my subconscious, a message from God, or a mix of both, it was what I needed. Prayer will make God both my strength and my shield. I still have fears sometimes, but I move forward despite them. *But none of these things move me, neither count I my life dear unto myself, so that I might finish my course with joy, and the ministry which I have received of the Lord Jesus, to testify the gospel of the grace of God (Acts 20:24).*

Real leaders in the church don't just talk to people. They get to work! We aren't just called to charity. We are called to go into all the nations and heal the sick, baptize people, and perform miracles in the name of Christ! If your ministry is more of a financially beneficial career than a mission to help those who need it, then you need to reevaluate your approach (*Matthew 6:24*). *Luke 10* and *Matthew 8-10* are notable examples of how Christ went around and ministered. Obviously in the modern day knocking on a stranger's door can get you shot, and we have been given tools to be able to connect with people all around the world without leaving our homes. However, we cannot allow ourselves to lose the spirit behind the reason he instructed us to minister as he did. Do not lose the purity of your ministry to capitalism and administration. In modern times, we are bound by financial necessity, but it does not dictate our ministry.

Since my testimony is part of my attempt to set a positive example, I will share openly how I have addressed this. Currently I am employed outside the church covering my daily life expenses, though I have no savings and live paycheck to paycheck. The sales from this book will go to support my living expenses. If the book becomes popular enough for there to be extra, I will donate to charities with it.

However, literally everything else I offer at this time through *Peace Is The Road* is not like that. I accept donations for life coaching services, and if someone is moved to contribute in that way the money is forwarded to charity. I keep none of it. There is no obligation to do that, so it is a free service. That way someone coming to me for help is helping others at the same time. To me, this is a great way to emphasize loving your neighbor as yourself. Personal growth benefits society.

I also accept donations outside of coaching if anyone would like to contribute, because I get involved in volunteer projects and make videos about them to support the cause. We also contribute to people in need when able and try to do random acts of kindness, so there is a fund set aside for that and only that. Any donations made to it are then separate of my personal life and all go to causes. Once that gains traction I intend to publicly post the ledger on my website (*blotting out names of those donating for privacy*) so people can trust where the money comes from and goes to.

Down the road there are other projects I would like to pursue. For example, I would love to record a five song album of me singing Christian songs. I think a couple would be covers of favorites and a couple would be written by me. After expenses are covered, all proceeds from that will be donated to charities. Recording is just something I would like to cross off my bucket list, and if I can use it to help minister and be charitable at the same time, then I say everybody wins. This is the logic I have behind all my endeavors. If my employment situation changes, I will still do everything I can to maintain this level of integrity and not be ministering to accumulate wealth or fancy things.

At the end of the day, I don't know why I was blessed with the ability to see the things I have seen or understand what I do. It could have been anyone else. It doesn't matter why, though. I have a responsibility to share. Maybe God knew I wouldn't ignore Him. If he can see into our hearts, perhaps He saw that I valued helping people enough to act. Maybe He wanted to prove that He can send His message through someone as insignificant as a plain Jane single mother who survives at the poverty line (*1 Corinthians 1:27*). I just don't know.

I've shared what I know and will continue to share what I continue to learn. I could write books upon books of my own thoughts on the Bible, but that is not what I felt called to do. I was called to guide you towards forming your own thoughts, to wake you up to thinking for yourself instead of being led by the world. I want to inspire you to use that brain God gave you to its most divine and pure potential. I pray that I have fulfilled that successfully.

In the space below, write what you think makes a good leader regarding this higher level of responsibility. Weigh your strengths against your weaknesses, and don't hold back honesty. Do you feel called to this? If so, are you ready, or is there still work to be done?

Reflect on past times where you have attempted to lead in any capacity. What worked? What didn't? Are there skills I didn't cover that you can carry over from those experiences? Pray and ask God to guide you to a clear understanding of what He wants from you.

_____
_____
_____
_____
_____
_____
_____
_____
_____

Leadership Test

  The life of a peacemaker on a mission to help people through faith is hard sometimes. It can be high pressure and result in being friends with everyone but often feeling like you have no friends at the same time. I can enjoy the company of just about any person I meet, and they often express fondness for our friendship. Many have started reaching out to me asking how I would handle their situation if it were me. I'm basically always busy and trying to connect with as many people as I can. I don't get much time to be social enough to build close friendships where we stay in touch several times a week and are deeply bonded. I do have some of those friends, just not a ton. I am content with that, though.

  As a Christian, you are told to be in the world but not of it. That's basically how I feel. Sometimes leadership feels like making a claymation movie, stepping in to help people readjust, then stepping back and appreciating it, then moving to the next frame. I know I'm in this world still. I'm completely aware of reality and it's many horrors and joys. But my heart lives in this future version of reality where we have triumphed the wilderness, emerged to live in peace, and people understand how to communicate without always escalating to conflict.

  In this future world, people all choose to learn the lessons and have a sincere desire to be a good person, the best version of themselves they can reach to be in a happy, healthy way. People there value wisdom and truth. They seek understanding and a deeper experience in life. Somehow we aren't there yet, and I've been trying to fine tune the best ways I can help without being some forceful egotistical authoritarian. I've been trying to identify what the best way is to do things differently than I once did and be the maximum level of truly effective.

  I personally have interpreted that to mean I seek to plant seeds of thought. I present people with questions they have to answer for themselves. That feels like wisdom. I don't have to tell you what to think. I just have to encourage you to think. The rest can handle itself with the guidance of Christ and the Holy Spirit if the right questions are asked.

  Inherently I do believe everyone has good in them, but it's understandable how the pain and suffering that can arise in a world of choices and lots of contrasting people can leave scars, distracting us from pure truth. That means the best way I can plant a seed of positive thought without being confrontational is to simply demonstrate compassion to anyone I meet. This is how empathy will heal the world. The real question then is *can empathy be learned*?

Can anyone change into a person that sincerely cares for others? I think yes. That is what the Holy Spirit does when it awakens within us. It is a spark of Christ in our hearts that makes us feel more deeply. It convicts us about what it means to live a life that doesn't harm others or ourselves. That conviction teaches love and corrects our missteps towards righteousness until it becomes our character. It is not just walking alongside Christ hand in hand. It is walking with his essence inside ourselves, mirroring his message in our personality. I look ahead, and it makes me want to help Christ create this better world.

That task is so grand that it feels like some large thing bursting its way into reality out of my dreams. Sometimes even pure intention and love can breed negatives like ego out of the pure desire to see the best possible outcome, so I constantly humble myself in thoughts of God. This is how I'm able to be a peacemaker, because even though I'm bouncing around from person to person, I never truly feel alone when God loves me. He really does hold you in the palm of his hand! Christ sits at the right hand of the Father. He is all and is in all. He is in us and we are in him and he is in the Father (*John 14:20*). How epic is that?

That is grace - to exist in His hand. It's not like anyone forced Him to outstretch His hand and keep it there so lovingly. To think about it makes you feel so tiny. How infinitely small are we in comparison to the planet, the galaxy, the universe? Look at how overwhelming daily life can feel, then consider how all that stress is a speck in the grand scheme of existence. The fact that God pays attention to any of us at all just feels like the most amazingly special thing. To feel like I matter in all of that is precious to be aware of. It's calming, peaceful. It soothes the soul like a lullaby.

This is the balance required for someone to be a good leader for the true and living God. Your ego must always be put in check by your own free will choice to do so, but you need to be able to think big and still see the meta perspective. Plus, you have to be able to still take those big concepts and explain them in those few simple words or actions while understanding the finer details so you can discern good from evil. This is a *huge* quest to undertake, but it is what makes a *true hero.*

It's not unrealistic to feel good about that kind of an accomplishment. When you look around and see so few people who care that much if even at all, you constantly have to remind yourself that this doesn't make you better than anyone else. You have to choose, and you must voice out that you're not judging people, otherwise you may unintentionally start to.

I'm being honest, because I want to see more leaders who care this much. I want to live in a world where people take the time to reflect on the impact of their choices yet still be decisive. I want to see people who are humble and equal with everyone else. This isn't just walking a tightrope. It's like walking on dental floss, or maybe even on air. This may just be a description of flying.

A part of me feels that is the spirit we had at the foundations of America. We chose the eagle as a national symbol. When an eagle sees a storm, they choose to fly above the clouds and avoid the turmoil. A person who flies is not choosing a side in conflict. They are choosing to rise above it by acknowledging everyone as best they can and seek a peaceful resolution. Just like Christ showed us, they can turn the other cheek when attacked, because they know any response of anger would be like endorsing the initial anger as acceptable. Instead, when they turn the other cheek, they plant a seed of a different path. The aggressor is forced to think about their actions and how they are being so much more hostile than those around them.

Turning the other cheek tells those who are angry that we will not play their game of hate. Love is better, and we *know* it. You'll know it too when you see it is an option. That is, if you can allow yourself to let go of the chip on your shoulder. *Can you?* Do you believe you can let go of rage in exchange for love? Do you believe you are capable of continuing to love when someone else is not yet living in this new kingdom of God with you?

I want to take you through a series of questions. None are intended to tell you a right answer. They are simply rhetorical and designed to help you paint a clearer image in your thoughts of the scale and complexity behind how to properly address a scenario. This can be viewed as a benchmark for you. After thinking through this at your own pace, step back and ask yourself how you would have instinctually responded to the exact same situation without having been guided through these thorough questions and given time to process it. Do you believe you are ready to carry this responsibility of comprehensive leadership? Do you have growing to do yet? Are you confident enough in the fundamentals that you could work your way through what comes?

Let's evaluate a common problem in the modern world. Ask yourself - you find out someone you care about has been abusing hard drugs like heroin, cocaine, or meth. They have been spending your money or money owed to you, lying to your face, manipulating everyone so precisely so they wouldn't get caught, and it ends in them hurting everyone including themselves. **How do you respond to that?**

Do you walk away for safety reasons, or stick by them because you understand their suffering that led to the mistake of drug addiction? If you stick by them, how much help do you give?
Do you refer them to rehab, counsel them through quitting, or break their trust and tell the people they lied to for the sake of the truth?
Do you try to pull those loved ones together for an intervention, or respect boundaries and not meddle in their affairs?
Do you involve the police since they broke the law, or do you try to help them quit and get clean without getting sucked into the revolving door system?
Do you think the scare of being caught by the legal system is the only thing left that will snap them out of their bad behaviors?
Would you respond differently if this was a stranger that you walked by on the street, or would empathy still compel you to try and help?
If you do help, how many chances do they get to mess up before you have to draw a line and back away from them to protect yourself from becoming collateral damage?
Or do you never give up on them to demonstrate unconditional love in faith that it will guide them out when they're ready?
Is your faith so strong that you believe praying for them and giving them space is all they need so they can learn to stand on their own two feet?
Or do you feel the Holy Spirit pull you towards putting your hands on their lives?
Can it be both?
If you are capable of jumping to one answer quickly without having to evaluate all these different possibilities, then did you really love

your neighbor as yourself?
Or has wisdom become your true character to a point of instinct and trust in God to guide you?
Are you fully aware of the massive amount of strength and fortitude required in the long term to help someone in this state of being who cannot see themselves as clearly from the inside as you can from the outside?
Or instead of being the helper in the scenario, do you still feel more like the person who fell into the trap of drugs, because you battled depression, anxiety, lack of fulfillment, or other life challenges that pushed you too far?
Are you the person who made a mistake and maybe wants to change but is scared, because you feel you're in too deep?
Do you feel justified in lying, because you feel it will protect those around you?
Do you push away those closest to you out of the guilt of hurting them with your actions or the pride of wanting to handle things all by yourself?
Are you aware of the effect the drugs have on your ability to think and act rationally?
Do you realize they might be triggering your nerves in a way that makes you feel more irritated or like everything is a bigger problem than it is?
Do you feel blind or think you're finally seeing clearly who your true friends are, because you found a way to justify pushing people away by thinking they all betrayed you?
Have you shown any care for how people have responded to your struggle?
Do you feel in control and not see your life spiraling out in chaos, or does it just feel like a new chapter in life?
As the helper, if we cannot understand the perspective of the user, can we truly ever be effective at helping them no matter what we do?
Do you really think there are ever going to be any political policies that could fully address the complexity of this kind of problem fairly and successfully, especially on such a wide scale with so many different variables?
Obviously they can be written to dramatically help the situation even if they can't completely cure it, but will those helpful policies ever be written if the hearts behind the legislation and our votes don't reflect this level of care?

Is healing ultimately going to come down to individual efforts?
Is it truly a matter of the heart?
Could quality communication skills on the parts of everyone involved have prevented someone from feeling the need to use drugs in the first place?
How much less awful could this situation have been for everyone to handle if preventative measures had been in place?

So… take a moment…

You just learned that someone you care about is abusing hard drugs. They have been lying to you and others and are on a destructive path. *How are you going to respond* that reflects God first, yourself and your loved one second, and society third?

_____
_____
_____
_____
_____
_____
_____
_____
_____
_____
_____
_____
_____
_____
_____
_____
_____
_____
_____
_____
_____
_____
_____
_____
_____
_____

End Time Prophecy

    I wanted to add one more subsection here before we complete this journey. This is going to be about prophecy. Before we dig in, I would like to share a story with you to garner a sense of perspective. Hear me out.

    In mythology, Cronus was a titan - Saturn, the god of time. His wife was Rhea. He came into power after overthrowing his father Ouranos - sky, Uranus. Cronus was given a prophecy that he too would be overthrown by his son. In fear of this prophecy, he swallowed each of his children as they were born. Rhea grew weary of losing her children, so she conspired to save her son Zeus by tricking Cronus into swallowing a rock instead. Zeus then recruited Metis - wisdom - to help him save his siblings. She gave Zeus a potion that caused Cronus to vomit up all his children, at which point the prophecy was fulfilled when Zeus defeated the titans with the help of his siblings and took his father's seat of power.

    The question I would like to pose to you is this - if he had not feared the prophecy he was given and responded negatively trying to prevent it, would it have happened? This is an age old question. Did hearing and responding to the prophecy create the circumstances that caused them to happen, or were they an inevitable fate? If Cronus had chosen to ignore the prophecy and not swallowed his children, could he have been a good ruler that nobody would have been angry enough with to overthrow?

    This is a thought exercise towards a purpose. I'm not suggesting that the book of Revelation is avoidable, but how you respond to that book defines who you truly are on a soul level. Are you going to kill, hide, or save people? Who are you really?

    What I'm suggesting is that if it *is* fated to occur and there's nothing to stop it, why would we let it change our behavior? The Bible clearly outlines what we must do to enter the kingdom of heaven and that those who are strong of faith will be kept safe. Christ can see into our hearts, and it is God's desire that all are saved. If we all simply strive to be our best selves daily and remain prepared, it won't matter when Revelation happens. We will be ready. Revelation says that the judgments will be deemed fair and just, so it really makes me wonder what will be seen in the hearts of the wicked to warrant punishment.

    If you had been Cronus, how would you have responded to

such a prophecy? Would you have been able to ignore it, or would you have obsessed over it? *Revelation* is *your* prophecy. We are all a part of it.

So many people get into a tailspin of emotion when they study prophecy. In the grand scheme of studying all end time prophecies from various cultures, that is called *eschatology*. Some worry they won't be ready, and they waste all their time trying to set dates instead of doing what they actually need to prepare. Some see the chance to grab at power, and they lose sight of the heart of the gospel message. Some become terrified and become doomsday preppers, ignoring the part where God promises to nourish and protect us and says not to store up things on earth. Just live the *message* - all the other things we talked about in this book - and Revelation will be what it will be. Sharpen your discernment, and you'll know the antichrist when you see him.

For example, it says that the antichrist will produce false signs like calling down fire from heaven. That is based on scripture as something that Elijah did in the Old Testament, but in the modern world all it would take is a satellite with a laser attachment of some kind. You can't be afraid to question things. It says that anyone who comes against the two witnesses will also die in fire and that they will be able to control plagues and weather, so if you see someone preaching the gospel, not calling themselves God, and surrounded by those signs, pay attention. It's not rocket science, but if you don't read to be aware about what's coming, you could easily be duped.

Character is a dead giveaway when words can be lies. I have seen many, many videos of people sharing visions about this time period, and they all suggest that Christ's army will be the ones helping people, healing, and saving them. They will turn to physical violence as a last resort.

Ultimately, the only way to survive a study in Revelation is to have built your strength as a person of faith first. Know that you are safe and secure in Christ, then look at the book as a tool to prepare you. It is intended for awareness. Enjoy each moment like it could be your last, prepare for the worst, and hope for the best. That way of thinking led me slowly to peace. Prophecy is not going to dictate my behavior. I will be my best self every day. Doing that will certainly lead me to wherever I deserve to go when I die, because I trust that the true and living God will be fair and just in his judgments for or against me.

My best self will undoubtedly set a positive example and work to help people be their best selves through love. I know that by developing my behavior to be righteous in the eyes of God, I will have done everything I am capable of doing to create the most positive outcome for myself and those around me. If prophecy is true, then I will have been on the team of the good guys without fear. If it doesn't happen in my lifetime, I will have lived a good life of high moral character and tried to leave the world better than when I entered it. Being my best self is all I can truly do in response to a prophecy like the book of Revelation. Whatever will be, will be.

Does this mean I don't seek to understand it and pay attention to what's going on around me? No, of course not! Not worrying doesn't mean not being aware. That's the balance necessary to carry with you in order to do an objective study on such a topic as end time prophecy. If you don't bring that mindset to the table, it will consume you.

When you read passages that say things like the sky will be rolled up or heaven and earth will be destroyed, it can feel scary. Finish reading to the end! We will get new heaven and new earth and a joyful eternity with God. When one door closes, another opens. The end of time is simply the beginning of eternity (*Matthew 7:20*).

The last thing I want to point out here is the realization this study brought to me. In truth, we all have the capability inside of us to be beauty or the beast. We can be both. We make choices every single day, and all choices have consequences. We know that even the best intentions can lack effective execution. Life is beautiful, but it is also fragile. Until we accept that darkness exists in us, we cannot remove it by filling it with light. Acknowledging it is the first step towards being freed from it.

There is a modern movement to encourage people to accept themselves as perfect just the way they are. I encourage you to realize that is flawed, and accepting yourself is step one in a process. Is someone perfect who desires to kill people? Of course not! Should they be allowed and even encouraged to believe they are perfect as they are as though the desire to kill is healthy? No, that would be downright dangerous. No person who believes in real love can accept evil behavior.

However, until that person with a desire for murder in their heart can acknowledge that this feeling is bad and accept that it is a part of them, then they will never be able to change it. You can't remove a tumor until you have been given the diagnosis acquired by seeing the x-ray, right? Once they can see it clearly as a bad thing, help can be given to bring them out of their darkness. This may be an extreme example, but the point stands.

While this person is in the phase of being blind to their emotional state, poking the bear with aggression won't help anything. Attacking them won't solve problems, in fact, it might provoke them to follow that desire to kill. Being capable of defending yourself while approaching in compassion would be the only way to help this person see. Even that is built on a balance! We prepare for the worst case scenario but lead hoping for the best (*1 Thessalonians 5:3*). Apply this to your understanding of the overall concepts of prophecy and judgment, and I'm sure you'll be fine. Below I have left space for you to take notes if you feel moved to undertake a study of this nature. I pray you find clarity and peace.

17. Freedom to Live

> *Jesus answered them,*
> *"Verily, verily, I say unto you,*
> *Whoever committeth sin is the servant of sin.*
> *And the servant abideth not in the house forever,*
> *But the Son abideth forever.*
> *If the Son therefore shall make you free,*
> *Ye shall be free indeed.*
> John 8:34-36

To get to the heart of a matter means to get to the point at the core or center. That point is that love cannot exist without free will. You are free to choose, but you are not free from the consequences of your choices. Christ came to free us from the bondage of sin and death. He did that by teaching us the love of God in his life and by his death. *That is perfect.* I realize through his sacrifice for us that I would rather die for choosing love than live without it. Perhaps that is part of why he did not fight back as he carried his own cross.

Without free will, we would all be robots. With it, we have the chaotic potential to become pure evil just as much as pure good and everything in between. It has been suggested that the ability to make choices was God's crowning glory of the creation of man in His image. I agree, because real love could not exist without free will. Perhaps going through all of this was about defining what is a healthy application of it so love can flourish to its greatest potential. Can you really think of a better way for humanity to learn and develop such a crucial concept than what has occurred through history?

It started with the rebellion of Lucifer followed by the disobedience of Adam and Eve. It ends with our choice to accept God completely. Humanity has covered the entire spectrum from oppression where nobody could meet the standard and all faced wrath, to a free will system like we have today where one chooses in a chaotic sense to do whatever they want focusing on unconditional love and forgiveness. We went from small population to large, and inequality to at least a general level of equality.

The kingdom of heaven revolves around the balance of all these factors. If balance is so important, how can we identify where center is if we do not know where the edges are? The extremes and outer darkness may be where evil lies (*Job 10:22, 1 Samuel 2:9, Matthew 22:13, etc.*), but humanity had to go to them to collect the data of their reality in order to learn, understand, and calculate balance accurately. How can you appreciate light if you have never seen darkness (*1 John 1:5*)?

Once you find the absolute perfect balance of free will, you then have to ask yourself how wisdom applies to that precise knowledge and understanding. Is perfection all it's cracked up to be? I imagine if every single person on the planet was totally perfect, life would get remarkably boring. We would experience no range of emotions which is what creates the depth of our feelings. No mistakes would mean not learning from them anymore. Feelings are a huge benefit of free will. There is an anime called *One Punch Man* that explores the downfalls of perfection and how monotonous life could be without any challenges. Check it out.

This means that true, technical, calculated perfection is imperfect by its nature to allow for beauty in variation. God is a melody, and His children are a harmony to the same one song. To live exactly perfect, even as a natural extension of your character, would create too much pressure to maintain it and not enough joy for it to be worthwhile. That is why wisdom applies feelings to knowledge. The heart understands the essence of life, the intangibles. Being a true Christian is like speaking a new language, one of the heart. A hero for perfect love understands, accepts, forgives, learns, appreciates, shares, and brings joyful peace.

Something was really bothering me for the longest time. I was asking myself why eating from the tree of the knowledge of good and evil was so bad for Adam and Eve if the ability to discern it is now so crucial to our salvation. We *must* be able to decipher truth versus lies and good versus evil so we are not duped into following the devil. After much prayer and reflection, it eventually came to me.

Everything in the garden was *good* at first. Eating from the tree added evil. The universe exists on a balance. Before, good balanced against itself. Adding evil changed that, and suddenly the way the balance was structured reflected balancing good against evil. They are the epitome of duality and division. The fact that good and evil are opposites is now what most defines them. We are attempting to walk in two clashing concepts when we focus on good *and* evil.

That's why true balance in God who is good is the only answer. When we remove the darkness from our lives and balance everything that remains as best we can in Him, nothing is in conflict, and we are free. We rid ourselves of the darkness and become centered in the light (*Daniel 12:3, Isaiah 60:19, Colossians 1:13-14, Revelation 21:23*). Good and evil no longer exist. Only peace exists which is inherently good. It leads me to think that may have been God's divine plan all along - a return to the peace of the garden. It was good before, and it can be good again.

The benefit of learning about it, deeply studying, and developing a moral code is to garner appreciation and understanding of why peace is best. Experience is a lesson. Christ will come in division to test us, teach us, and separate the wheat from the tares. The tares will be burned away, and the wheat will be stored in the barn (*Matthew 13:24-30, Revelation 14:14-20*). The wheat that remains will be all that fall in that center third of the spectrum of love and free will. The extremes will be gone and peace will be established in the kingdom (*Hebrews 12:25-27*). We will come full circle to the idea that God was right all along, and He patiently waited for us to figure it out.

Balance still contains all things. They just don't fight each other in that state. That doesn't mean we shouldn't face problems and work to resolve them. The power is in refusing to escalate the situation. We learn to choose our words appropriately, adjust our tone and body language, not rise to anger, not judge, keep things to facts, lean on the wisdom of God, and not delay. We become efficient at problem solving. We develop smart hearts! That process takes time and patience. Experience that teaches will involve trial and error and lots of self awareness.

We are not God and never will be. His eternal knowledge, wisdom, patience and love will always be well beyond our grasp. That doesn't mean we can't ponder and postulate about His reasoning as it applies to us. I find it healthy to at least try to understand *why*. In my journey of study followed by the eventual writing of this book, I couldn't help but develop guesses as to the purpose of all of this. Here are some possibilities I pondered.

I imagine that the best way for an eternal being at the scale and magnitude of God to study and find the best balance of free will and love versus authority would be to live it through others. Maybe we are all as a whole God's self-reflection process, and we should mirror back to Him our best selves. That would imply that every individual one of us analyzed it all ourselves and took some of the work off His shoulders.

Maybe love cannot be learned without interaction, so God made creation to learn it for Himself. Life is defined by self awareness, and the ability to interact ties closely to that. If there was only one being in all of existence that was self aware and nothing else existed, would that really be called life, or stasis?

Maybe He already knew all of this, but He also knew we had to experience it to be able to understand and appreciate the level of responsibility on His shoulders. It's hard to have companionship with those who don't understand anything about you. Family is precious.

It's sort of like the super computer in *Hitchhiker's Guide To The Galaxy* built to try and calculate the meaning of life. The computer answers forty-two and everyone is confused, so they are then told to seek the ultimate question. Earth is then created to find that question. *Spoiler Alert:* In the book, it turns out forty-two is the sum of all sides of a pair of dice, because the computer believed it was random chance.

I don't agree though. Perhaps God Himself came into existence by chance, but life as we know it is so intricate and perfectly designed, there just had to be hands behind it. I see no possible way that random chance or even evolution could develop the systems of our body or brains capable of the advancements we have made. It's too perfect, too orderly, too organized and patterned to be chaos and random chance.

Maybe this is the process by which He perfected man in a way higher than technical perfection on paper. Before that, maybe everything was more computer styled, cut and dry existence. Did our presence then awaken the joy in His heart? God clearly needs other life. Again, if there's no other life than you, what's the point of living, and who are you the God of but yourself?

Existence of life creates purpose for the God of life who doesn't want to be lonely. Deep down, even if we were all a tiny piece of God staring at our own reflection in a mirror, everyone just wants to be loved. We can make that hard for everyone, or we can make it easier. That choice is up to you.

That's a **lot** of *maybe*, but in a section about freedom and where we go from here, it's fun to explore. I have absolutely no clue what God's motives are for creating life, but it doesn't hurt to contemplate. It seems to me that this is the logic that will bring us back to the state of life before Adam and Eve ate the fruit of the tree (*Matthew 12:25, Genesis 6:3*).

My musings here might not be the truth, but it sounds pretty logical to me. Love and companionship, being happy and healthy - those are reasons I can understand. I can respect that motive from God who has proven to be steadfast in His love, because there's not a single person on this planet who could live alone from birth to death (*Luke 14:15-24, Matthew 22:1-14, Revelation 19:7-9*). It's a commonality for all of us. I can accept that reasoning for existence, because I feel it in myself. We all want to be loved and solve the big problems. We all need some freedom and some responsibility. We all need compassion if we aren't going to kill each other.

The time has come to get it right. It's time to follow God. If it will lead us to true, healthy peace, is there anyone who is against that? Be still, and know (*Psalm 46:10*). The truth will set you free (*John 8:32*). The truth is Christ.

> *Stand fast therefore in the liberty wherewith*
> *Christ has made us free,*
> *And be not entangled again with the yoke of bondage.*
> Galatians 5:1

Heavenly Father,

Thank you **so very much** for this journey! We love you with our whole hearts, minds, and souls, and we are sorry it took us so much time and effort to truly learn. Life is such a gift, even when we face struggles. Thank you for all the blessings, the moments of joy, the tears both happy and sad, and the miracle that is creation.

Use each and every one of us to fulfill your will to bring peace through the balance of law and love. Please continue to guide our paths to be straight. Empower us to share your message in truth and wisdom, and help us stay strong and patient in each step we take. Help us to be better at the action of love, both for ourselves and for others. Let that be a light among all people that leads them to you.

I send up this prayer in the Spirit and name of Christ,
Amen!
4-17-18

Let's Connect!

Ann Lenaers

Ann.PeaceistheRoad@gmail.com

www.peaceistheroad.org

www.facebook.com/peaceistheroad

Like, subscribe, interact, and let's come together in Christ!

The purpose of this book is first and foremost to help people and bring them to God. I encourage you to pass this book along if you know someone who could benefit from it.

However, it is a workbook, and I understand you may not wish to pay forward your private information. I prefer that the book be purchased if it can be afforded in order to support my living expenses and charitable causes, but if you know someone who cannot afford it, please provide them with my email address. I will send them a pdf copy free of charge — no questions asked. I trust that if you have reached this page of the book, God will put it in your heart to enact this offer with integrity.

Love,
Ann